# *Towards the Digital Library*

## The British Library's *Initiatives for Access* programme

edited by Leona Carpenter, Simon Shaw and Andrew Prescott

THE BRITISH LIBRARY

For Alex

© 1998 The British Library Board
First published by
The British Library
96 Euston Road
St Pancras
London NW1

ISBN 0 7123 4540 X

Designed and typeset by Andrew Shoolbred
Printed in England by Henry Ling Ltd., Dorchester

# Contents

# Foreword

**Sir Anthony Kenny**

Once upon a time, the role of a library was easily defined. Its functions could be summed up in three words: acquisition, preservation, and access. For centuries, this meant getting hold of books, looking after books, and placing books in the hands of readers. At the end of the 20th century the three principal tasks of acquisition, preservation and access remain fundamentally unaltered: but their scope is expanding and methods of fulfilling them are multiplying. This book describes the ways in which The British Library is aiming to carry out its traditional tasks in a world profoundly modified by information technology.

First, there is acquisition. We must first dismiss the fantasies of those who say that in the 21st century all information will be stored and transmitted electronically, and there will be no more books to be acquired. New printed monographs have continued to appear at a rate of more than 60,000 a year in the UK alone, in spite of the boom in electronic publishing, so that there is no reason to foretell the death of the book. The digital revolution is often, and justly, compared with the introduction of printing. But printing supplemented, and did not supersede, handwriting. Libraries have continued to collect manuscripts, and every child learns to write in school, more than 500 years after Gutenberg.

Alongside the continuing stream of books, however, libraries like The British Library will have to acquire, in ever increasing quantity, information published in electronic form. Moreover, even if monographs continue to thrive, economic factors make it likely that many of the 126,000 journals now published world-wide, if they are not to founder, will have to be distributed only in electronic form. If the national published archive is to be maintained, the legal obligation on publishers to deposit their products in The British Library, which at present only applies to print on paper, will have to be extended to material distributed in new media. The Library has presented proposals for the extension of legal deposit which were benevolently received by the previous government, and has good hopes that the appropriate legislation will be passed during the life of the present Parliament.

The acquisition of non-book material will bring new challenges. In preparation for meeting these the Library has undertaken a number of demonstration projects. One of these explored the problems in the cataloguing of CD-ROMs. After 60 CDs had been catalogued and submitted to authority control, it was discovered that on average each of them took up to four times as long to catalogue as a printed book, because of the time taken in installation, and the need to check for viruses. Moreover, the identification of authors, editors, and compilers is a much more complex matter when electronic products are in question. However, having learnt some salutary lessons from the demonstrator project, the Library feels confident of its ability to handle any CD-ROM material that comes its way.

Such products of electronic technology present new problems for cataloguing; but of course the technology itself offers new kinds of assistance in the actual cataloguing process. Several examples are described in the present book.

Thanks to Excalibur's Electronic Filing System, which permits fuzzy matching, the unwieldy 19th-century catalogue of British Library seals, and the early 20th-century catalogue of manuscript music, were both converted in an astonishingly short time, with a minimum of curatorial intervention, into searchable electronic form. Other small collection lists, if not the mainstream catalogues, may soon hope to benefit from conversions which are similarly electronic in their process as well as in their output.

The Library possesses an extensive collection of images of various kinds, a collection likely to grow with the extension of legal deposit. For some time it has been exploring appropriate electronic methods of cataloguing this archive. Here the demonstrator project was the British Library Electronic Photo Viewing system, (popularly, if not euphonically, known as PIX). This is a database containing over 13,000 rare images, such as early photographs, reproductions of illuminations, Indian miniatures, rare stamps and sheets of music. A chapter in this book describes the process of image capture by PhotoCD and the structure which makes possible keyword and textual searching. The system is not designed to produce hard-copy reproductions, though it can produce acceptable postcard-sized prints. 'The provision of photographic negatives from digital images' the author observes 'is only a stop-gap measure as people are weaned off bits of plastic with heavy metal particles stuck on it. There is very little future in film.'

The second duty of libraries is to preserve their collections once they have acquired them. The progress of science has provided libraries with new, remarkable, and expensive methods of maintaining and restoring books whose paper is brittle and whose bindings are damaged. But 'preservation' has come to mean not only the physical conservation of a readable artefact, but also the transfer of its contents to a surrogate, such as a microfilm. The 17th- and 18th-century newspapers and broadsheets of the Burney collection are among the most frequently consulted holdings of The British Library. When consulted in their original form, they were gradually being worn out by the fingers of readers. Some years ago, therefore, they were systematically microfilmed and all preliminary consultation of them now takes place on film. But readers do not enjoy using microfilms, which are less pleasant to consult than the originals, and offer no compensatory advantages in facilitating research. It can be wearisome to pursue a search through reel after reel of unindexed photographs.

Here is a case where digitisation offers the best hope of preservation. The section of the Burney microfilms which deal with the years of the French Revolution has now been scanned onto optical disk, as have two illustrated 17th-century collections of ballads. This project was finished in March 1996, and though it moved slowly at its inception, it speeded up to a point where it would now take only nine further months to complete the scanning of the entire Burney collection.

Among The British Library's most valued possessions are its illuminated manuscripts. For historical reasons, there has hitherto existed no detailed listing of these manuscripts, many of which are scattered among several of the Library's foundation collections. In preparation for the move to St Pancras it was essential to have a thorough survey of each volume at the shelf. Ten thousand manuscripts have been identified as specially significant and coded summary descriptions have been made with SGML tags. Here is another way in which electronic technology has come to the aid of preservation, by providing the structure and links of a specially targeted catalogue.

Digitisation has been taking place in the aural as well as the visual field. Between 1993 and 1995 in the Library's National Sound Archive many wax cylinders, acetate-backed tapes, and LPs which had been in heavy demand were converted from analogue into digital form. Here digitisation had become essential for conservation and back-up.

After acquisition and preservation, we come, thirdly, to access. It is here that technology is most profoundly affecting the way in which libraries carry out their traditional role. Once, it was enough if a library provided its readers with a desk to which books could be brought, and, under the same roof, a written catalogue of its holdings. Now, a great library's catalogue is expected to be available far beyond its own walls, and the information contained in its holdings is pursued by many who will never set foot in its reading rooms.

For some time the library catalogues of a number of American institutions have been available online to scholars in this country, through the Internet. The British Library's Online Public Access Catalogue (OPAC), which first went live in its London reading rooms in 1993 was launched in April 1994 on the Joint Academic Network, JANET. This meant that students in any university in the UK were able to search the catalogues at their desks. More recently OPAC 97 extended this service freely to researchers all over the world via the World Wide Web. OPAC includes records of some eight and a half million books, in many languages and several scripts, scattered through several different collections in the Library.

But the ambition of scholars is to have access not just to the catalogues but to the actual holdings of the world's great libraries. The Library already deals with three and a half million requests from offsite readers from its Document Supply Centre in Boston Spa. Hitherto, most requests have been satisfied by the loan of duplicates within the Library's holdings, or by photocopies of the originals. With the cooperation of publishers, the Document Supply Centre began in 1992 to explore the possibility of switching to electronic storage and delivery. Forty-eight journals were scanned onto disk, indexed, stored and made available for delivery in response to live requests. Many lessons were learned from this project, but there is still some way to go before large-scale electronic delivery can be introduced: once possible this will be much faster and will give the end-user enhanced facilities for searching.

In the meantime, information technology has been used to speed up and improve traditional document supply. *Inside* is a system designed to combine remote digital access to collection catalogues with an efficient direct order facility. The 20,000 journals most in demand from the Document Supply Centre at Boston Spa are catalogued to article title level and then entered into a database, along with individual papers from the 16,000 conferences which the Library monitors annually. The database was first published on two CD-ROMs launched in April 1996; updates have since been issued monthly, each carrying six months' worth of data. In January 1997 *Inside* was launched online. Titles enter the database within 72 hours of receipt into the Library, and photocopies can be ordered directly.

On the Library's Holborn site, more than a million current patents from the UK, US, and European Patent Offices are held on CD-ROM jukeboxes for instant despatch to inquirers. Initially, the patents were delivered by fax in response to touch-tone telephone requests, but the Library is moving towards a completely paperless document system, which already allows e-mail ordering, and will eventually permit a delivery over the Internet. The Holborn library now possesses 27 jukeboxes, each with 100 CD-ROMs; this is the largest such jukebox installation in Europe.

It is not only current scientific material which will benefit from being made accessible in electronic form. So too will some of The British Library's antique possessions. When a library possesses items of rare interest and beauty, two different kinds of access are needed. Treasures must be placed on view to members of the general public to fascinate them with their beauty; but scholars also wish to scrutinise them in detail, page by page. These two kinds of demand, as things are, get in each other's way. Now that digital surrogate colour images have been produced of items such as the Sforza Hours and the Leonardo Notebook, it is possible for scholars and visitors to see magnified details, and to look at openings other than those on exhibition. Even the illusion of turning the pages has been created within this virtual library of treasures.

One of the most remarkable of current British Library projects is the digitisation of the manuscript of the 1000-year-old epic of Beowulf. This manuscript, of uncertain date, is the sole source of our knowledge of the poem, and it has had a catastrophic history, having been damaged in a fire in 1731 and subsequently obscured by the interventions of Victorian restorers. The manuscript was photographed by high-resolution cameras under various kinds of light, and reproduced in digital form under the academic direction of two American experts. The computer images enabled scholars to see for the first time erasures and fire-damaged passages hidden from the naked eye. Test images were made available over the Internet, and a CD-ROM publication in 1997, a year ahead of schedule. Scholars all over the world will benefit. No doubt their number is limited, but the scanning of Beowulf, apart from its intrinsic interest, presents a challenging test case for the new technology. If you can digitise Beowulf, you can digitise anything.

The Beowulf project was an outstanding example of transatlantic co-operation. A more recent similar collaboration between The British Library and the University of Washington in Seattle has as its goal the digitisation of a set of 80 Buddhist texts from Gandhara, perhaps 2000 years old. These, when acquired by the Library, were unrolled birch bark scrolls, which had to be flattened under glass if they were to be read and preserved. They are written in Kharoshti, an obscure script closer than any other sources to the original language of the Buddha. Their scholarly and religious significance is enormous: they have been described as the Buddhist equivalent of the Dead Sea Scrolls. Because the originals are too fragile for further manipulation, prolonged study of them would be impossible without the creation of a digital surrogate.

In all these ways, contemporary techniques are both supporting and modifying a library's traditional functions of acquisition, preservation, and access provision. Indeed, information technology is breaking down the boundaries between the three functions. A university library wishing to provide for the needs of its academic users may, instead of purchasing a volume to hold on its own shelves, decide that it is more cost-effective to procure access to a text held elsewhere, either by inter-library loan or by online delivery. According to the American Commission on Preservation and Access, the exploration of the uses of digital technology for preserving the deteriorating printed documents of the past has taught us that in the digital world, preservation is access, and access is preservation. The provision of access is emerging, as we reach the end of the 20th century, as the dominant partner among the triad of library functions.

It is for this reason that The British Library gave, to the collectivity of its digital projects, the title *Initiatives for Access*. A score of different projects were undertaken in order to exploit information technology in ways to enhance and extend access to its collections. Information about them was furnished to the world of research through Portico, the Library's online information server on the Internet. Portico is The British Library's home page, but is also a host to a number of home pages, built up, department by department, to a common standard. Each month a third of a million transactions are logged, and the site is often cited as a model of national library online information service.

I had the good fortune to be Chairman of the Board of The British Library during the years when all these initiatives were in progress. Though I was kept informed about them, and had many opportunities to visit the teams which were working on them, it was only when I read this book that I fully grasped the variety and complexity of the problems to be tackled, and the frustrations and exhilarations involved in overcoming them. The writers of the individual chapters have been very successful in communicating a lively feeling of what it was like to be involved, hands-on, in these pioneering projects. The authors' detailed descriptions of technical devices and projects, and especially their candid accounts of mistakes and blind-alleys, will make the book of great value to experts in other institutions and other countries working in similar fields.

Everyone in The British Library can feel proud of what was achieved by these initiatives. Great care was taken to ensure that the programme was driven by the Library's genuine needs, rather than by the desire to experiment with technology for technology's sake. The complaint has been made, as Andrew Prescott observes wryly, that 'the programme was insufficiently experimental, in that all the projects proved to be successful. There were no completely wild proposals which failed completely'. All those involved can be pleased if that is the worst criticism that can be made of *Initiatives for Access*.

# Introduction

**John Mahoney**

The fundamental purpose of any research library is to provide access to the organised record of knowledge and ideas. That purpose goes back through history to the great library of Alexandria and beyond. It is the fundamental purpose of The British Library, whose unparalleled collection includes every known written language, covers all subject spheres and embraces every era of recorded knowledge.

Great changes are happening in the ways that knowledge and ideas are communicated, recorded and accessed. Several factors are contributing to them. Many of the changes are driven by the development of information technology and by the convergence of computing, telecommunications and other communications media. It is often said that we are witnessing a revolution in communication comparable with the invention of printing. At the same time, libraries have begun to take a much more proactive stance to their role. They are recognising the potential that exists for them to play a central part in addressing the opportunities the technological changes are bringing, and are positioning themselves to do so, rather than taking a purely reactive stance as collectors and preservers.

The timespan of The British Library's collection gives an important perspective to current changes. The medium of recording and the mode of access to the record of ideas has changed several times. The oldest thing in the collection was written 3500 years ago on a piece of oxbone. Between that time and now, there are papyri, vellum, parchment, paper – all containing writing and drawing. There are sound recordings on various media, there are photographs, microfilms, and of course an enormous amount of print on paper. The late 20th century has added to this already large repertoire of access technologies with the hugely greater potential of digital recording, digital delivery and digital organisation.

It was to explore, to learn about and to demonstrate the potential of digital materials and digital modes of access to contribute to the broad and unchanged fundamental purpose of the Library that we launched the *Initiatives for Access* programme in 1994.

## Strategic considerations

The Library's Strategic Objectives published in 1993 made clear, as had been apparent for some time, that the use of information systems – computing and network telecommunications – would have fundamental impacts on all those whose business or research is concerned with the generation and use of information and ideas. The following objectives encapsulate what the Library intended, and intends, to do.

'By the year 2000, the British Library will be a major centre for the storage of and access to digital texts required for research.'

'By the year 2005, our digital collection will be enormous and growing at a huge rate.'

'... becoming a major centre for the capture, storage and transmission of electronic documents...'

' ...we are seeking to make our collection better known and more widely available by exploiting the increasing use of computer networks...'

The Library decided to take these broad objectives forward in two complementary and parallel but relatively different ways.

First, it took the classical top-down business planning approach of moving from vision to action, where broad strategic objectives are amplified and detailed, and then used to develop action plans for implementation of the broad objectives. Based on its strategic objectives, the Library developed a formal Information Systems Strategy through an extensive process of consultation and analysis looking both inside the organisation and outside. Associated with that strategy it developed a relatively detailed implementation plan and a very detailed set of initial project implementation plans.

Secondly, and in parallel with the early stages of formulating that Information Systems Strategy, the Library launched the *Initiatives for Access* programme. It was intended to be creative, open and challenging. It was predicated on the recognition that we did not and legitimately could not possibly understand all the implications of the fast-changing technology and creative environment being generated by the development of digital techniques and global computer networking.

The *Initiatives for Access* programme therefore set out to learn about new ways of working, to demonstrate those new ways to staff within the Library and to people in a broad range of constituencies outside, and to embed understanding of and enthusiasm for the new technologies within the staff in general. In all these ways it aimed to open the way for further, faster, more effective and more creative change.

We were very clear that the programme was not technology for its own sake. We took pains to try to communicate it in terms of the benefits to library services and collections.

Electronic Beowulf is a good example. A highly sophisticated digitisation of the earliest known manuscript of a work originating from the oral communication tradition has helped illuminate the past while at the same time generating insights into the future. The technical challenges of dealing with the manuscript generated insights that were of use in other projects working with quite different materials. The scholarly achievement is of significant value in its own right. And the project generated helpful publicity and awareness in the national and overseas press and media.

We were clear from the beginning that for The British Library, and probably for most libraries, being a digital library would emphatically not mean being an exclusively digital library. Information technology has unprecedented potential to deepen our understanding and help us to learn. Like many other new technologies it will enhance and add value to the pattern as a whole; it will supplement, not supplant. Looking back one can see that the introduction of printing by moveable type in Europe in the 15th century did not replace writing, any more than writing replaced speech, or indeed any more than speech replaced hand gestures. Printing was obviously better suited to some applications than writing, yet writing remains as important in the era of printing's maturity as ever it was. In other applications, printing enabled new things to happen that previously were impossible, even unimaginable. In the same way digital techniques will replace (have already replaced in some cases) the use of printing. It also seems very probable that digital technologies will allow people to do new things that we do not even yet have in our imagination.

While technology change is rapid and increasing, and while creativity is burgeoning in its wake, there seems not to be the same speed of change in intuitive understanding that most people have of printed media. Arguably the novel is a form of art and communication ideally suited to the printed form yet it was several hundred years, and many human generations, from the development of printing to the maturity of the form. It is interesting to speculate on what new forms of art, literature and communication will develop within the possibilities of digital modes. If it takes as many human generations as did the novel, today's new CD-ROM and Internet products will come to seem as difficult and remote as the incunables of early printing.

## Outcomes

The *Initiatives for Access* programme as a whole was a resounding success. If there is any regret it is an unusual one to be voiced by a senior manager of an institution such as this: there were no failures. All the projects met their basic objectives and many of them succeeded far beyond our initial hopes and expectations. The fact that none of them failed suggests that perhaps we were too conservative, or at least not quite as bold and imaginative as we might have been in thinking up new schemes and new ways of working.

The programme generated enormous enthusiasm and commitment from our own staff, from our partners and from our suppliers. Some of that communicates itself through the pages of this book. While it was certainly an objective of the programme to generate ownership and insight, the outcome was self-reinforcing because people became committed to achieving and bettering expectations and worked very hard to achieve that.

## An environment of change

Changes in the broader environment informed work on the programme. We hope the programme in its turn has informed and is helping to shape those changes themselves.

These changes were and are of two kinds: those driven by needs and expectations of users of library and information services, and those driven by changes in technology.

The needs and expectations of users for information and library services are growing more extensive and diverse. People are coming to expect faster access to more complete sources, delivered in a more timely way. In most of the developed world, computer literacy from school to workplace and into the home is becoming a reality. The Internet has experienced unprecedented growth. In North America, and increasingly in Western Europe and in the Japan / Pacific region, it is an accepted business, educational and personal tool. There is clear evidence that researchers in academia and industry, and educators and learners at all levels, will increasingly want to use digital materials alongside traditional materials and will want access from their desktop whenever they want and wherever they are.

In parallel with these user-driven changes, there are strong IT-driven changes. They have an interesting and powerful dual effect because they both force coherence and enable connections within and between services and organisations. For example, when many services from a single organisation can be experienced at the same point via a computer network, there is a strong incentive to make those services consistent and inter-operable. In other words, the technology forces coherence. Moreover, by enabling connections between different services, and between different organisations, the technology has potential to allow more useful and valuable services to be produced than have previously been practicable. In The British Library's case one example is a pilot digital image browsing system developed as part of the *Initiatives for Access* programme. It allows paintings, drawings and photographs from many different parts of the collection to be seen and explored in juxtaposition for the first time. The value of that juxtaposition as well as the simple fact of ready availability has already raised appetite and expectation among users.

In a similar way, IT is driving convergence between several previously separate business and industry sectors: computing and communications, publishing and media, education and entertainment. One can already see new communication forms like interactive television beginning to emerge, and educational materials are being created which combine tuition and fun in game-like learning tools. While all these forms will offer great potential for improving access to library resources, they also pose significant challenges as sources which themselves need to form part of future library archival collections.

All service industries, and particularly those such as libraries whose core asset is information, need to respond creatively and dynamically to all these changes. The *Initiatives for Access* programme has helped The British Library to begin to do so.

**Partnerships**

The Library also wanted to use the programme as part of its continuing commitment to work with other organisations in the UK and overseas. We therefore sought to establish a number of joint projects, some focused on technology and some on particular collections or special materials. In the later stages we worked closely with the Follett Implementation Group for IT (FIGIT) of the UK Higher Education Joint Information Systems Committee, which had begun work in closely related areas. The development of joint standards was particularly helpful, informed as it was by a substantial body of experience that the *Initia-*

*tives for Access* programme had already documented. Overall, the programme has helped develop a number of important relationships with other libraries, with publishers, with the public and higher education sectors in the UK, and with some important sectors of the technology community.

**Vision**
The results of the programme have informed the Library's vision of itself as a digital library. The nine-point vision in summary is this:
- integrated access to The British Library and other digital collections
- organised/indexed for access
- integrated with traditional collections and services
- increased access – more people, more material
- continued availability – digital archives
- staff 'digital competencies'
- digitisation for conservation and access
- balance between Intellectual Property Rights and 'fair dealing'
- substantial investment – The British Library and partners

The vision is amplified at the end of this book by Brian Lang in *Developing the digital library*, and then set in a broader context by Lorcan Dempsey in the afterword, *Places and spaces*.

The *Initiatives for Access* programme itself is now closed. It has met its objectives because we have learned, we have shown, we have generated enthusiasm and we have opened the way for change. The challenge that lies ahead is likely to be an even more difficult one as we turn what were previously pilots and experimental projects into mature and stable operational services. At the same time we must not shut off the creativity and openness the programme has created to considering new ideas and new ways. Certainly these will continue to be enabled as far ahead as one can see by the growth in technology and the richer and broader creativity that it is bringing with it.

# The Initiatives for Access programme: an overview

**Michael Alexander and Andrew Prescott**

*In this ideal text, the networks are many and interact, without any one of them being able to surpass the rest; this text is a galaxy of signifiers, not a structure of signified; it has no beginning; it is reversible; we gain access to it by several entrances, none of which can be authoritatively declared to be the main one.*
Roland Barthes, *S/Z*

## We have been here before

In 1881, the economist William Stanley Jevons wrote to Richard Garnett, the Superintendent of the British Museum Reading Room, expressing his alarm at recent innovations there. He was horrified by these and considered that they posed a serious threat to the Museum and its collections. 'I believe you have simply admitted the Trojan Horse', he declared. The development which so alarmed Jevons was the introduction of electric lighting into the Reading Room of the Museum. Gas had been for many years prohibited in the main Museum buildings, for fear of fire. Jevons was convinced that the risk of fire from electricity was even greater, and felt that it should not be used in the Museum building until it had been rebuilt to incorporate the latest fire precautions. The electric lights in the Museum were powered by an experimental generator under Holborn Viaduct, which was powered by steam traction engines, and was both expensive to run and unreliable. The gas companies sniped that 'electric light can never be applied without the production of an offensive smell which undoubtedly causes headaches and in its naked state it can never be used in rooms of even large size without danger to sight'. The introduction of electric light into the Reading Room was nevertheless a great success. It allowed the Reading Room to open in the evening for the first time. Moreover, until the electric lights were provided, the Reading Room had to close whenever one of the 'pea-souper' fogs of Victorian London occurred, and in the winter could be closed for days at a time.

The introduction of light into the British Museum Reading Room could be seen as the first great initiative for access. The lighting scheme was the brainchild of Edward Augustus Bond, who was Keeper of Manuscripts from 1866 to 1878 and Principal Librarian from 1878 to 1888. Bond was a remarkable man, who took an almost schoolboyish delight in new technical developments which could help make the collections for which he was responsible more widely available. He was a pioneer in the production of photographic facsimiles of manuscripts, establishing the Palaeographical Society, which produced a huge 'databank' of photographic images of manuscripts from many different collections. He introduced photographs into the exhibition displays in order both to reduce wear and tear on original artefacts and to allow visitors to see different pages of the volumes on display. It was during Bond's time that the idea of a 'flying press', an early type of mobile shelving which almost trebled the amount of shelving available, was implemented. Bond represented the best aspects of the intellectual traditions of the old British Museum Library, which were characterised by a very practical and down-to-earth willingness to exploit the latest technical and other aids in helping to ensure that the collections were as comprehensive as possible, that readers could easily find what they wanted, and that the collections were made as widely available to the public as possible.

This tradition of exploiting technology in support of access to information was not confined to the British Museum Library. It was a characteristic of all the various institutions which came together to form The British Library in 1973. The most startling embodiment of this is the remarkable inter-library lending factory established by Donald Urquhart at Boston Spa in the 1950s. Although Urquhart's philosophy of librarianship was to a large degree a formidable intellectual challenge to the traditions of Bloomsbury, in some ways his work can be seen as a modern revival of the outlook of the great 19th-century Principal Librarians of the British Museum like Bond and Panizzi. In Urquhart's vision, the technology of the factory was used to streamline the process of getting books to users. The visitor to Boston Spa is confronted by conveyor belts and dispatch bays which are more reminiscent of a mail order outlet than a library. But the aim remains the same as it was for the great Victorian librarians – to use every available technical aid to give the quickest and cheapest access to information.

The British Library has continued to develop and extend the pioneering work of its component organisations. Although BLAISE may now seem very venerable, it was in the 1970s one of the first online catalogue services. In converting the massive General Catalogue to machine-readable form in the early 1980s, pioneering attempts were made to use Optical Character Recognition (OCR) technology to create automatically computer records from the hard-copy catalogue, using the only OCR facility then available in Britain, at the DHSS in Newcastle. The experiment was ahead of its time, and in the end keyboarding had to be used, but it pointed the way towards technologies that have now assumed great importance for librarians. Almost every area of the Library has been involved in technical innovation of various kinds. The Library's preservation service developed the first overhead photocopier which reduced the damage to books involved in photocopying them. The Manuscripts Department established in the 1980s one of the first systems for the automated cataloguing of manuscripts. Various areas of the Library have been involved in pioneering work for the handling of non-Roman scripts by computers.

**A wider initiative**
The *Initiatives for Access* (IfA) programme represents the most sustained programme of technical innovation so far undertaken by the Library. As new

digital and networking technologies began to become available in the late 1980s, it was evident that they not only offered opportunities to develop new services based on the Library's collections but would also radically change the way in which information was used and disseminated, so that the role of all libraries would be transformed. Although the IfA programme belongs to a long tradition of technical innovation in libraries, the programme was very different from earlier kinds of technical experimentation. Most of the examples of technical innovation already noted were limited in scope and range – somebody noticed that a particular invention might assist a certain type of work in the Library. By contrast, the digital and networking technologies offered the prospect of change in almost every area of the Library. The development of OCR technology, for example, might not only assist cataloguing but also offer the prospect of converting the books themselves into searchable texts which could be used by researchers in completely different ways. The World Wide Web might not only help in spreading information about the Library and its collections, but might change the nature of the collections themselves, as more and more research findings are disseminated through the Web. The same kind of imaging technology which might be used to support improved document supply of scientific periodicals might also be used for the forensic investigation of ancient manuscripts.

IfA was intended to help the Library come to terms with this technology by offering both library staff and users hands-on experience. The nature of both the technology and the wide-ranging character of the Library's services meant that it had to be a multi-faceted programme. The intention was in the first instance to produce a series of demonstrators. Some of these might become full-blown services. Others might simply offer an opportunity to appraise the validity of a particular technical approach in a 'live' situation. Whatever the outcome, the programme would assist the Library in intelligently appraising the best way to exploit the new opportunities that technology is increasingly offering.

An experimental phase of this kind is probably an essential prerequisite to the successful exploitation of the new technologies. A similar pattern may be seen in many other programmes. Thus, the e-Lib programme developed by the Higher Education funding councils in Britain is in many ways similar in concept to IfA. It is admittedly more generously funded and on a much larger scale than IfA, but, like IfA, is producing a number of important demonstrator projects in a variety of fields. Just as with IfA, the issue of how one moves effectively from these demonstrators towards a more integrated form of digital library provision is starting to become a very important one for the e-Lib programme. Likewise, the various projects undertaken under the auspices of a number of funding programmes in the United States, the most prominent of which is the National Science Foundation Digital Library programme, can be seen as creating a series of very large-scale demonstrator projects, and the recent formation of a National Digital Library Federation, involving a number of major US libraries and agencies, can be seen as representing a first attempt to draw together these diverse initiatives.

## New lessons, new practices

IfA was, of course, an internal British Library programme, and much more modest than great national initiatives like the e-Lib programme. However, the various IfA projects explored in depth many issues which will be of central importance in the development of a digital library. The purpose of this book is to draw together and record these lessons, in the hope that they will be of value in the development of larger-scale projects. The impetus for IfA came from the Library's Computing and Telecommunications (now Information Systems) directorate, which channeled the funding for capital investment and technical support. The programme was directed by a Digital and Network Services Steering Committee (DNSCC) comprising senior management from many different areas of the Library.

This in itself provides a first lesson of the programme – patterns of development of services using the new technologies will be different for different kinds of libraries and for different kinds of collections within libraries. In university libraries, the impetus for exploiting the new technologies has often come from users, particularly in scientific disciplines, who are in close contact with new developments and, working closely with subject librarians, are well placed to ensure that their libraries respond to new opportunities. National libraries are, despite every effort to reduce the gulf, inherently at a greater distance from their users, and the impetus to experiment with new technical solutions to service issues consequently has to come from within the Library. IT departments are well placed to provide this impetus, since they are often staffed by people who are both librarians and technicians. They can therefore see new opportunities and identify services which might benefit from them. A similar pattern is evident in other national libraries. The pattern of uptake of new technologies in public libraries is again completely different.

The experience of the IfA programme suggests that it is inadvisable to see IT departments as merely providing a technical infrastructure. Librarians operating in service and collection areas will frequently have a relatively restricted view of the technical possibilities available to them. A narrow focus on the issues presented by single services means that new service opportunities will be missed. In large libraries, successful exploitation of the new technologies requires an active dialogue between IT departments and those areas concerned with collections and services. One of the most striking features of IfA was the way in which it opened up and extended such a dialogue. And here it behoved the two IT teams involved in the programme, the Document and Image Processing team and the Network Services team, led by Michael Alexander and Neil Smith respectively, to be as imaginative and as creative in their response to curatorial colleagues' requirements as they could be.

It may be objected that this approach will result in technology for technology's sake. The IfA programme did not fall into this trap, largely because of the way in which the programme was initiated. Service and collection areas were invited to propose projects which seemed relevant to their areas. The C&T directorate was happy to accept the role of catalyst in this process, and did not insist on trying to fit all the projects into a procrustean technical bed. The overriding intention was for library curators, conservators and information technologists to learn together how to make the most effective use of the new technologies for the benefit of the Library and its users. The result was a wide range of projects which might, at first sight, appear bewildering. However, this flexibility of approach is essential if the opportunities offered by the new technologies are to be exploited. It is easy to assume that the magic word 'digitisation' means simply obtaining image files of items in a library's collection, whilst forgetting that it also means a radical change in the type of information which libraries receive from the outside world or that it might offer new approaches to handling text documents for both librarians and researchers. The 'digital library' is more than a huge image databank. It is a whole range of new approaches to information for providers and users of information.

However, the flexible nature of the new technical possibilities in a programme such as IfA could cause projects to run out of control. Not only can the various projects fly off in different directions in pursuit of distant technical chimeras, but the fact that many issues concerning the effective application of emerging technologies to image or network projects are as yet little understood (by IT personnel as much as by librarians) means that projects frequently do not go to plan. It is quite likely that an image capture station carefully selected after a rigorous tender process and configured according to the best technical advice will prove, when it goes into action, to be underpowered. Indeed, the experience of the IfA programme suggests that this will almost certainly happen. Clearly, an upgrade will be needed, but this will create pressure constantly to upgrade the system. To keep such demands under control, rigorous project management techniques were used for all the IfA projects. The methodology used was PRINCE, which was employed throughout The British Library. Each stage of all the projects was carefully documented and the roles of each participant in the project carefully defined in advance. The use of PRINCE not only kept the progress of each project under control, but also ensured that each project produced a detailed report, summarising the issues which had arisen in the course of the project. Many of the articles in this volume are based on these reports.

The avowedly experimental nature of the programme was sometimes difficult to convey to outsiders. It was occasionally assumed that, because a particular method of image capture was being used by one project, this represented a corporate British Library approach to digitisation. This was not the case – the key feature of IfA was the exploration of a variety of technical approaches to different service issues. Thanks to the quiet encouragement and gentle persuasion of the Information Systems teams, the result was in fact an extremely well-balanced programme of technical exploration. In the case of the imaging projects, for example, all the main means of image capture were explored: flatbed scanning, scanning of microfilm, scanning of photographic transparencies, PhotoCD, and direct scanning. Similarly, a number of different types of data storage were examined, ranging from Digital Audio Tape (DAT) backup to network transfer of data to mass storage systems. Moreover, the different projects dealt with a very wide range of different materials in the Library's collections.

Likewise, the projects concerned with text-handling and network services also represented a well-rounded programme of a variety of different technical possibilities.

## No single solution

Despite the diversity of projects, some common themes emerged, which will be important in further developments. The first and most important is that the digital library cannot be reduced to a single technical infrastructure. There is no one means of creating and exploiting the digital library. It will be based on a range of different technical approaches, and the particular approach used will depend on the immediate service requirement. Again, this is strikingly demonstrated by the various IfA imaging projects. Where there are no major conservation constraints and the emphasis is on speed and quantity of scanning, as with modern scientific periodicals, flat-bed scanning may offer the best solution. For rare material available only in surrogate where the concern is to provide a more manageable surrogate than microfilm, microfilm scanning may be a solution. PhotoCD may be useful in making available to casual browsers large collections of photographic transparencies, but direct scanning may be preferable for more forensic examination of a particular object. In the case of delicate art objects which cannot be directly scanned on conservation grounds, high-resolution scanning of large photographic transparencies may be the best way of proceeding. The well-equipped national library of the future will be able to offer a range of such facilities in order to meet all its different service needs, and will not rely on just one such approach.

The importance of this 'horses for courses' principle can also be seen in the different projects concerned with text handling and catalogues. Extensions of existing MARC records might offer one approach to dealing with growing collections of digital materials. However, in the case of existing complex catalogue records, such as illuminated manuscripts, SGML-based approaches might be more appropriate. Novel software solutions, such as the Excalibur Electronic Filing System, may be appropriate for the conversion of existing hard-copy records which, for one reason or the other, may never be keyboarded. The varied character of the technical approaches described in this volume may seem to be due to the experimental nature of the IfA programme, but it is also inherent in the technologies themselves. It seems likely that this diversity will become greater, and this will need to be taken into account in the creation of digital libraries. In developing digital libraries, the key to success will be not to rely on a single strategy but to develop structures which will allow the greatest flexibility of approach.

It was pointed out during a meeting discussing the programme that it was perhaps insufficiently experimental, in that all the projects proved to be successful. There were no completely wild proposals which failed completely. All the projects were able eventually to achieve their aims and showed that they could make a real impact in a variety of different service areas. However, for many of the projects, the path to success was a hard and stony one, littered with changes in configuration to equipment, the latest software not proving up to the job, vital components not performing as well as they should, and insufficient availability of vital technical information. This was due simply to the difficulties of dealing with cutting-edge equipment and software. Although these problems were all resolved for the purpose of the limited projects of the programme, it is a worrying lesson for the creation of larger digital libraries.

There seems to be a common assumption that, having achieved satisfactory results on small-scale projects, all that is necessary to create the digital library is to secure more capital investment and scale up the experimental work. However, it may be the case that larger investment will simply create on a bigger scale technical problems of the sort encountered in the IfA programme. Much more work needs to be done on relevant system architecture before taking the leap in the dark of creating the grand 'digital library'. In any case, it may be that the rush to create large-scale systems misses the logic of the technology. What is exciting is not that we can hold images, video, sound and text in common formats, but that this material can be made accessible in different ways; most importantly that they can be transmitted across networks for the benefit of remote users. The system requirements and economics of a distributed library network will be different from those of huge central datastores. This might obviate the need for large-scale single-site investment, or at the very least, change the pattern of investment required. Possibly, instead of thinking of a digital library which, by amassing large amounts of information in a series of digital stores, merely replicates the 19th-century universal library in a digital environment, one should be thinking of a series of discrete small-scale projects which embody different approaches to information storage and manipulation, but which are linked together to form a wider resource. After all, the model of the digital library most readily available at the moment, the Internet, follows this approach.

However, this path will not be an easy one to follow. It presupposes a commitment from all participating projects to the common goal of *inter-operability*. This cumbersome but important term encompasses the ability of existing and future digital library developments to share information with each other for the maximum benefit of their users. It demands that the technical infrastructures developed adopt common technical standards for the capture, storage and transmission of digital material. It also demands that the manner in which this material is described and identified should have a commonality across the entire digital domain. Such an approach will require a commitment to co-operation both at institutional and supra-institutional level which is very different to the 19th-century model of 'splendid isolation' of major research holdings and we will return later to the question of large-scale co-operation in the library and information world.

**Data storage – the new collection management issue**
Of the various technical issues highlighted by the IfA programme, the most important was data storage. Although various methods such as direct scanning or scanning from microfilm can quickly generate large quantities of information, backing up the data proved a huge bottleneck. Most of the imaging pro-

jects found that backup could take as long as the original scanning. The problem can be moved out of sight by using a large-scale storage system such as that at the University of London Computing Centre currently used by the Library to store its digital collections. This makes the preparation of back-ups less of a day-to-day nightmare for individual projects, but the use of such facilities can be expensive, and does not get rid of the overhead. Moreover, the responsibility for organising and controlling this data still lies with the Library.

At a seminar at the University of London Computing Centre in 1994, a speaker from the Meteorological Office gave what was for listeners from other disciplines a chilling presentation describing the data storage issues confronted by the Office. It was not simply a question of the massive quantities of data involved – thousands of satellite images and other data occupying many terabytes – but also the sheer number of files which the Office needed in its day to day work – rainfall, sunlight and temperature records from thousands of places all over the world. Simply naming and organising all these files was a terrifying prospect. The message of the speaker was that before long all organisations using computers will confront problems such as these. The petabyte will soon become as familiar as the gigabyte. Many of the issues of managing such huge quantities of data are unresolved. The Meteorological Office found the architecture of proprietary large-storage systems inadequate for its needs, and had had to enter into direct discussion with manufacturers to improve system architecture. New means of finding data were needed to cope with the millions of files. The relatively modest amounts of data generated by the IfA programme has already caused great data management and storage problems for the Library. Some of the issues raised by the Meteorological Office speaker will have to be addressed before we proceed further.

Again, the experience of the IfA programme confirmed that the manpower problems of indexing and cataloguing data will be a major stumbling block for the creation of the digital library. Finding adequate professional resources to feed the voracious appetite of the digital computer was a problem for all the projects. The C&T funding was able to help with paying for technical support, but the expert help needed to, say, catalogue images of oriental paintings or stamps could not be so readily bought in. This was a problem for each of the imaging projects. For example, the Digitisation of Ageing Microfilm (DAMP) project showed that digital images provided a more manageable surrogate than microfilm for use in reading rooms. However, the level of cataloguing required for microfilms is relatively crude, simply consisting in labelling the different reels. By contrast, with digital images each file, equivalent to a frame of microfilm, needs indexing. Likewise, the PIX project demonstrated how an image database could be used for browsing banks of images, but in order to search effectively these images, database records needed completing for each image, a task which could in many cases effectively amount to re-cataloguing the collection.

This issue was not confined to imaging projects. A major issue in developing network services such as the Library's World Wide Web server, Portico, was in ensuring that collection and service areas could provide full, accurate and up-to-date information about their work. This had to be undertaken in addition to conventional activities. It would clearly be desirable that the Library should offer a full e-mail inquiry and ordering service. However, it has difficulty in adequately staffing its telephone service. This is a major difference between the first wave of library automation, in which computers were used to make more efficient very labour-intensive tasks such as cataloguing, and the present technological changes, in which the technology offers the possibility of creating additional services which will initially run side-by-side with more conventional activities. Finding the additional staff resources to develop these extra activities will prove a major stumbling block for many organisations.

The IfA projects suggested some ways around these problems. The first is that, as new projects develop which would otherwise have been undertaken by conventional means, they will make use of new technologies in ways that will make the work less costly. Thus, the Survey of Illuminated Manuscripts is an essential activity in preparation for the move to St Pancras. The use of SGML for the preparation of catalogue entries is intended to make these quicker to produce, and thus less resource-intensive. The other approach which will reduce the resource requirements in developing new activities is greater co-operation. A notable feature of the IfA programme was the way in which it acted as a stimulus to external co-operation, and this is evident from the number of external contributors to this volume. Academics are anxious to make use of the new technologies to work more closely with primary materials held by the Library, whether it be images of a medieval manuscript or textual information. In the case of the Beowulf project, the assumption was from the beginning that the Library would have neither the expertise nor the resources to undertake the detailed preparation of a massive image edition, and the work has been undertaken by an external academic editor. Similarly, the concept of the York Doomsday project is to work with scholars expert in the field to realise a novel research and teaching vision. The Library's agreement with the University of Sheffield has enabled it to undertake detailed testing of the Excalibur Pix-Tex project which would not otherwise have been possible.

### Mapping the digital landscape

Readers of Umberto Eco's *The Name of the Rose* will recall the gripping description of trying to find one's way through the labyrinthine stacks of the monastic library. One is forcibly struck by how much more strongly that image applies to the task of negotiating the web of information in the digital environment. There is a strong need for librarians, archivists and others to remember that achieving the satisfactory use of the technology is not the only issue. What makes any library collection valuable is the way in which the information about it is organised and presented to the users of that collection. The creation and maintenance of the library catalogue is such a self-evident activity for librarians that it scarcely seems to need a mention. However, it is vitally important to remember that none of the digital material, either re-created from another medium or published only in digital form, will be identified or identifiable within any form of datastore unless it has been catalogued in a usable way. A major requirement of the researcher, one which has spurred librarians to heroic efforts of bibliographic compilation, particularly in the past 150 years, is the requirement to have an accurate description of an item and its existence. This requirement obtains even more pressingly in the digital domain where the objects exist only as binary digits in a computer's memory.

## Descriptive and substantive data

So in order to work effectively a library collection needs to provide two forms of information for its users. One form consists of the items that constitute the collection: books, manuscripts, journals, maps etc. These items may be termed substantive data, since they are the essential parts of the collection which are sought by the user. The other form of information may be termed descriptive data. Its function is to facilitate the correct identification and location of items within the collection. It is typically exemplified by catalogues, indexes and other finding aids. However, the interesting point about this form of data is that despite its apparent secondary function as a finding tool, it can also be a form of substantive data as well. The mere presence of a bibliographic record for an item in a catalogue list may be quite sufficient for the needs of a researcher. Librarians and bibliographers have sought over the years to systematise these forms of description, both to ease the path of the researchers in providing information for them in a uniform way and to enable the freer interchange of bibliographic information between institutions: an early form of inter-operability.

Recognition of the importance of this form of data for digital library collections can be seen in the increasing amount of debate and discussion within the community of digital library developers concerning a suitable method of systematising this descriptive data, or 'metadata' as it has increasingly come to be known. The authors must here admit to some prejudice against the use of the term metadata in this context. The word had previously been used in computing by database developers to indicate the data structure within a particular database. Through its appearance as a tag in HTML and by using the rather loose definition of the term, *data about data*, the digital library community has come to affix it to some particular forms of data content, descriptive data, rather than data structures. This we believe to be mistaken. However, the use of the word in this situation has now become so widespread and acceptable in this context we must reluctantly accept that metadata has become synonymous with *descriptive data*.

## Agreed standards

Within the world of information technology standards have had and continue to have a chequered profile. The term 'technical standards' can be used to apply to anything from the pin configuration on a plug to the way in which user documentation is laid out. Some forms of standard have the force of national or international agreement through the work of national standards agencies and their parent body ISO (the International Standards Organisation). Others are simply examples of 'best practice' which gain general approbation within the industry. While others again are the result of an individual IT company's product or method gaining sufficient market dominance to become the norm. In debate about the value and applicability of standards the word is sometimes used as a talisman, its presence apparently guaranteeing that a project is bound to succeed. This is of course very far from the truth. Some international standards are so arcane and complex that their implementation proves almost impossible. In such situations most IT developers, whose vision tends for the most part to be short-term, will take the most practical route to successful implementation, even where that means proprietary systems and closed architectures. The 'standards' which count most in such a situation are Quality Standards which primarily address the issues of effectiveness in meeting requirements and efficiency in terms of resource-usage. Two particular concepts which can assist here are 'fit for purpose' and 'future proof'.

It is as well to remember how very recent is the practical use of this technology within the Library and Information Science (LIS) community and that many of those people will still regard the large-scale application of this technology with suspicion. This is not, in our belief, simply technophobia. Despite the stereotyped image which persists in the public consciousness, the LIS community, as the opening paragraph has shown, has a long and robust tradition in the innovative use of technology to solve problems – often well in advance of the wider world. The real issue is 'the long haul'. Librarians and archivists, and particularly those responsible for large research collections, have a strong sense of professional responsibility for those colleagues and library users who will come after them. They aim to do everything which will maintain the collections, and make them more rather than less available in years to come. On occasions this has not always been to the benefit of succeeding generations, but as a whole the efforts of collection managers to tackle issues such as paper degradation, the use of high-quality microfilming and other conservation techniques have been successful and will continue to pay dividends in future. It is in that context that justifiable concerns are raised about the viability of digital materials in years to come.

Some steps are being taken by librarians and archivists in Europe and North America to address these issues and this is not before time. Even if material from existing collections was never to be digitised, the publishing world is gradually going digital, and this technology will inevitably intrude itself into research collections. In fact as the research world also begins to go digital the researchers will increasingly expect material to be accessible in this form, including existing material for which the surrogates of reproduction and photography are currently acceptable alternatives. This means that LIS professionals will have to become more deeply aware of the implications and functionality of the new digital and networking technologies, just as in the past they absorbed the chemistry of paper, the physics of photography and the data structures of MARC records. They have shown the ability to do so and should do it boldly, while retaining their professional caution intact! The British Library, in particular, is fortunate to have its own in-house computing staff, who understand the Library's business requirements, and can advise their colleagues from a position of knowledge. Not every institution has this possibility but it has to be recognised from the outset that digital information is inseparable from its IT environment and that representatives from the two disciplines need to work closely and continuously together if the material is to remain usefully available. Librarians and archivists need to think out clearly and deliberately the role of this new medium in their collections and make that very clear to their IT colleagues or suppliers.

Information technologists must understand that the material within the systems they are developing will last far longer than data in traditional business processing systems has been expected to survive. (Archivists would of course rightly argue that this in itself has been a mistaken attitude and will cause future grief when researchers come to try to analyse business developments from late 20th-century records.) The formats, structures and systems they implement must be adequately documented with clear forward-migration paths. Librarians and archivists need to plan how these new materials and new ways of delivery will fit into the existing collection management paradigm (for the bulk of existing material may never be digitised). They also need to be prepared for the inevitable cost and reorganisation of methods which these will bring.

If the combined talents of librarians and archivists and digital technology experts are successfully used to create changes in the use and handling of information, it will be partly because such resource issues create an inexorable pressure towards greater co-operation. Already, within the IfA programme, changes in the relationship between different types of professional expertise can be seen. These skills have to be more closely integrated, and this will change the relative roles of the professionals. In all the imaging projects, the skills of photographers and reprographic operators remain as important as ever. The photographer's understanding of lighting and colour is more vital than ever. However, as new types of light are used and primary materials are subjected to more demanding processes, the conservator has to work closely with the photographer. Moreover, the technical expert has to work with the photographer to help understand how the technology is treating the image – to what extent the use of different platforms will affect appearance, how different software packages may affect the lighting and colour value established by the photographer, or what type of control the software package allows over the image.

With a conventional photographic service, the external academic has a purely passive role. He or she is a consumer, and will passively pass on the images to those who consume his or her scholarship. With a digital image, the scholar will be seeking actively to explore or transform the image – to make faded sections more legible by changing brightness, contrast or colour, to juxtapose different parts of a volume, or to explore parts of the image under high magnification. The need might therefore be more than an accurate representation. The user might prefer a higher-resolution image whose colour does not reach the standards demanded by a professional photographer, or might prefer a brighter lighting which does not give such good colour. In short, the external scholar will cease to be merely a customer, but become actively engaged in the creation of the image.

Within all this, the role of the curator or librarian changes to become a catalyst in promoting this dialogue. Again, the role is more active than is implied in the common image of the keeper of the gateway. It is perhaps more that of the entrepreneur, who sees a match between issues presented by the collections for which he or she is responsible and the technical possibilities whose range and potential increase daily.

The IfA programme was perhaps the most exciting programme of investigation yet to occur in the Library. The enthusiasm which it generated from both the Library's staff and users was extraordinary. It is to be hoped that this book conveys something of this sense of excitement, of new vistas of activity opening up daily and a new sense emerging of what the Library can potentially become. It is also to be hoped that, as the Library moves towards the creation of a digital library, this sense of excitement will be retained.

# Digital Imaging

Images are generally seen by most people as at the heart of any digital library collection and were one of the most distinctive components of the *Initiatives For Access* programme. The projects in this section are indicative of the wide range of issues raised when digitising collections as diverse as those of The British Library. **Constructing Electronic Beowulf**, **Digitising the Gandharan Buddhist Scrolls**, and **The York Doomsday project** are case studies in the digitisation of original collection items using high-end digital photography; the first two exploring the technical and conservation issues associated with material of this type, and the last examining the issues which arise in building a primarily scholarly electronic archive. All three showed how effective the new technologies can be when allied with detailed scholarly research in exploring ancient materials. The scanning of the Gandhari fragments extended this approach to a completely different type of material but also illustrated the need for close collaboration with relevant scholars to obtain the best possible results.

Scanning of less conservationally sensitive material is illustrated by the **Image Demonstrator Project**, using the capture device most obviously associated with digitisation, the flatbed scanner. It showed that a number of difficult organisational issues need to be resolved if such an activity is to be undertaken in support of an operational document delivery service.

Microfilm has for many years been an effective access surrogate for many of the Library's materials. However, the quality of much early microfilming is now poor by contemporary standards and microfilm is a cumbersome medium for users. Unfortunately, much material which was subject to early microfilming is no longer in a condition to permit refilming. The **Digitisation of Microfilm** project has demonstrated very effectively that digitisation from existing microfilm can produce images of a satisfactory quality for the viewer without further interference with the original material.

Over time, any colour photographic image will fade, thus diminishing its value as a facsimile record. By digitising the photographic facsimile while it is still new, a more stable image can be retained for long-term use, without further damage to the original item. Such an approach is particularly apposite to exploitation of images of the Library's most famous volumes, and was explored in the **St Pancras Treasures** project.

**PIX project** (in this section) and **Project Digitise** (Document Management and Descriptive Data section) case studies address both data capture and data management and access. PIX project has served to highlight the very important place which photographic expertise has in enabling the capture of images at a quality appropriate for both the picture researcher and the general viewer. It also illustrates the need for good descriptions to accompany this material if it is to be assembled into an effective database retrieval system. PIX project used a variety of sources, primary and intermediate, with PhotoCD as a transfer and access medium. Project Digitise was not concerned with image capture, but can be seen as closely related to these projects, since it is in effect the PIX project realised in sound rather than in pictures. Just as PIX project took early photographic material such as sepia photographs and glass plates, and converted then to a digital form to facilitate their preservation, so Project Digitise took early recorded material, such as wax cylinder and tapes, and converted the information to digital form.

The various projects in the *Initiatives for Access* programme thus explored all the chief approaches currently available for image capture, and allowed a balanced appraisal of the issues associated with their use in a variety of different contexts. **Gallery applications and educational multimedia** illustrates the development issues which arise in using the digitised images in multimedia products: using digital images in innovative displays; making differing choices for differing purposes; and adding value through complex animation.

# Constructing Electronic Beowulf

**Andrew Prescott**

In 1992, Dr Andrew Prescott of The British Library's Manuscript Collections attended on the Library's behalf a conference at the University of Wisconsin in Madison to discuss a project to produce a microfiche edition of all surviving Old English manuscripts, the Anglo-Saxon Manuscripts in Microfiche project. This conference initiated a very successful project, which is in the process of producing not only inexpensive high-quality microfiche reproductions of the entire manuscript corpus of Old English but, just as importantly, is providing new and up-to-date descriptions of all these manuscripts. For all its virtues, this project may in future years come to be regarded as one of the last gasps of a microfilm technology which, since the Second World War, has served scholars very well in providing access to manuscripts and other rare source materials on a large scale, but which was always cumbersome to use, prone to deterioration and offered images which were a pale shadow of the original. The high-quality colour images which digital cameras can now produce will, once scholars become accustomed to their use, make them unwilling to settle for anything less (providing that libraries make reasonable charges for them).

Digital cameras offer colour images which show more clearly than microfilm or black and white facsimiles such key details as abbreviation and punctuation marks or erasures. The images will not degrade with use. Details can be magnified, and different parts of the manuscript (or different manuscripts) compared side by side on the screen. However, these advantages come at a cost. In particular, the large size of image files means that users require very powerful computers to access them, and storage and transfer of the files can be a difficult task. Already in 1992, some scholars were suggesting that the Anglo-Saxon Manuscripts in Microfiche series should be based on digital images rather than microfilm. The difficulties the editors of this series have encountered (and heroically overcome) in obtaining permissions from many different manuscript owners and arranging for their manuscripts to be filmed suggest that this is an unfair criticism. If the series had been burdened with the additional need to cope with the use of digital imaging techniques which are still in their infancy, it would never have achieved its primary aim of rapidly making available affordable and easily accessible reproductions of all Old English manuscripts. However, the microfiche project did, indirectly, give a great fillip to the use of digital technology in medieval studies in that the initial meeting in Madison proved to be the starting point of the Electronic Beowulf project.

At Madison, Dr Prescott met for the first time two of the world's most eminent Old English scholars, Professor Paul Szarmach and Professor Kevin Kiernan. Professor Kiernan is Professor of English at the University of Kentucky and is the leading expert on the history of the Beowulf manuscript, Cotton MS. Vitellius A.xv, one of The British Library's greatest treasures. He wrote a controversial study of the manuscript in 1981 which for the first time gave a detailed account of its history and proposed that the composition of the poem was contemporary with the manuscript (the prevailing view had been that the poem was considerably older than the manuscript). He also published the first full analysis of the important early transcripts of the manuscript by the Danish antiquary Thorkelin. Professor Szarmach was at that time at the State University of New York and the author of a number of important studies of Anglo-Saxon manuscripts. As the editor of the *Old English Newsletter*, he was renowned as one of the great academic entrepreneurs of Old English studies, a role which he has been able to extend considerably since his appointment in 1994 as the Director of the International Medieval Institute at Western Michigan University, Kalamazoo.

During the Madison conference, Professor Szarmach asked Prescott (during a conversation in the men's lavatory, of all places) how he felt The British Library would react to a proposal to digitise the Beowulf manuscript. Knowing that The British Library was starting to take an interest in investigating digital imaging, Prescott replied that he thought that the time was just right for such a proposal. Further discussions with Szarmach over a Thanksgiving Day lunch during a visit by him to London in 1992 gave added impetus to the proposal. The first action of Szarmach and Prescott was to get in further contact with Professor Kiernan by establishing an e-mail link from The British Library, at that time still an unusual facility in the British Museum building. At first, all this achieved was the circuitous relay of dramatic descriptions of winter weather in New York by Szarmach, but as it became possible to discuss the project in greater detail, it proved to have more exciting possibilities than at first realised.

The crux of Kiernan's 1981 book was that the Beowulf manuscript was more complex in character than might have been expected if it was assumed that the poem was transmitted by word of mouth and not written down until some time after its composition. He drew attention to one folio which he argued might have been a palimpsest folio – one in which the original text had been erased and replaced with something else. This suggestion was not well received by the scholarly community, but it is evident that something very strange has happened to the manuscript at this point. Kiernan suggested that digital image processing might reveal what was going on, and as early as 1984 had experimented with making videotapes of readings under particular lighting conditions to provide input to a medical imaging machine. Three years later, he invaded the Department of Manuscripts of The British Library with massive medical imaging equipment to see if this would assist in interpreting the manuscript. This experiment improved the legibility of some sections of the page and raised some doubts about accepted readings, but by no means resolved the problems raised by this folio. However, Kiernan was conscious that, as the technology improved, it might assist in investigating these numerous doubtful or uncertain points in the manuscript.

Moreover, these were not the only points at which it seemed that digital technology might assist in exploring the manuscript. The manuscript had been badly damaged in the fire which in 1731 ravaged the library formed by the 16th-century antiquary Sir Robert Cotton. Eighteenth-century conservation techniques had proved unequal to the task of stabilising the condition of the manuscript, and it was left unprotected for over 100 years. Following its transfer to the British Museum in 1753, use of the brittle and smoke-stained manuscript led to serious textual loss, with pieces probably being left on the Reading Room floor every time it was used. It was not until 1845, when the binder Henry Gough, working under the supervision of the Keeper of Manuscripts, Sir Frederic Madden, mounted each leaf of the manuscript in a protective paper frame, that the condition of the manuscript was stabilised. However, in order to have a retaining edge for the paper frame, Gough was forced to cover letters around the edge of the verso of each leaf, obscuring hundreds of letters from view. This may seem unfortunate, but at least these letters did not disappear in a dustpan, as would otherwise have happened.

This conservation strategy was triumphantly vindicated by Kiernan in 1984, when he showed that by using a powerful fibre-optic light, which would not harm the manuscript, the concealed letters could be deciphered. However, it was not possible to produce a facsimile of the hidden letters. In order to read the letter, it was necessary to hold the fibre-optic cable at an oblique angle, and the letter could quickly disappear from sight as the angle at which the cable was held changed. Kiernan guessed that, with a conventional camera, it would be impossible to know, by the time the shot had been taken and the film processed, if the elusive reading had been correctly captured. Subsequent tests showed that this was indeed the case and that these hidden letters could not be recorded with a conventional camera. Given the contentious nature of Beowulf studies, where discussions of single readings can generate great academic controversies, and bearing in mind that some of the hidden letters represented part of the only known record of some Old English words, the need to find a method of recording readings made with fibre-optic lights was pressing. Kiernan was anxious to see how far a digital camera could help.

The project was, then, quickly progressing beyond the simple production of straightforward electronic scans of the manuscript of the Beowulf poem itself, which was what Szarmach and Prescott had envisaged in their original discussion in the Madison lavatory, and which Prescott had, at one point, optimistically suggested would only take a few weeks to complete. In order to understand the context of the Beowulf section of the manuscript, it was clearly necessary to provide scans of the rest of the section of the manuscript in which it is contained, known as the Nowell Codex. It would also be worth exploring how far the concealed letters in the rest of the Nowell Codex could be recorded. Cotton MS Vitellius A.xv in fact consists of two separate and unrelated manuscripts, bound up together, probably by Sir Robert Cotton. The other manuscript in the volume is known as the Southwick Codex, and it would be helpful in conveying the full context of the Beowulf text to provide an electronic facsimile of the Southwick Codex as well.

Because of the fire damage to the Beowulf manuscript, transcripts and collations of the poem made in the 18th and early 19th centuries provide vital evidence of the text. The earliest sets of transcripts, dating from the 1780s, belonged to the Danish antiquary Grímur Jónsson Thorkelin, and are in the Royal Library, Copenhagen. The first, known as Thorkelin 'A', was made for Thorkelin by an English copyist who was not familiar with Old English script but made a brave attempt to reproduce the appearance of the letters in the manuscript. The second, Thorkelin 'B', is in Thorkelin's own hand. These transcripts record many words and letters which afterwards crumbled away. Thorkelin published the first edition of Beowulf in 1815. Two years later, John Conybeare made a detailed comparison of Thorkelin's text with the original manuscript, recording his findings in an interleaved copy of Thorkelin's edition, noting which letters had vanished in the time since Thorkelin looked at the manuscript. This, the first collation of Thorkelin's edition, was in the possession of Professor Whitney Bolton of Rutgers University. Professor Bolton kindly donated this fascinating volume to The British Library to facilitate its scanning, a generous gift for which The British Library would like to record its thanks. A more accurate collation of Thorkelin's edition with the manuscript was made in 1824 by Frederic Madden, afterwards Keeper of Manuscripts at the British Museum. Madden's collation, prefaced by an eerily realistic drawing of the first page of Beowulf, is now, with other annotated books and transcripts by him, in the Houghton Library at Harvard University.

The scope of the project, then, grew in the course of our initial discussions, from an electronic facsimile of one section of a manuscript into a collection of images of all the primary evidence for the Beowulf text. This implied not so much the production of an electronic edition as the creation of a digital archive recording the history of Beowulf. As this view of the project developed, it suggested a different approach to the electronic edition to that espoused by other kindred projects. In such well-known textual electronic editions as the Canterbury Tales Project and the Piers Plowman Project, conventional editions are being prepared in a SGML-tagged text. It is hoped in both cases to use computers to compare the different witnesses of the text in order to establish an authoritative original text, an ur-text – a very conservative view of the aim of the editorial text. In the case of the Beowulf project, the aim is not to arrive at a definitive text, but to expose the layers of evidence for the text, which are obscured in printed editions. The Electronic Beowulf in essence seeks to dissolve the text into its constituent parts. While the Canterbury Tales and Piers Plowman projects will include images of manuscripts, these are ancillary to the main purpose of both projects. By contrast, the Electronic Beowulf seeks to confront the user with the different types of evidence on which his understanding of the text depends, so that it is the images which are central to the project, not their interpretation into SGML-tagged text. One way of describing Electronic Beowulf might be as a diplomatic edition done with pictures instead of words, but even this does not convey the radical nature of the edition.

The Electronic Beowulf is therefore not simply an experiment in applying new technology to a famous manuscript. It represents a coherent and subversive challenge to the tradition of editing texts. In this respect, it reflects the views of Professor Kiernan as to the nature of the Beowulf text and draws together themes he has been developing in his work for nearly 20 years. Kiernan has not only provided the intellectual vision behind the project, but has also been the main driving force throughout and, above all, has undertaken an immensely complex editorial task in splicing the different images into a coherent whole. The project, however, has involved a much larger team of people both in America and England. Indeed, one of the most exciting aspects of the project has been this Anglo-American collaboration.

The British Library provided the equipment for image capture and the necessary technical, curatorial, photographic and conservation staff to supervise the scanning of the manuscripts. This was complemented by a similar investment by the University of Kentucky, which gave Kiernan access to its Convex mass-storage system to store the images, provided him with a powerful Hewlett Packard UNIX workstation to work on the image files, and also gave essential technical support. It was evident from the beginning of the project that The British Library would never be able to provide the curatorial resources to undertake detailed work on the images. Integral to the concept of the project from the beginning was therefore the assumption that external funding would be sought to provide Kiernan with time to put together the final product. This funding was provided by the Andrew W. Mellon Foundation which gave Kiernan a grant to release him from teaching duties for a year. The National Endowment for the Humanities also helped fund Professor Kiernan's costs for one major session of scanning under special lighting conditions. One of the chief lessons of the *Initiatives for Access* programme is that it will be difficult for libraries to find the extra staff resources to undertake projects using the new technologies. The Electronic Beowulf suggests that one way of avoiding this problem is collaboration with external partners. A collaborative approach is strewn with pitfalls. That it was successful in this case has been due to the enthusiasm and commitment to the project of both the partners on both sides of the Atlantic.

As a result of these preliminary discussions, it was possible to put a detailed proposal to The British Library's Digital and Network Services Steering Committee, which directed the *Initiatives for Access* programme, in the summer of 1993, and the committee agreed to provide initial funding for the project. It is interesting to note that the initial documentation for the project assumed a completion date of 1998. The CD-ROM is now scheduled for release in 1997, a year ahead of schedule. The Library funding allowed the appointment of John Bennett of Strategic Information Management to manage the purchase of equipment and establish the procedures for image capture.

### Choosing a digital camera

The most urgent question was selecting a suitable camera for use in the project. In general, the best route appeared to be a digital camera. Anything that involved direct contact of the scanning device with the manuscript was unacceptable on conservation grounds, which ruled out flatbed scanners. (It should be noted, however, that where photocopying of documents is permitted, as in large modern archives, there would be no objection to the use of flatbed scanners, and this would be a perfectly acceptable way of scanning large quantities of loose modern documents.) Scanning from photographic negatives might have been an acceptable way of proceeding if all that was envisaged was a simple digital facsimile of the manuscript, but such an approach would not have permitted the shots under special lighting conditions, such as the fibre-optic shots, envisaged in the project.

Moreover, the consensus among textual scholars who have worked with digital images is that direct scanning gives a more legible reproduction of the manuscript than any process involving a photographic intermediary. Peter Robinson, for example, in comparing images of the same manuscript, points out that such details as faint hairline abbreviations or damaged text appear more clearly on images made with a digital camera than on equivalent PhotoCD images: 'The detail, accuracy, and range of the colour [in the digital camera images] were such that in every case it was as if one were reading the manuscript itself, but the manuscript enlarged and printed on the computer screen.' By contrast, text that was readable in these images became unreadable on PhotoCD: 'The PhotoCD images also seemed flat, lacking in colour range and contrast... Overall, the effect of the PhotoCD images was that one was looking at a very good reproduction of the manuscript, equivalent to a good microfilm or a well printed facsimile'. Robinson ascribes the limitations of PhotoCD to the resolution limits of the Kodak scanner, so that it 'cannot give an image better than that provided by the best colour microfilm'. Against the better quality of the images produced by direct scanning, however, must be set the greater wear and tear on the original object produced by this process.

In early 1993, David Cooper and Peter Robinson of Oxford University arranged the demonstration in the Library of a high-resolution image capture system manufactured by a company called Primagraphics. This offered very high resolutions (in theory, up to 5000 x 7000 pixels), but the demonstration immediately showed that the colour quality was poor. Moreover, focusing of the camera was dependent on very cumbersome histogram adjustments and access to the images required expensive custom-made programs. At the same time, Professor Kiernan had made an investigation of the digital cameras available in the United States. A very successful demonstration had been arranged at Kentucky of the ProgRes 3012 camera manufactured by a German medical imaging company, Kontron, marketed in America by Roche, and Professor Kiernan set up a demonstration of this camera at The British Library. This camera produced a slightly smaller resolution than the Primagraphics system (3072 x 2320 pixels; an upgrade offering 4490 x 3480 pixels is now available) but produced full 24-bit colour. Moreover, the Kontron camera had a convenient real-time focusing facility similar to adjusting a conventional camera, with areas of over-exposure indicated on-screen. A feed was also provided to a black and white monitor which was of great assistance in setting up shots under special lighting conditions. The camera could be used under all the three main operating systems, PC, Mac and UNIX. The camera had been used in the remarkable VASARI project at the National Gallery, which had demonstrated the ability of digital images to provide a superior record to conventional photography of the condition of ancient artefacts. As a result of Kiernan's recommendation of this camera, it was not only used for the Electronic Beowulf project, but was discussed very favourably in Peter Robinson's guide to *The Digitization of Primary Textual Sources* (1992) and was purchased by the University of Oxford and the National Library of Scotland. It has also been the preferred camera of the ACCORD group in the United States, which has established a listserv discussion group devoted to issues associated with scanning manuscript materials using this camera.

### Digital photography, lighting and conservation

The technical features of the camera have been lucidly described by Peter Robinson in *The Digitization of Primary Textual Sources*, so the discussion here will concentrate on the practical lessons which have been learnt from its intensive use in the Beowulf project. An immediate issue was lighting. Flash lighting is usually preferred for manuscript photography, as it provides the best colours with minimum exposure of the manuscript to light and heat. Since the Kontron camera, when used on a Windows 3.1 platform, requires a 15-second scan in which the charge coupled device (CCD) arrays move physically down and across the image, flash lighting could not be used. The photographer assigned to the project, Annie Gilbert, recommended that fluorescent lighting would not produce good colours, so the decision was made to use two 2KW photoflood lights similar to those used for video filming. The use of such intensive light is obviously a major issue for the conservation of the manuscript. Exposure to light and heat (measured according to the international unit of lux) will accelerate the decay of a vellum manuscript. Not only will the light bleach the ink, but the vellum will visibly move in the heat of the light. When manuscripts are exhibited, the British standard (BS5454) and international convention require that a manuscript should not be exposed to more than 50 lux. The photofloods required for scanning with the Kontron camera produced thousands of lux.

A detailed analysis was made by the Library's conservation staff of the effect on the manuscript of exposure to light during the digitisation process. It should not be assumed that, simply because light levels are much higher than the 50 lux in the exhibition galleries, this will automatically damage the manuscript. After all, the ambient light in, say, the Library's Manuscripts reading room is about 500 lux, so that every time the manuscript is used by a reader, it is exposed to higher light levels. Moreover, since the issue is one of ageing over time, it is not light levels from a single exposure which are important – annual light exposure is a more important consideration. Display in the exhibition galleries subjects the manuscript to an annual light exposure of approximately 180,000 lux. It was calculated that, during the digitisation of the manuscript, the light exposure would be equivalent to five years' display in the gallery. However, since a photographic facsimile of the Nowell Codex has been available for some time, there has not been much photographic work on the manuscript in recent years, making the extra light exposure acceptable. Viewed from another angle, the scanning of the manuscript involved an exposure to light equivalent to about a year's continuous use in the higher light levels of the reading room. If, as is hoped, the provision of an electronic colour facsimile substantially reduces the frequency with which the original manuscript needs to be consulted by readers, then the digitisation process will have had no discernible effect on the overall life of the manuscript.

It will be evident from this discussion that the various factors that have to be taken into account in considering the effect of light exposure on the manuscript are very complex, and need to be considered on a case by case basis. Illuminated manuscripts are, for example, generally too delicate for scanning of this kind. Maps with wash colouring would also be prone to damage. This is a serious limitation, as these are categories of material for which digital images would be particularly useful. Because of these considerations, close conservation supervision of the process has been required throughout. We have been exceptionally fortunate, in that the supervising conservator, David French, has become deeply interested in the techniques of digital scanning, and has effectively provided the main technical support for the project. Nevertheless, the requirement for conservation control has helped make the scanning extremely labour-intensive, and conservation issues have limited the range of material which can be scanned with the camera.

Thus, the advice offered by Peter Robinson, 'one should digitize from the original object wherever possible', is simplistic in that it takes no account of the conservation issues involved in scanning the object. Ideally, one would want to use a different light source with the Kontron camera. The best possible arrangement, from a conservation point of view, would be to use a fluorescent light source, but the experience of Oxford University in using such a set-up has not been encouraging. The Oxford project for the scanning of early Welsh manuscripts found that, owing to the construction of the CCD, the use of cold lighting with the Kontron camera created a 'Newton's ring' effect, causing patterning on the image. The Oxford University team, led by David Cooper, were able to remove this pattern by post-processing of the image, but clearly this is unsatisfactory as a long-term solution to the problem. The Oxford project found that images comparable in quality (and indeed with the possibility of higher resolution) could be created with a digital back device, a scanner mounted on a conventional camera. Recent work by the Manuscripts Photographic Studio at The British Library has also shown that digital back devices work very well under such a light source. Currently, Kontron continue to recommend that fluorescent lights should not be used with the ProgRes camera, and this problem is likely to limit the usefulness of this camera for large-scale direct scanning.

Conservation issues of this kind are bound to continue to be a major determinant in developing projects involving direct scanning of manuscript materials. Although fluorescent light sources are generally described as 'cold', the powerful lights required for scanning still generate a great deal of ambient heat, and the length of time required for the scanning process means that the light exposures involved are still much higher than for conventional photography. Moreover, there is a risk that the development of the technology will create greater pressure to rescan the manuscript, not less. Every time a manuscript is rephotographed or rescanned, it is subjected to more light exposure and general wear and tear, shortening its overall life. Although a digital image (if properly stored and maintained) will not degrade like a conventional photographic negative, it is likely that in, say, four years' time a 400 dpi shot generated by a Kontron camera will look very crude by comparison with images produced by the latest generation of digital cameras. There will therefore be a demand to scan the manuscript again. Trying to balance conservation issues against a wish to provide the best possible surrogate images of a manuscript will be a major concern for the custodians of the manuscript.

Despite these conservation issues, the images produced by the Kontron camera throughout the project have been outstanding. The camera has been exceptionally reliable and versatile – the only piece of equipment at the London end of the project with which there have been no problems. The performance of the camera was particularly impressive for shots under special lighting conditions. Although for conservation reasons other devices might now be preferred to produce straightforward colour images of manuscripts, these have yet to be tested with the arduous work undertaken by the Kontron camera in the Beowulf project, and it seems likely that they will be too cumbersome to undertake this kind of highly specialised work.

It has been known for a long time that ultra-violet light enables erased or damaged text to be read. Indeed, among the first experiments in ultra-violet photography were attempts to read damaged portions of the Beowulf manuscript in the 1930s. Conventional ultra-violet photography characteristically requires very long exposure times, sometimes as long as 15 to 20 minutes. This is hazardous for both the manuscript and the operator. It was found that ultra-violet images could be made with the Kontron camera in the normal 15-second scan time. The camera needed to be recalibrated under ultra-violet light to take these shots, and fairly powerful ultra-violet light sources were required. Since the Kontron camera only takes colour images, the first results were little more than a murky blue patch, but when the contrast of these was adjusted and they were transferred to grey-scale, clear images of readings under ultra-violet light were obtained. Similarly, the camera is very useful for infra-red photography. Infra-red light is not very helpful with the Beowulf manuscript, but can be essential for other types of material. The Library possesses a collection of more than 4000 Greek ostraca (potsherds with writing on them), many of which can only be read under infra-red light. It was found in tests that the Kontron camera produced very clear images of these under infra-red light. The only complication in producing these shots was that the infra-red filter in the camera has to be removed.

Where the Kontron camera showed its greatest versatility was in taking images of the sections of vellum concealed beneath the paper frames protecting each folio, revealed by fibre optic lights positioned behind the frame. Considerable experimentation was required to arrive at the best procedure for taking these shots. Initially it was hoped that an A4 fibre-optic pad, laid underneath the folio, would reveal large areas of concealed text, but this light source was not sufficiently powerful. Eventually, it was found necessary to use two or more fibre optic cables clamped into position behind each letter or group of letters (fibre optic cables conduct the light from a remote light source, producing very intense light, but not creating any heat which would damage the manuscript, see Plate 1). The camera had to focus on a small area of very powerful light, but produced very readable images (see Plate 2). Subsequent image processing made the lost letters even more legible. Under the direction of Professor Kiernan, hundreds of such images have been shot, very demanding work as the light had to be set at a very precise angle to capture the hidden letters.

The acquisition by The British Library of a video-spectral comparator (VSC) in the 1970s, which enables manuscripts to be examined under a variety of precisely controlled light wavelengths, marked a break away from traditional manuscript conservation work, which focuses on the physical repair and preservation of manuscripts. For the first time, conservators started to become involved in using technical aids to recover further information about a manuscript which could not be seen with the naked eye. The use of the Kontron camera in the Beowulf project marks a further important step in the development of this activity. The project has barely begun to explore the possibilities of this technology. The Kontron camera can, for example, be mounted onto microscopes and magnifiers, which will enable very fine details of manuscripts to be recorded and investigated. This application of the camera has not so far been tested. At present, there is no means of mounting the Kontron camera on the VSC. A frame-grab facility has been installed on the Beowulf equipment, which allows digital images of readings obtained by the VSC to be made, but these are low-resolution, grey-scale images. A link between these two pieces of equipment which would allow high-resolution images to be taken under particular light settings would be a desirable next step in the development of the digital conservation studio which is gradually taking shape in the Library.

## Computer platforms and software

The Kontron camera operates on a PC, Mac or UNIX platform. It was decided to run the camera for the Beowulf project on a PC, running the latest version of Windows (3.1, and later 3.11). This was a purely pragmatic decision. Although it was recognised that UNIX and Mac offered a superior environment to the PC for the handling of images, Mac and UNIX support in the Library was very limited at the time that the project began, and it was felt that it would be difficult enough to learn to use a new camera without having to master a Mac or UNIX machine as well. In fact, despite the frustrations involved in the use of a different platform in London from those used in America, this was a worthwhile experiment, since the experience of regularly transferring images across from PC to Mac or UNIX gave a good insight into the perils of using different operating platforms.

The uncompressed TIFF produced by the camera operating at full resolution is 21 megabytes in size. This required the use of much larger PCs than were commonly available in 1993. Indeed, at that time the suppliers of the camera in Britain, Image Associates of Thame, did not often use the full resolution and were operating the camera on a 486 machine under 16 megabytes of RAM (upgraded to 32 megabytes for a demonstration in the Library). Initially, the PC purchased from Image Associates to run the camera was a 486 DX2/66, with an EISA bus board, with 96 megabytes of RAM, a 1-gigabyte hard disc and DAT drive. A 486 system was preferred as Pentium machines were then only just becoming available, and the suppliers were unable at that stage to confirm whether the camera would run on a Pentium machine. A Matrox 1-megabyte 1024 video card was used, with a 21-inch monitor. This PC was subsequently upgraded to a Pentium P60 (the first in The British Library) running a local VESA bus board, and the hard drives have been progressively upgraded to the present 5 gigabytes on the image capture machine (split 3, 2; the 3-gigabyte drive is further split 2, 1, because of the difficulty DOS has in addressing anything more than 2 gigabytes). Two similarly configured PCs were acquired for off-line processing, giving a further 10 gigabytes of local storage.

The camera ran initially on WinCam, a fairly simple proprietary image capture Windows programme supplied by Kontron, running on a 16-bit pri-at card. The image-handling software available for the PC at the beginning of the project was very limited. Halo Desktop Imager was initially used, at the recommendation of Image Associates, because it could load the full TIFF and was less memory-intensive than other image-handling packages available at that time. Adobe's Photoshop was released for the PC shortly after the project began and is now the standard tool within the project for handling images. During 1995, Kontron produced a plug-in allowing images to be captured from within Photoshop. This ostensibly gives much more sophisticated control over the images than WinCam, but problems have been found with the colour of images made using this plug-in. It is to be hoped that the plug-in announced by Kontron for Photoshop 4.00 will prove more reliable.

Broadly, the PCs were satisfactory for simple capture and viewing of images, but unsuitable for quality control and image manipulation. The DOS/Windows architecture does not address all the RAM available in the system, and this makes the performance slow and prone to locking when processor-intensive operations like rotation or the display of a number of different images are involved. The large hard discs were also initially physically unreliable and prone to failure. The most spectacular hard disc problem was probably a complete failure during the first visit of a journalist to the project in early 1994. The off-line machines have recently been upgraded to an NT4 server workstation and client, and the improvement of performance was immediately evident. By contrast, the HP UNIX workstation at the University of Kentucky, with 128 megabytes of RAM, 5 gigabytes of local storage and Ethernet access to a large scale Convex storage system, has proved extremely stable and reliable in its handling of large image files, as have the various powerful Macs used there.

More serious have been the problems in colour. Since Windows 3.11 is not a 32-bit operating system, it does not display the full 24 bits of the colour images. Although it was found the local PCs could be successfully calibrated to match the colours of the manuscript, these were displayed differently when transferred to the UNIX and Mac machines at Kentucky. By trial and error, a calibration was found which gave the best results at Kentucky. However, it was clearly unsatisfactory from the point of view of quality control that the operators in London could not be exactly sure how the images would appear when viewed in America. It is hoped that the implementation of an NT4 platform for image capture in London will eventually resolve this problem.

The contrast in display of the images between the PCs in London and the UNIX or Mac machines in Kentucky has been dramatic. The images look good when seen on the PC in London, but viewed on the UNIX machine in Kentucky, they look majestic. The difference between PC and Mac has also been evident in presentations of the project, where the superiority of the Mac images in presentations prepared at Kentucky over the PC images from presentations prepared in London has been (embarrassingly for the London representative) obvious. In general, the feeling of The British Library team involved in the project is that if there is one change they would have made in the way the project was organised, it is that they should have come to grips with using a Mac or UNIX machine to run the camera in London.

### Data storage and transfer

The other major technical issue has been the storage of the large quantities of data produced by the project. The scan time of the camera working on a Pentium machine under Windows 3.1 is about 15 seconds (this is reduced when Windows NT4 or Windows 95 is used). This means that the speed of scanning can potentially rival microfilm, but something has to be done with the data – over 2 gigabytes can easily be produced in a normal working day. The Library does not possess a large-scale storage system for data, and some kind of local storage capable of dealing with these gigabytes of data (and, even, new words encountered early on in the project, terabytes and petabytes). This was a problem encountered by all the *Initiatives for Access* imaging projects, but an additional problem faced by the Beowulf project was that it was necessary to transfer all this data to Kentucky for Professor Kiernan to work on it. Kentucky could store the data on its Convex system, but somehow the data had to be got there.

Initially, it was felt that the best solution was to copy the images onto 120-megabyte magneto-optical discs and gradually transfer them to a machine which could be used to check the quality of the images and, when sufficient data had been accrued, back them up onto DAT tape. DAT offers large amounts of storage very cheaply – in 1993, 2 gigabytes for less than 20 pounds. However, the process of copying the images onto optical disc was tiresome – every time six images had been shot, it was necessary to stop work and wait for half an hour while the images were copied. Moreover, the optical drive proved extremely unreliable. Experiences with the DAT tapes were equally unsatisfactory. The back-up procedure was extremely time-consuming. It could take three times as long to back up the images as to shoot them. DAT proved very unreliable as a long-term storage medium. The cartridges needed checking every six months, a very time-consuming process, and it was often found that they had failed. DAT proved equally troublesome as a means of transfer to America. The proprietary DOS software used in The British Library could not be run on the UNIX machines in America. Although a utility enabling the PC to create UNIX tar back-up files eventually made the transfer easier, it had to be admitted that the cheapness of the DAT was a false economy. The length of time spent in maintaining and recovering data from the DAT wiped out the savings achieved through the cheapness of the tape.

It was observed during a discussion of a presentation of the project in 1994 that these problems were not so much ones of storage as of bandwidth, and indeed they eased as the capacity of the networks improved. The University of London Computing Centre (ULCC) was at that time investigating the development of a national data archive based on a Convex Emass tower. They suggested that this might provide a suitable home for the British copy of the Beowulf data, and the existing data was transferred on DAT tape to the ULCC archive. As the high-speed SuperJANET link became available, it was possible to transfer image files across the network directly to ULCC. At first, attempts to transfer images across the network to Kentucky proved very frustrating as the images took an extremely long time to be transmitted across the small-capacity lines then available, frequently triggering time-outs in the file transfer protocol (FTP) software, which cut off the transfer before it was completed. A programme called 'split' was developed in Kentucky to break down the files into small components which could then be transferred, but such an elaborate procedure was only suitable for small numbers of files. As transatlantic network capacity has increased, however, it has finally proved possible to transfer images by FTP from ULCC to Kentucky, and this is currently the normal method of transfer.

Network links are still, however, not as reliable or as speedy as one would like, and, while in theory they provide the simplest link, in practice other methods might yet prove to be more efficient. One obvious procedure would be to link a CD-writer to the PC operating the camera and transfer images by CD-ROM. The project has not yet had access to a CD-writer in London to investigate this, but experiences with the *York Doomsday* Project in Lancaster suggest that this may be an efficient approach. The images made with the Kontron camera for this project have been stored at ULCC then transferred via SuperJANET to Lancaster, where they have been placed on CD. This is a time-consuming process, and by no means yet entirely reliable, but nevertheless over 20 gigabytes of data have been stored on CD in this way. The directors of this project can now sit at home in Lancaster and access quickly from CD colour images of whole manuscripts in the Library's collection – a heady experience when it is confronted for the first time, and perhaps the most dramatic illustration of what the *Initiatives for Access* programme was intended to achieve. The likely increase in CD capacity in the near future (to perhaps as much as 6 gigabytes) and the availability of cheaper and easier-to-use external hard drive devices may make direct physical transfer of images in this way of greater importance in the short term than network transfer.

## Making the digital archive usable
Knitting together the many different layers of the Electronic Beowulf proved to

be a further difficult problem. The idea was to give the user hyperlinks between each different level of the images. The user would be able to click on the appropriate part of an image of a folio from the original manuscript and be able to see hidden letters and ultra-violet readings in their appropriate place. With a further click, he or she would be able to call up images of the relevant sections of the Thorkelin transcripts or Conybeare or Madden collations. We were anxious that the package would be available for UNIX, Mac and PC platforms. A UNIX programme which provided hyperlinks between all the different types of images was developed in Kentucky. A Mac programme, called MacBeowulf, was also developed under Professor Kiernan's supervision, which he successfully demonstrated to the International Medieval Congress at Kalamazoo in 1995. However, development of a PC version proved very difficult because of the variety of types of PC available, and Kiernan despaired of ever being able to produce a workable interface for PC users. Moreover, it was not clear how this software would be supported. Worst of all, it seemed likely that the editorial work would have to be done three times over, once for each version of the CD.

While the issues associated with this development work were being investigated, the network browsers had made great strides forward. Netscape version 2.0 for the first time offered the ability to display frames containing different images side by side, precisely how we wanted to display the Beowulf materials. With Netscape 3.0 came the Java programming language, which allowed tools to be developed which would help the user of the images, such as a tool for zooming in on different parts of the manuscript. Brooding on the problems of providing a user interface for Beowulf while he was on holiday in South Carolina, Kiernan suddenly realised that the network browsers in fact offered all the necessary functionality. The only problem was that the networks did not have the capacity to handle very smoothly the large image files, even when in a compressed JPEG format. In fact, even though the image files will be distributed as JPEGs, it will be difficult to fit them all on two CDs. However, the network browsers not only read networked files but also files held on a local disc. So the final CD-ROM will use Netscape 3.0 as a front end to read HTML files and images held on a local CD – the kind of hybrid approach which is likely to be increasingly common until network capacities are substantially increased. This offers a number of advantages. The materials on the CD-ROM will essentially be independent of the software. It will also be very simple to make the package available on the Internet when network speeds improve. The CD-ROM is currently scheduled for publication in 1997.

Of course, this by no means exhausts all the problems we have had to confront in creating the Electronic Beowulf. To obtain images of the Thorkelin transcripts in Copenhagen and the Madden collation in Harvard, we had to transport the camera, PC and other equipment to Denmark and America, a considerable logistical exercise, comparable to arranging a film shoot. Assistance in undertaking this shoot was generously given by the University of Kansas and Harvard University. When shooting was ready to begin in Copenhagen, the large photoflood lights blew out the electrical circuits of the Royal Library three

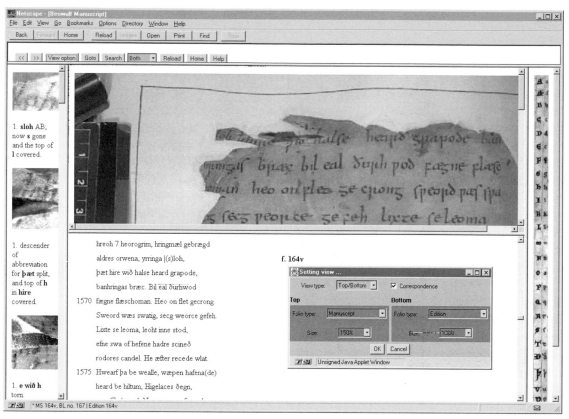

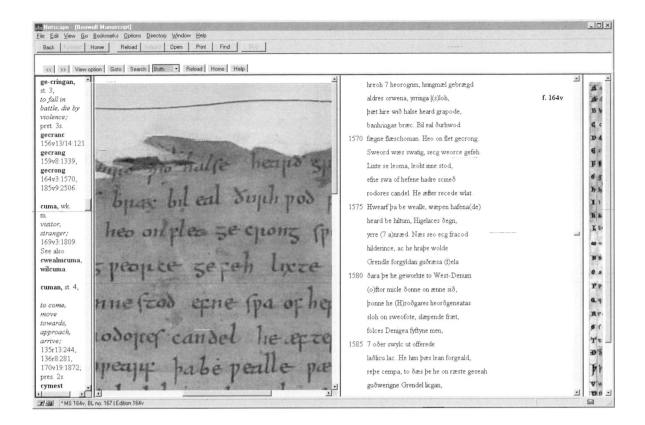

**Opposite top:** Prototype CD-ROM of Electronic Beowulf, showing how the Netscape interface allows the letters 'hidden' by the paper inlay, which have been recorded using the digital camera and fibre optic light, to be displayed to the left of the relevant image from the Beowulf manuscript itself.

**Opposite below:** The original intention was to include a full SGML edition of the text of Beowulf in the package, but the limitations of existing browsers meant that the decision was made to develop a customised search engine working with an HTML text. This search engine was implemented using Java. This image shows a prototype of the search engine in use.

**Above:** In this screen from the prototype CD ROM of Beowulf shows how a specially compiled glossary can be used with images of the manuscript.

**Right:** This is the 'home page' of the Electronic Beowulf CD ROM, which uses an image of the cover of the original manuscript.

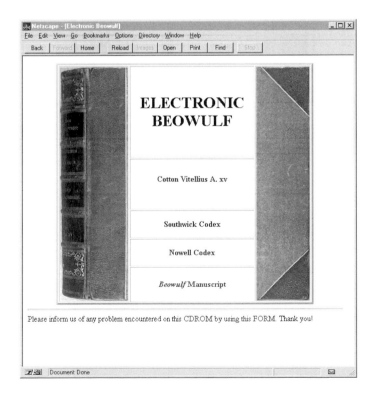

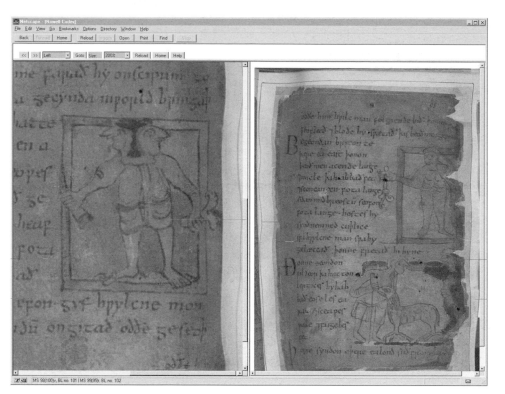

The Java tools implemented in the Electronic Beowulf CD ROM allow images to be magnified and compared in different ways. This example shows two images from the Wonders of The East section of the manuscript magnified and displayed side by side.

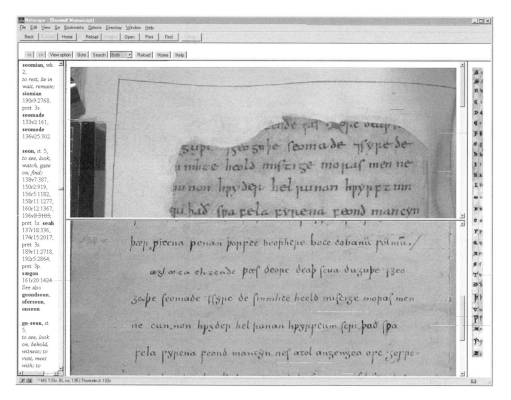

In this example, the original manuscript is being compared with the 'Thorkelin A' transcript, while the glossary is being consulted.

The package will also include images of two collations of Thorkelin's first edition of the poem with the original manuscript. Users can check these collations afresh against images of the original manuscript. Here, the manuscript is displayed with Sir Frederic Madden's collation, now at the Houghton Library.

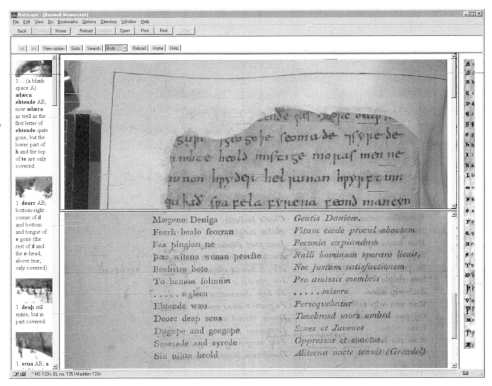

In this example, the manuscript is being compared with John Conybeare's collation.

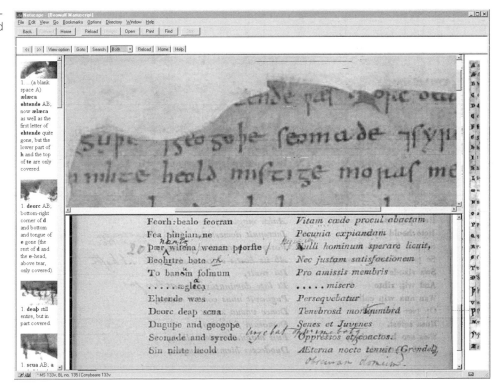

times. The demands of finally working all the digital materials into a publishable form have been immense. The lot of the editor is made much harder by the new media. These responsibilities have been borne by Professor Kiernan, who has had to sort, rotate and crop hundreds of images. He has had to prepare thousands of complex HTML documents linking together the images and associated scholarly apparatus. He has been valiantly assisted in this huge task by his pupil, Danette Shupe, and by other members of the University of Kentucky. The compilation of the glossary, which will be an important feature of the package, has been the work of Michael Ellis.

It will be evident from this discussion that the digital path is by no means a simple one. There sometimes seems to be a confident assumption, almost Whiggish in its optimistic expectation of the inexorability of technical progress, that the kinds of issues described here will vanish as computers increase in power and programs become more sophisticated. Some will certainly disappear as the technology improves and we become more proficient in the use of it. Some difficulties have indeed eased in the course of the project. At the beginning of the project, it was a major exercise to move a 21-megabyte file outside a British Library building, which ran the risk of wrecking e-mail systems and crashing online systems. Now we make such transfers routinely. Other problems, such as the conservation issues involved in direct scanning or the inherent additional cost of backing up data, may not vanish so easily. The concept of the *Initiatives for Access* programme is that the new technologies will make the Library's collections easier for remote users to consult. In its experimental stage, this is not necessarily a valid assumption – if all we had wanted to do was to make colour images of the Beowulf manuscript more easily available, it would have been simpler and cheaper to have published a conventional colour facsimile. The extra cost of using digital technology is only justifiable because it enables us to see the great textual universe contained in a library such as The British Library in new ways. Thus, the Electronic Beowulf does not simply present us with colour images of the manuscript but reveals features of the manuscript which cannot be recorded in any other way and draws together widely dispersed information about the history of the manuscript. In short, the Electronic Beowulf contains information of solid research value which could only have been assembled by the use of digital technology. For the humanities scholar, digital technology is interesting not simply because it potentially offers easier access to source materials but also because it provides a wholly new research tool and produces results which are almost priceless in their value. There is a terrible risk that as digital libraries enter a phase of commercial development this will be lost sight of. The only way of ensuring that the kind of research-orientated approach which the Electronic Beowulf has pioneered continues and develops is to maintain and build on the close co-operation between scholar, curator, conservator, photographer and technical expert which has provided the basis of the success of the Electronic Beowulf.

Further information on the history of the Beowulf manuscript and the restoration of the Cotton library can be found in the following:

W. F. Bolton, 'The Coneybeare Copy of Thorkelin', *English Studies* 55 (1974), 97-107

K. Kiernan, *Beowulf and the Beowulf Manuscript* (2nd ed., Ann Arbor: University of Michigan Press, 1996)

K. Kiernan, 'The Thorkelin Transcripts of Beowulf', *Anglistica* 35 (Copenhagen: Rosenkilde and Bagger, 1986)

K. Kiernan, 'The Coneybeare-Madden Collation of Thorkelin's Beowulf' *in* P. Pulsiano and E. Treharne, eds., *Anglo-Saxon Manuscripts and their Heritage* (Aldershot: Scolar Press, 1997)

K. Kiernan, 'Alfred the Great's Burnt Boethius' *in* G. Borstein and T. Tinkle, *The Iconic Page in Manuscript, Print, and Digital Culture* (Ann Arbor: University of Michigan Press, forthcoming)

A Prescott, '"Their Present Miserable State of Cremation": The Restoration of the Cotton Library' *in* C. J. Wright, ed., *Sir Robert Cotton as Collector: Essays in an Early Stuart Courtier and his Legacy* (London: The British Library, 1997), 391-454

A. Prescott, 'The Ghost of Asser' *in* Pulsiano and Treharne, op.cit., 259-95

# The York Doomsday Project

**Meg Twycross, Pamela King and Andrew Prescott**

### Multimedia and medieval drama

One of the striking features of the *Initiatives for Access* programme was the prominence assumed by The British Library's medieval collections. It is understandable that great masterpieces of late medieval art such as the Sforza Hours should be prime candidates for digitisation. More surprising is the way in which textual manuscripts, such as the Beowulf manuscript, have also been a focus of the Library's initial digital experiments. This is partly because medievalists have always been particularly anxious to stress the appearance and characteristics of their original source materials. It is also because digital technology enables the different types of evidence used by medievalists to be integrated and juxtaposed in ways that are not feasible with analogue technology. (See Plate 3.)

The possibilities of multimedia are particularly exciting to specialists in medieval theatre. The teaching of this subject has always been essentially multimedia, drawing heavily on all the resources of audio-visual support units – often weighing teachers down physically with large equipment. Now at least they have the possibility of involvement with only one large and temperamental piece of hardware. But the real excitement lies in the potential of multimedia to present the source material for medieval drama in completely new ways.

Mystery plays, telling the story of the world from Creation to Doomsday, were one of the prevalent dramatic forms of late medieval England. Their performance on pageant wagons, sponsored by the trade and craft guilds in cities, was an adjunct to the great late medieval feast of Corpus Christi. The Mercers' play of Doomsday was the spectacular finale to the York Cycle and the materials used in the performance are recorded in a surviving indenture from 1433. On the basis of information in the indenture and the play, attempts have been made to reconstruct the physical circumstances of performance. Multimedia allows modern scholars to place the reconstructed pageant wagon alongside the indenture and the play text so that the reconstruction can be assessed. Moreover, the indenture can be placed in a wider context, alongside the Hull customs accounts, for example, which clarify the trading activities of the guild. As well as allowing for the easy comparison of pictorial and written material, through a multimedia package different aspects of the play can be explored: the route of the pageant wagons can be mapped out on the city streets; video of a modern performance can be added to the package; and the iconography of the play can be explored in sources ranging from wallpaintings to prints.

Possibilities such as these prompted Professor Meg Twycross of the University of Lancaster to propose in 1992 the creation of an electronic teaching package of the Doomsday play. In 1993-4, Joanne Lomax, a pupil of Professor

Twycross, prepared an M.A. dissertation on the *York Doomsday* play, written in Asymetrix Toolbook. This brilliantly demonstrated the potential of simple multimedia techniques to give a completely new perspective to the study of medieval drama. However, the preparation of this project also showed that active co-operation of librarians, archivists and museum curators was needed to obtain good-quality images and that a better technical infrastructure than that commonly available to humanities scholars was required to achieve the full potential of this approach. A presentation of the thesis to Andrew Prescott of The British Library encouraged him to see how far the Library could help achieve the grander vision, leading to the establishment of a full-scale project, the *York Doomsday* Project.

The aim of the *York Doomsday* Project, which began in 1996, is to bring the resources of recent advances in multimedia computer technology to the development of new directions in interdisciplinary research and teaching on the English mystery plays. The project is a co-operative venture directed by Meg Twycross at Lancaster University and Pamela King at the University College of St Martin, also in Lancaster. The chief British Library contacts for the project have been Andrew Prescott, David French and Joanne Lomax (who joined the Library on a temporary contract to help further the Project). The British Academy has provided major research funding for the Project's first year of operation, which has enabled the directors to visit their chief sources of materials and to employ Paul Williams as Project Officer to design and set up storage and transcription facilities for the Project's archive. Olga Horner has since joined the team as Project Associate, assisting in the search for and description of sources.

**The multimedia book and the digital archive**
The potential of the multimedia book (published on disc or CD-ROM) for making rare artefacts and documents accessible to a larger audience has already been widely recognised. Broadly speaking, currently available products all exploit the fundamental properties of multimedia that allow for text, image, sound and moving image to be integrated on screen, and of hypertext that allow the reader certain freedoms in choosing his or her own pathway through the material so that the forming of a book's many possible narratives becomes a collaboration between author and reader in which the reader takes the initiative. Conventional libraries in higher and further education are being supplemented with 'resource centres' holding machine-readable books and study-aids. This is seen by some as a necessary evil, a way of managing the move to mass higher education on the cheap, but for the less cynical it recognises the potential of electronic media as well as capitalising on the technological skills which are fast becoming commonplace in the modern school-leaver. We intend producing customised electronic packages as one of the spin-offs of the project. We are also under way with the first electronic facsimile of a medieval theatre script, the surviving Coventry pageants, edited by Pamela King. However, the *York Doomsday* Project is not simply writing a multimedia book on CD-ROM about mystery plays, but is using information technology as a powerful research tool in data assembly, ordering and interrogation. A key

stage of conventional academic research in many humanities disciplines has usually been the visit to the archive or library and the lengthy transcription of selected 'primary' sources. The *York Doomsday* Project is exploring ways in which new technology can change this process. The first phase of this is the formation of a machine-readable archive. The procedure for assembling the archive is relatively simple. Images are taken using The British Library's Kontron ProgRes 3012 camera, are copied by file transfer to the Library's digital store at the University of London Computing Centre (ULCC), then transferred across SuperJanet to Lancaster, where they are copied to CD-ROM. Copies of the archive are therefore held by The British Library on the ULCC server and by the Project directors on CD-ROM at the University of Lancaster. Direct scanning of manuscripts has been preferred wherever possible (conservation considerations mean that illuminated and illustrated manuscripts have been scanned from photographic transparencies). Our experience has confirmed that direct scanning in 24-bit colour gives a better record of such critical details as punctuation and hair-line abbreviations in the original manuscript. We have also found that, for the same reasons, it is essential while preparing presentations based on the archive to have access to the original uncompressed TIFF files. Inevitably, the apparently straightforward process of creating the archive has not been as smooth as might be expected – images taken by the Library on a Windows 3.11 platform sometimes look different when viewed at Lancaster on Windows 95, there are delays in obtaining essential bulbs and fuses, hard discs have failed, or network connections have sometimes been inexplicably slow. Nevertheless, already images amounting to about 20 GB or the equivalent of 35 CDs have been assembled from The British Library alone, making the Doomsday archive already one of the largest electronic archives in Britain.

This archive, like any conventional physical assemblage of materials around a particular theme or topic, is not designed for publication in its entirety. Quite apart from the problems posed by copyright and control that publication or any other form of open access would create, the archive will be so huge that it will require a very powerful search-engine to manipulate it. It is, therefore, unlikely that many individuals or institutions would have either the technical means or the necessary storage space for it. In any case, it is extremely unlikely that anyone would want it all. Access to it will necessarily be restricted to the members of the Project, therefore, although the owners of the originals of its parts will be given machine-readable full-size file copies of the relevant parts on CD-ROM.

The purpose of the archive in this phase is not, therefore, general access, but the creation of a databank of conservation facsimiles of the highest quality currently attainable. The electronic medium in which the facsimiles are stored renders them less vulnerable to natural disaster than their physical originals – some of the most important York city records have already suffered damage as a result of floods in the city, and the creation of electronic surrogates will be a safeguard against further loss. Another advantage intrinsic to the medium is that an electronic archive has the capacity to be 'intelligent', that is, able to be searched and interrogated in new ways. For example, shapes can be matched to assist the palaeographer or iconographer. More conventionally, all text sources will be stored with transcriptions which will be machine encoded using SGML to create a complementary bank of electronic diplomatic editions. The archive is, then, the ultimate in resources facilitating a variety of research outputs in later phases of the Project.

The rationale behind the selection of materials that form the archive is primarily to assemble a complete spectrum of evidence to the material culture of the York play of *Doomsday*. It is intended that the treatment of the *Doomsday* play will also form a framing shell for equivalent collections relating to the York Cycle as a whole. The selection, therefore, falls somewhere between capturing all surviving evidence of life in 15th-century York and the more selective approach represented by the Records of Early English Drama project which during the 1970s sought to assemble a collection of specific references to drama in medieval records. The *York Doomsday* Project is assembling a variety of witnesses to the social and economic milieux in which the plays throve, a variety of texts and images that illustrate the devotional context in the north of England in the same period, as well as pan-European intellectual, iconographic, literary and theatrical materials which supply a wider aesthetic context.

For example, from the resources of The British Library alone, the Project has not only been able to commission scans of the entire York Register (Additional MS 35290, the 'script' of the York Corpus Christi play, a register against which the performance was checked to ensure that each guild had done its part), but has also obtained images of the records of a number of York guilds, such as the Corpus Christi Guild, the Bakers' Guild and selections from the Guild of Barber Surgeons' Book. Service books of late medieval York use are being scanned as well as Yorkshire manuscripts of such 15th-century English devotional texts as The Prick of Conscience, The Lay Folks' Catechism, and Cursor Mundi. The archive also includes images from the celebrated Additional MS 37049, a 15th-century devotional miscellany compiled by a Yorkshire Carthusian house, which is enlivened by cartoon-like drawings whose vigorous style and iconography provide an insight into the visual culture of the mystery plays. To these have been added selected examples of northern European illuminated manuscripts illustrating the evolution of the iconography of Doomsday. Plans are far advanced to add to this collection from the sources available in York itself, as well as in Oxford, Cambridge, Glasgow and York's trading partners in the Low Countries. To the literary, devotional and iconographic materials assembled so far will thus be added the wider documentation of civic life in late medieval York, from council memoranda, guild accounts and indentures, to the wills and inventories of individuals associated with the play, and records of the goods which they imported, exported, owned and handled as part of their daily life.

## Exploring the torus

The Project has already given rise to a number of research spin-offs, to be published in the short and longer term. For example, exploring the Freemen's Register and the shipping accounts of York Mercers through Hull has led us to adjust our view of the number of alien merchants who were integrated into

York society, and the number of York merchants who spent much of their careers living abroad. The exploration of mercantile devotional tastes has led to a review of the date, ownership and provenance of York's most famous lay book of hours, the so-called Bolton Hours (York Minster Library, Additional MS 2). Items in the 1433 York Mercers' indenture have taken on new significance in the light of a closer exploration of the Hull custom accounts. Comparison of hands across a number of York-produced mid 15th-century manuscripts has brought us closer to knowing who wrote down what in the city, and given us a sense of how the process of recording city business was managed, who was content to muddle along, and who was a new broom – and incidentally told us which of the late 15th-century civic officials could write their own names.

It should be emphasised that research findings are not incidental to the Project: the processes by which materials are selected, included and catalogued are a research project in their own right, and recognised as such by the British Academy for this initial year's funding. We did, of course, have a firm idea when we embarked of primary categories of material to be included, but to have circumscribed the archive at that stage would have been bad historical practice. Three neutral parameters – geography, chronology and subject matter – set the criteria of relevance, but the process of drawing boundaries is endlessly recursive as we visit and revisit materials in an evolving context. The focus of our research lies, therefore, in a process of constant re-negotiation of the criteria for inclusion. As the archive expands, huge but imperfect amounts of raw data configure themselves to form new arguments for the relevance and significance of individual items.

It is for these reasons that we feel that a research enterprise such as the *York Doomsday* Project works best with a small executive team with a comprehensive supporting panel of expert consultants, as the development of the archive is a rolling process which evolves as data is examined, discussed, selected and stored. In this way, the Project differs significantly from previous projects in humanities computing, such as the Sheffield-based Canterbury Tales Project, where the raw material is self-defining so the various processing activities may be safely and efficiently farmed out to a number of individual scholars working in a large team, or as in products of the giant Teaching and Learning Technology Programme.

So, although the directors of *York Doomsday* Project began with a shopping list of items for probable inclusion, this was essentially provisional. What underpins the Project more securely is a theoretical concept of the shape of the archive which has been in place from the beginning. Initially this was conceived as a simple ring-doughnut, where the hole in the middle was the original sequence of irrecoverable unique performances in the streets of York, and the ring was made up of different types of indirect witness listed above, including the register of the play which was not privileged over any other record. As the archive has progressed, the principle of that ring has survived, but in the more geometrically sophisticated form of the torus, a three-dimensional object amorphous in all respects except that somewhere there is a hole through it. Thus, just as all tori share certain topological properties, so too, although the selection of materials for inclusion in the archive is constantly being modified, conceptually it remains fixed.

Nor does each item in the body of our conceptual torus justify its inclusion because of a simple relationship to the hole in the middle, the play itself. Each small part of the archive is potentially linked to a number of other pieces of information. Thus the body of the torus is made up of items that can be inter-linked using hypermedia with one another to explicate both one another and the play. The possible links are always multiple and dependent upon the point of view from which they are encountered. In practical terms what this means is that no single homogeneous reading of the play is imposed on the material. Nor is there a single fixed evolutionary narrative, as the archive can be sliced chronologically and the evidence assembled, for example, for any given decade in the history of the play's performance. With the electronic medium we can also create links between, and facilitate comparison of, physically remote materials for many purposes, for example palaeography. Individual items can be pulled up on screen side by side, or even overlaid upon each other.

The distinction between text and image, and between script and records, which conventional print collections impose, is broken down by the electronic medium in which the archive is being assembled, as every item is preserved as a facsimile artefact. The physical appearance of each item in the archive is then part of the evidence it offers. Hence the Mercers' 1433 indenture, for instance, becomes less a transparent list of now missing objects relating to the perfor-mance of *Doomsday*, but is itself an object which conforms to a particular shape, has a particular status, and has its own physical history, having passed through a number of identifiable, and not yet identifiable, hands. The archive throws us into the world of manuscript studies, and wider areas of conserva-tion archaeology, as the technology which is being used to capture the images foregrounds old texts and images as artefacts in a way which nothing but han-dling the originals can. The unadulterated images of real objects can be repro-duced in such high resolution that it becomes possible to distinguish the hair from the flesh side of a manuscript. Then the pages of that manuscript can be viewed in close-up, or can be turned in a simulation of their three-dimensional reality. Moreover, the circumstances in which the scans are made allow for the use of sophisticated lighting techniques that have already recuperated lost let-ters from the margins of the Beowulf manuscript. This is particularly useful for materials which have suffered wear and tear, for example the 1415 Ordo Pagi-narum, a key document in one of the York civic records, some parts of which are now virtually illegible with the naked eye.

The same technology also allows for the integration of video and sound material into the archive. Hence records of actual reconstructions of those irre-trievable original performances can be linked to the evidence upon which they were based. Materials relating to the ground-breaking production of the cycle for the Festival of Britain in 1951, including lantern slides and unique sound recordings, form part of the E. Martin Browne archive, which is the property of the journal *Medieval English Theatre*, and can now be digitised. Video footage of the 1988 Joculatores Lancastrienses production of *Doomsday* in York will be incorporated also. Beyond that still, the pageant-route through the streets of 15th-century York can be reconstructed in three dimensions using the techniques of virtual reality so that the geographical and topographical locations of the original performance become a readable text, extending the experience of the 1988 and 1992 productions, when our ideas of how the play might have exploited its setting were revolutionised. In this way, using photographs of surviving buildings interspersed with grid outlines of now missing ones, the viewer will be able to move with a wagon along the known pageant route. And objects known to have been involved in performance, from pageant-wagon to stage property, can also be speculatively reconstructed and stored as a different type of readable text.

### Fakes and their dangers

As we move from the actual to the reconstruction, all of which can be included in a collection that is not subject to the usual hierarchies of information, we move into what are probably the most controversial, if the most technologically exciting, aspects of the Project. Everything in the archive is really just a string of machine codes that can realise a temporary two-dimensional image on screen. In such an environment where damaged texts can be invisibly mended and the circumstances of actual performance replicated, a decorum for signalling fakes has to be carefully observed. There is a line that can be crossed in manipulating images in this way, whereby it is possible to 'improve' on the original, by increasing the contrast between darkened vellum and faded ink, by restoring old paste-downs to their original position, or by 'tidying up' a particularly crabbed hand. Some of these techniques have no place in an archive such as this; other aspects of image manipulation, which involve speculative reconstruction, however well-founded, must always be scrupulously and prominently recorded. Where image manipulation improves the legibility of a manuscript, the tidied-up version can be offered, but only for comparison with the unmediated version. Equally the status any reconstruction can have is the status of an interpretation only, and must always be presented as such.

Although interpretation will, in the form of reconstructions, inevitably creep into the archive if only to make it a complete record of the after-life of the plays, the overriding status of the whole will be as a neutral resource. Its real potential for the generation of new readings of the York plays will be realised fully in independent later phases when its potential begins to be exploited in secondary scholarship. Three broad dimensions to output are currently envisaged. First, conservation facsimiles will be copied to the owners of the collections from which the originals are taken. As well as being a highly secure means of storing facsimiles of vulnerable and unique objects, the superb photographic quality and the hypertext architecture of these will allow for them to be exploited in ways far more flexible than conventional photographs or microfilms. The control of access to individual items will then become a matter of co-operation between the owners and the Project, including The British Library interest, in which customary legal rights will necessarily be respected on both sides. Owners of records who depend for revenue on giving access to unique materials and to consequent spin-offs may understandably be nervous of the loss of control that high-quality electronic copying such as the Project proposes might bring them. We believe, however, that the Project will if anything increase interest in the originals and their repositories. While the preliminary work and casual curiosity that leads to wear and tear can be minimised as scholars and students are able to check the precise nature of the original without physically calling it up, greater general intimacy with the nature of the originals should increase informed interest. The availability of high-resolution digital scans will increase both the quality and flexibility of derivative products. This does not rule out more commercial exploitation by the owners or the Project, subject to contractual constraints on both sides.

Secondly, there is a clearly defined demand for a call-order system whereby scholars will be able to procure from the Project, with the permission of copyright owners, elements of the archive in machine-readable form for their research. A catalogue of the contents of the archive will be published to this end, in both electronic and conventional print-media forms, as a priority. This is being produced in two stages. First, there is a neutral listing of scans by file names, with cross-identification to the manuscript shelfmark and folio number. Next there will be a much fuller descriptive database of each image. For this, we are experimenting with the Document Type Definition developed by Richard Masters for The British Library's Survey of Illuminated Manuscripts. Again release of materials will be strictly regulated, and further reproduction will be controlled, much as it is in print media. Materials released in this way would generally be in compressed form, for ease of manipulation on the currently standard-specification personal computer, so would not be at the level of resolution of the originals. This in turn would create the usual generational problems for anyone tempted to generate illegal further reproductions. Finally, the directors of the Project themselves, as well as publishing fresh research findings that arise from the process of forming the archive, aim to draw on its raw material to write hypertext books for target markets within the education sector.

Ultimately the strength of an archive such as this lies both in its level of security, capturing unique artefacts for posterity as data that can be perpetually refreshed and is not tied to a single location, but also in its future utility for research and other purposes in ways as yet unenvisaged.

# Digitising the Gandharan Buddhist Scrolls

**Simon Shaw and Andrew Prescott**

The Electronic Asia project was established after The British Library acquired 80 fragments of Buddhist text which will help trace the earliest history of Buddhism and clarify its earliest developments. The manuscripts are believed to originate from the Gandhara region – what is now northern Pakistan and eastern Afghanistan. Estimated to be nearly 2000 years old the scrolls were supposedly found rolled up inside the clay pots bearing dedicatory inscriptions which permit a dating as early as the first century AD. This establishes the scrolls as not only the oldest surviving texts of Buddhist literature, but also the earliest South Asian manuscripts of any type.

The texts are recorded on fragile and crumbling birch bark scrolls. Birch bark is probably the most fragile material that has ever been used for writing. The task of unrolling the scrolls was a delicate and complex one for conservators at The British Library. The scrolls were carefully unravelled after being moistened overnight in a bell jar and tweezers were then used to flatten them out and place them under glass. Even though the fragments are between glass, they have to be stored in a carefully controlled environment, and cannot be made generally available in the Library's reading rooms.

Given these restrictions, the creation of a digital surrogate for use by readers was an obvious course. Moreover, the text of the fragments can only be deciphered once they have been unrolled and placed under glass. It was impracticable to consider rearranging the fragments within the glass sheets once they had been fully identified, so again the use of digital images seemed to offer a potential aid to cataloguing and arranging the material.

The transcription, translation and interpretation of these texts is being undertaken by Professor Richard Salomon and his research team at the University of Washington in Seattle. To facilitate this work, the Early Buddhist Manuscripts project has been set up between The British Library and the University of Washington. Apart from the delicate nature of the fragments, a further problem in cataloguing them is that they are in a very obscure script, namely Kharoshti. The Gandharan fragments bring us closer than any other sources yet unearthed to the 'original' language of the Buddha himself. The original language of the Buddha is presumably no longer recoverable, but it may well be possible to discern features of the underlying language or dialect from which the Gandharan translations were made.

In order to assess the viability of digitising these texts, Professor Kevin

Kiernan gave a demonstration of his work on the Electronic Beowulf to Professor Salomon and curatorial staff from the Library's Oriental and India Office Collections. Test scans of some of the Gandharan fragments were also made in the course of this demonstration. This showed how digital images could be used to reassemble fragments in their correct order and magnified to examine details of the script. The use of backlighting techniques to recover text obscured by curling of the bark was also demonstrated.

It was not desirable to transport the entire collection of fragments to Bloomsbury for scanning, so an image capture workstation was set up at Orbit House on Blackfriars Road, where the Oriental and India Office Collections are currently located, to allow the Kontron camera to be used there. This comprised two large PCs similar in configuration to those used for the Beowulf project, one for image capture and the other for quality assurance. As with the Beowulf project, the PCs ran under Windows 3.11. Owing to potential conflicts with the Library's network, use of Windows 95 or NT was not at that stage an option.

It has already been noted that lighting is a major problem with use of the Kontron camera. For the scanning of the Gandharan fragments, two 2KW photofloods were again used, as in the early stages of the Beowulf project. However, the vulnerability of the birch bark meant that exposure to these intense lights had to be even more restricted than with the Beowulf manuscript. This created serious difficulties because the glass frames containing the fragments were very large. Ideally, to keep light exposure to a minimum, each frame should have been scanned just once on each side, but this would have resulted in very low-resolution images, because of the distance between the camera and the object. As a compromise, therefore, separate images were made of the top and bottom halves of a number of frames. The aim was that each image would be taken at more than 300 DPI, but this was difficult to ensure under these conditions.

As a result of these problems, it was found when the images were sent to the United States that a number of details of the script could not be clearly read when magnified. This difficulty was compounded by problems with focus. Focusing a shot of an object in a glass plate is in any case a difficult process. The Kontron plug-in to Adobe Photoshop 3.0 was used in shooting the images (see Plate 4). Although focusing the Kontron camera using this package is much easier than with many digital cameras, it is still difficult in that a shot which appears well focused on the monitor may prove, when viewed at full size, to be slightly blurred. This is because the image for focusing purposes is adjusted to fit the size of the monitor. Moreover, it was difficult to ensure that the camera was focusing on the fragment rather than the top sheet of glass. The colour handling of the Photoshop plug-in is also a problem. The 32-bit emulator (Win32S) used when running Photoshop under Windows 3.11 means that images look acceptable on the PC, but the colours are distorted when viewed on other platforms.

The result was that, although the images seemed acceptable when made in London, when they were transferred to the United States, Professor Salomon and his team found that some key details were not as visible as they had hoped.

The lesson of this is probably that, when digital images are made to support detailed academic research of this kind, effective quality control can only be exercised by the ultimate user of the images. Part of the reason for the success of the Electronic Beowulf project was the very close supervision over all stages of the image capture process exercised by Kevin Kiernan. It is impossible for anyone other than the expert in the field to know whether the images will do everything that is required.

Ideally, the answer to these problems would be to re-shoot the images under Professor Salomon's supervision, perhaps mounting the camera on a microscope for the capture of particular details. However, the delicate nature of the fragments limits the amount of re-shooting that can be undertaken. Instead, some of the fragments are being re-shot with a digital back device which uses colder lights and produces images of higher resolution than the Kontron (although it should be noted that an upgrade is available to the Kontron camera which will increase the resolution). Even when so-called 'cold' lights are used, the conservation problems should not be underestimated. These lights still create a great deal of ambient heat. The ideal solution would be a large fibre-optic device which transmits light from a remote light source, so that the heat generated by the light source can be kept well away from the manuscript. Such a device, though technically feasible, is not, however, commercially available.

Transfer of the images to the University of Washington was less fraught than the early days of the Beowulf project, but still not without its difficulties. The images were sent to Washington in the form of Iomega Jaz disks which have the capacity to hold 1 gigabyte of information. They are also cross-platform, which is particularly important for this project, as The British Library is using PCs and Professor Salomon and his team work on Macs. The British Library is also sending files via file transfer protocol (FTP) to the University of London Computer Centre, which will enable the Washington end of the project to download images directly by FTP.

The University of Washington is purchasing three computer workstations for the project and has created two new positions for research assistants. The first publication emanating from this project, a summary analysis and description, will come out in 1998. The editors also envisage a series of publications that will contribute to re-evaluation of the early history of Buddhism.

# The Image Demonstrator Project

**Cindy Carr**

The Image Demonstrator Project was an experimental electronic store of images from journals and was designed to support document supply to remote customers. The decision to create an image demonstrator was taken by the Library's Document Supply Centre (DSC) in 1992. The establishment of the project was similar to other electronic journal initiatives being taken elsewhere, such as a project that INIST, a French document supply company, were undertaking to scan a number of their most highly used serial titles and store them on optical disk; and the ADONIS project, where a consortium of publishers created an electronic document store in the biomedical subject area. This study of the Image Demonstrator Project gives a general overview of the Project and describes the lessons that were learnt by The British Library during the course of the Project.

The major objectives of the project were:

- To provide a demonstrator system for the electronic scanning, indexing, storage and retrieval of articles from a set of 48 journal titles, for which The British Library acquired electronic storage rights from the publishers. These rights were acquired for the duration of the Project only, the agreement requiring The British Library to delete the images on completion of the Project.
- To use this platform to form a mutually beneficial working relationship with rights holders, namely publishers. The Image Demonstrator Project aimed to show that The British Library, in exploring the technologies needed to store and use documents in digital form, was committed to negotiating rights to use the material.
- To develop expertise in the areas of scanning and indexing, image storage and retrieval.
- To work towards achieving the objectives laid down in The British Library's strategic plan. These state that the DSC will double the number of requests it handles by the year 2003 (to six million) and provide the services required by its customers by exploiting to the full the opportunities offered by information technology to provide faster, more efficient and more comprehensive services.

An invitation to tender (ITT) was issued in November 1992. IBM was awarded the contract and subcontracted the work to Martec Imaging Ltd (based in Chester). The system was delivered in 1993. The scanning workstation comprised one IBM 2456 flatbed scanner, one IBM PS/2 processor, and one IBM 8508 screen displaying at 100 DPI. Processing was carried out by an IBM RS6000 system running AIX, the IBM flavour of Unix.

The images were initially stored on four IBM 7204001 magnetic discs, at 1 gigabyte each, and then transferred on to optical disks stored on a Reflection Systems RF20JM Jukebox, which gave an additional 16 gigabytes of storage, also managed by an RS6000 system. There was also a Reflection Systems optical drive to use for back-up in case of jukebox failure. Output was from a retrieval workstation that comprised one IBM PS/2 processor, screen keyboard and mouse. The images were then printed using an ATI high-speed laser printer, accessed by a DOS server. Only paper copy was used for the duration of the Project but it had initially been intended to use fax or file transfer protocol (FTP) as an alternative to postal delivery.

There were three basic levels of software. Both retrieval and input front ends were the same and were written in Visual Basic, by Martec Imaging. The original front end was adapted from a system used for processing invoices for a car hire company. The experience of the Project suggested that, in the end, it might have been easier to develop this software from scratch. The set-up of the original system meant that every journal part had to be indexed individually with full cover information such as journal title, size, ISSN details, shelfmark and name of publisher. The latest upgrade enabled the operator to input this information only once per journal and then to recall it for future issues.

On the retrieval side, when searching for documents by volume and page number only, the system originally retrieved only one document per search (usually the first scanned on to the system). As the database grew this meant that negative results were found for documents that were actually on the system. Upgrades to the software mean that a list of 'hits' was produced and the operator could select from this by highlighting the appropriate one.

The scanner was driven by Image 6000 software, produced by SGS Informatica, a company based in Italy. Each page was indexed separately, using index fields from the BRS search engine that was part of the Image 6000 software. This also handled searching and retrieval. During the course of the Project two versions of the software were loaded. The second, version 6.1, was loaded in the autumn of 1993 and was generally an improvement except that the rotation of images when scanning was an extremely slow process.

Forty-eight titles, some covering 1993 and some 1994, were selected for scanning using the following criteria:

- The size of the journal had to be A4 or smaller. This was because of the printer that was to be used. A decision was made not to reduce the image size to fit A4, or to enlarge it to A4 either.
- The title had to be on the Inside Information database (DSC's contents alerting service) and where possible in the top 1000 most used titles. The most highly used titles were selected to allow useful evaluation of document supply.
- Titles on the ADONIS system were excluded, to avoid duplication of material already stored electronically.

The journals were scanned from cover to cover at 300 DPI, the lowest resolution that could be used for a high-quality image which could be transmitted electronically using such methods as FTP if required. In the event FTP and fax delivery were not used and the images were printed and sent out as hard copy by post, so 200 DPI would have been acceptable.

The operator was able to scan a document as text, black and white image or colour image. For each of these, a light, medium or dark setting was available, giving the operator a total of nine settings to choose from. Each page was indexed as a separate image. The images were passed to the processor and stored on magnetic media, transferring to optical storage after quality control procedures. CCITT Group IV compression was used for text and PackBits for grey-scale images. These were used to obtain the best possible image using the most efficient compression available on the system and thus using the minimum amount of storage space. Hindsight tells us that we should have explored other possibilities for compression.

The documents were retrieved, printed on an ATI printer and dispatched. A cover sheet was attached giving bibliographic details and a copyright statement.

The journals had to be scanned without cutting the spines, as an additional copy was not purchased. A further requirement was a swift turnaround so that the journals could be used for the standard document supply service. Consequently, the quality of the images had to be better than, or at worst as good as, a photocopy image. Each page had to done as a single pass scan (this meant that pages containing both photographs and text were scanned as photographs and those with just text as text).

Indexing was done manually by staff who were not trained typists or cataloguers. The following standard information was entered for each issue:

- Journal title. This was quoted in full.
- Year
- Volume number
- Part number
- DSC shelfmark. This enabled document supply to the system, and allowed routing of requests via the Automatch system (DSC's automated post sorting system). The shelfmark is a DSC unique identifier for all serials with that title.
- International Standard Serial Number (ISSN). This was initially for usage information. Although usage information was subsequently derived from the publisher field, the ISSN nevertheless continued to be entered throughout the project.
- Publisher. The Publisher field was added after the project had been going for three months so that full usage statistics could be given to the publishers involved in the project. Publishers required a confidentiality clause so full usage statistics down to article level were only given to each individual publisher for their own titles.
- Size. This indicated whether the journal was A4, A5 or other. In the case of 'other', the book was measured and the length and width put in. This was done to allow black border removal and to cut down on the storage space.
- Article and Author (of the individual article). In order to reduce the amount of indexing, entries were limited to the first five words of the article title and a maximum of four authors. This did not cause any problems with retrieval and decreased the time spent on input.

Contents pages were used as a guide, so classified advertisements were omitted, if they were not paginated. This was because it was unclear how they should be indexed for retrieval (by product or by manufacturer? Questions were raised here about advertising revenue for publishers – if this policy were adopted for a full-scale project, how would publishers feel about it?). Conference alerting details, editorial board membership lists, subscription details and instructions for authors were also not included. Abstracts caused problems as there could be at least six abstracts on one page. If they were individually listed in the contents the same page would have to be scanned six times and indexed six times, but usually they came under sub-headings in the contents, which were used. Where possible the author index was also scanned (so that it could be referred to if a customer quoted an author of an abstract without giving the page number).

Supplying documents from the system, in response to 'live' requests, started in April 1994. A success rate of 70% was achieved by supplying 813 documents from the system. The figure was low because 1994 issues were being loaded as an ongoing process. In fact 53% of the failures were because the journal had not been loaded on to the system. The routing of request forms was done indiscriminately. This meant that *all* automated requests for *any* journal on the system, for 1993/1994, were routed to the IDP (and included in the requests received figure). It should be noted that, since DSC offers a loan and a photocopy service, some of these requests were for loans. Loans were not offered from the system, since customers want the original item, so these requests were routed to the stores where the hard copy is held. Requests received by post were not included as this would have caused unnecessary delays in processing. As in the case of supply from hard copy the 'b' copy of the request form was sent out with the document, so that the customer could easily match their records.

Basic usage statistics were kept noting the publisher's name, journal title, article title and the number of times the article was printed, with a grand total per journal and publisher. These included the journal covers which were retrieved for demonstration purposes. Some of the journal covers were particularly useful for showing the quality of the images. There were 12,017 articles on the system. Given an average of 12 pages per article, there were 144,205 images on the system. A total of 1090 articles, covers or contents pages were retrieved from the system. It should also be noted that the statistics programme was not added until at least six months into the Project, and excludes many items retrieved during demonstrations at the start of the Project.

As with many projects, it took time to ensure that everyone was speaking the same language. This may sound like a very basic requirement, but was not as easy as it sounds. Certain things were not specified tightly enough in the ITT, such as actual speed required from the printer (not rated speed of the printer) and exact quality of images. It was recognised that whilst specifying quality on images was difficult, some benchmarks should be given. The suppliers had no knowledge of operational procedures and library terminology. Similarly the terminology used by the supplier was not always understood by DSC.

Complete reliance on the suppliers for every element of the demonstrator caused major problems. There were occasions when the system was unavailable for a number of days because of delays in supply of software updates or replacement parts (the scanner used was one of only two in the UK). Communication problems between the contractor and subcontractor caused further delays.

It was specified that the spines of the journals should not be cut to enable use of the automatic document feed on the scanner as the cost of rebinding them would have been prohibitive. The journals had to be returned to the storage areas quickly, to make them available for other document supply needs. With hindsight, the documents should have been cut up for scanning.

The design of the flatbed scanner meant that every other page had to be scanned upside-down. This was because the lid and the automatic document feed get in the way (this was not unique to the IBM scanner as most were designed in the same way). The images were rotated on screen before storing them. Initially it took up to 45 seconds to index scan, rotate and process a 782K image compared to 18 seconds to index scan and process a 45K image without rotation. The time difference was due to the time it took to process each image, as scanning and indexing were pretty constant. Modifications were made to the software that reduced the times considerably; these were 25 seconds for a 911k grey-scale image and 19 seconds for a 102k text image.

Manual indexing and scanning meant that the process was very slow. The amount of typing to be done was reduced by only indexing the first five words of the article title and up to and including four authors. This was still a laborious task as some of the words in the technical journals were as long as whole titles in the management journals! It was concluded that a possible solution would be to extract the data from our Inside Information database and download it directly into the index. Unfortunately time and budgetary restrictions did not allow for this to be implemented.

A considerable number of challenges were experienced in getting the correct user interface. The original was designed for an invoicing system and not suitable. Initially there were a number of errors with the set-up of the system, which meant that it kept failing. Problems occurred with indexing because of the link between BRS Search (the indexing software) and the user interface, written in Visual Basic by Martec. BRS has a number of stop or link words such as 'and', 'not', 'with', etc. When a title such as 'The British Library and the Image Demonstrator Project' was indexed there was difficulty retrieving it through the front end. It saw the 'and' as a syntax error, ignored it and so did not find a match, giving a 'no document' message. Similar problems with apostrophes, commas, full stops, spacing and so on were also encountered, which again caused syntax errors. These were all ironed out in time but it took nearly a year to rectify as one 'fix' created problems in other areas. This was particularly irritating as one of the main reasons for selecting the system was that it was based on BRS Search, a standard bibliographic retrieval package. This, on paper, looked ideal for the requirements of the system and should have been flexible enough for even the most difficult indexing problems.

When the project was first set up CCITT Group IV compression was used. This was efficient for text and produced very good images. It was found that when colour or black and white illustrations in the text were scanned as grey-scale images at 300 DPI and compressed as CCITT Group IV, the results were very poor. The pictures were either so dark that it was impossible to determine what the image was, or the image was distorted.

This was overcome by producing the images using a dither pattern (diffusion) for scanning and PackBits compression. Even with a single pass scan it was still legible and far better than a fax copy. Although CCITT Group IV compression was efficient for text, PackBits for grey-scale images was not. Even after compression, there were files on the system ranging from 32K to 950K! A full A4 page of text produced an average file size of between 90 and 120K, depending on the text. It was very difficult to select an average file size for grey-scale but compression could be as little as 21% for some of the larger images. This was very different to the average 50K per image originally envisaged. The miscalculation on image sizes had implications in terms of storage as the magnetic storage space was full within the first three months. This was a double-edged sword as it allowed investigation into the use of optical storage, which was not the original intention. Retrieval was slower from the optical jukebox, but when processing batches of requests this was only apparent for the first retrieval. This is assuming that all images in one batch were stored on the same optical disk. If the articles were newly scanned on to the system and had not yet been transferred from the magnetic storage to the optical, the procedure was even slower. The operator had to manually switch between the optical and magnetic media (this could have been automated had the project been longer term).

A considerable amount of time was spent on quality. The problems with grey-scale images were mainly to do with brightness and contrast and the distortion of images. Images were so dark that outlines were indistinguishable or so light that elements disappeared. The journals covered varied subjects and contained many different types of image. Text, graphs, diagrams and detailed line drawing, generally presented no problems and could be treated as text. Very few of these had to be scanned as grey-scale images.

Many of the photographic images (grey-scale) had very fine detail and were difficult to reproduce. They ranged from medical to materials science and were often x-ray images or minute details shown under a microscope. A great deal of time was spent finding the best settings for these, and achieved good results. This was done by using a dither pattern for scanning grey-scale images. Adjustments could be made to the contrast and brightness settings to improve quality, but this was very time-consuming. A considerable number of tests were carried out and nine optimal settings were selected. Had the system included delivery by fax, fewer options would have been included for this type of delivery as, to a certain extent , the images are only as good as the fax machine that they are to be delivered to.

Staffing costs for the system, including loading, retrieval and development came to £2.20 per article. Cost of everything else, such as hardware, software, consumables, and staff training came to £12.40 per article giving a grand total of £14.60 per article. Obviously hardware costs can be written off as development costs for the demonstrator. If costs of hardware, software and preparation were removed the figure becomes £3.56 per article (which was still high). It became obvious that the staffing input alone made the Project too expensive to adopt as a full-scale production system in that particular configuration.

The system as implemented was thus too expensive to consider as a full-scale production system. However, The British Library learned a considerable amount about specifying for new systems, handling suppliers, electronic document storage, scanning and indexing and retrieval during the period of the project. Lessons learned and questions raised from scanning included:

- Realising that hours could be spent on looking at quality of the documents when it could be speed and the content of the text that were of interest to the customer.
- How like a photocopy machine should a scanner be for ease of operation for the staff? We assumed that this should be the case as it was the staff who were operating the photocopy machines who would use a full scale production system. It has turned out to be the case in other projects that this was a mistake.
- Does a customer really care if the images are all the same way up when they get the printed copy? The answer to this was a resounding YES.
- Are flatbed scanners really designed for scanning bound books efficiently and cost-effectively? The British Library has since investigated the use of overhead book scanners which seem to hold some promise at least for ease of operation if not for speed.
- Is it worth scanning and storing at all? There is some evidence that some articles only ever get asked for once in their lifetime so the cost of scanning and storing is not worth while. Indeed The British Library has recently started to work on the Trial Electronic Documents Store, a project where articles are supplied in electronic format directly from the publishers

Many of the lessons learned from the Project have been put to good use in other projects, particularly in the scanning, indexing and compression areas. Working closely with publishers in this area has also proved to be of great value to the Library.

Trying to adapt what was essentially an office automation system to the needs of document supply was, in retrospect, a mistake. We learned that we should have been very specific about what we wanted and that we should, to a certain extent, have ignored what was already available. We also felt that we should have more control over the Project by involving some more of the Library's own technical staff. The lost time for parts and upgrades of software was very frustrating. It should also be remembered that the project used the most up-to-date equipment available at the time. We discovered that by the time the system was up and running other hardware and software were available which may have better suited our needs. Having said that, we had many visitors to the system who had been working in this area for some considerable time and who had not achieved such good results.

# The Digitisation of Microfilm

**Hazel Podmore**

The British Library purchased a Mekel M400XL microfilm digitiser in 1992 to experiment with scanning its large holdings of microfilm. In order to provide a framework for these investigations, the Digitisation of Microfilm Project was set up in autumn 1993 by the Library's Collections and Preservation Directorate as part of the *Initiatives for Access* programme. The Project had the following objectives:

- To identify the best possible uses of the Mekel equipment within the Library, contributing towards establishing a preliminary portfolio of digital texts.
- To examine the most appropriate storage medium for digitised material and the implications for its maintenance in the medium and longer terms.
- To examine the implications for staff resources and operations in producing digitised material and providing adequate indexing for access to it.
- To determine the technical and procedural implications of supplying material digitised from microfilm to readers in the reading rooms.
- To investigate microfilming standards and their importance for microfilm digitisation.

It was agreed that the Project should devote its efforts to building up a significant body of material that was coherent (i.e. from the same collection) and from a defined period. In consultation with curators in other parts of the Library, it was decided to focus on a collection of 18th-century newspapers, the Burney collection. There were several reasons for this:

- The Burney collection is a large and complex collection of newspapers, which were sold to the Library on the death of their owner, Charles Burney. They have never been individually catalogued, and the only index to them is a copy of a 19th-century manuscript, which does not necessarily reflect the order in which they were filmed.
- Because of their age and fragility the original newspapers are never issued. Readers are obliged to use the microfilm, and they are notoriously difficult to use in this format. Newspapers from this period are very rare, and the collection is in high demand by researchers from all over the world.
- It is probably fair to say that they are not the best-quality film the Library has ever produced. By their very nature the Burney originals are of poor quality. There is a considerable variation in print density from page to page and within each page as well. Many of the individual letters are broken and, of course, there are some unusual characters, most notably the long s. We

knew that they would offer a very thorough test of the Mekel and its associated software. If the scanner could handle this, it could handle most of the material we were likely to want to digitise.

- And last, but not least, copyright of the microfilm belongs to the Library!

The Project concentrated on one part of the collection, newspapers from the years of the French Revolution (1789-1791). When work on the chosen segment of the Burneys was completed in March 1995, we scanned two 17th-century collections of ballads, which expanded the challenges we had set ourselves, since these are pages of woodcut illustrations with text underneath. The handwritten catalogue of Sir Hans Sloane's manuscripts was also scanned, which provided experience of digitising microfilms of manuscripts.

The Mekel M400XL microfilm digitiser uses a high-resolution 5000 pixel CCD linear array camera to capture the image. It was linked to a Qubie 486 PC workstation with a NEC Multi synch 5FG high-resolution monitor. For most of the time the system has used Turbo scan V.4 software to control image capture. V.5 was implemented in March 1995. A scan optimiser allows the operator to vary certain scanning parameters to produce the best possible image.

The images are captured in binary TIFF format and compressed after scanning using CCITT Group 4 fax compression. Initial storage is to hard disc. When the disc is full the data is transferred to magneto-optical disc using a local network link.

The data is then downloaded to a second PC, a Dell 433 ME with another high-resolution monitor. At this stage the operator 'quality assures' the images. They are stripped of the black border around the edges of the frame of microfilm. This gives us at least a 10% saving in file storage space. At the same time images can be rotated and de-skewed if necessary.

When the digitised texts have been downloaded onto the optical disc drive and the changes to de-skew the image and reduce the unwanted borders have been applied, two copies of the final image are made and one is stored off-site. Two optical disc drives linked to two different workstations are used to access the material. Optical discs were chosen as the most suitable storage medium because of the high volume of data the digitised texts created.

As explained above, the Burney collection was chosen because of the thorough test of the equipment it would supply. Our first challenge was to see if the machine would be able to scan from the positive copy, or a duplicate negative. To begin with this was not achieved. Positive copies of microfilm contained sufficient loss of image quality to render the results unacceptable with the difficult material we selected. At first we were unable to use the duplicate negative either. The only acceptable results were achieved with the master, or archival negative. Although the Mekel is a well-designed machine and we had no problems with scratches or tears to our masters, we were still unhappy with using archival masters, since any damage to the master would mean that the volumes would have to be microfilmed again. Early tests on the 17th-century ballads were also disappointing. Either the illustration was visible but the text too faint to read, or the illustration was too dark and the text legible. This problem could not be solved even when using a first-generation negative.

Image of 18th-century newspaper digitised from microfilm.

It took some time to establish the best settings at which to scan. After initial tests with a range of different microfilms, the decision was to set a limit of 200 Dots Per Inch (DPI) as the scanning resolution. This was because the individual file sizes (each equalling one frame on microfilm or one page of text) become unmanageably large when higher resolutions are used. (The quantity of data and its storage is an ongoing challenge for this Project.) Very occasionally on particularly poor frames resolutions of up to 300 DPI are selected.

In addition we also found it difficult to use the continuous scan setting. This is where the operator sets up the scanning parameters at the beginning of each reel and the machine is set to run until all the frames have been scanned. Because of the great variation in the density of the frame's film, parameters had to be altered, in some cases on a frame by frame basis. This seriously affected our ability to maximise productivity. One of the advantages of scanning from microfilm should be the speed at which it works.

These problems were addressed by upgrades installed in March 1995, comprising a factory-refurbished Mekel, with Auto optimiser, and V.5 of Turbo scan, Turbo enhance and the two IP20 boards necessary to run the new software. The new scanner operates efficiently enough to allow scanning from a duplicate negative in most cases. Since acquiring the new scanner, the 17th-century ballads and manuscript catalogue of the Sloane collection have been digitised from duplicate negatives, all with excellent results. Moreover, all the material scanned since the acquisition of the new kit has been processed on continuous scan without any major difficulties. The increase in productivity is very great. At the start of the Project 3240 frames of the Burney collection were scanned on average in one month. At this productivity rate it would take approximately 129 months (nearly 11 years) to scan the entire collection. Using the new equipment we should be able to scan around 90,000 frames per month and it would take approximately 15-18 months to scan the rest of the collection. The size of the database generated by this quantity of data would (at a very rough estimate) be around 130 gigabytes.

Another issue was that, unlike microfilm, digital images require detailed indexing to make them accessible to a user. At the same time as the equipment upgrades were purchased, an indexing package was acquired from DP Advisers, a London-based firm who specialise in document image management packages. At present this is only licensed for one machine. It has been specifically designed for use with newspapers, but can be modified to use with other collections. It should be stressed that this package is for indexing and has not been designed as a search engine.

Mention has been made already of the 'difficult' nature of 18th-century newspapers and this carries over into the indexing of this type of material. Because of the poor print quality no current Optical Character Recognition (OCR) package can be used to convert automatically the digital images to machine-readable text. Some Burney files were used in the evaluation of the Excalibur PixTex/EFS product, and the results were unacceptably (but not surprisingly) too poor to be of any use. The majority of the 'articles' contained in the papers do not carry headlines in the sense we understand that term now.

Indeed, in many cases, there is only a paragraph break between one topic and the next. Together these rule out any form of free-text indexing, or subject indexing.

The Project proved that it is possible to create from microfilm an acceptable digital surrogate for use in reading rooms. A good clear image can be produced which is legible and, with a zoom capability, offers readers a clearer image of poor text than microfilm copy. The maximum productivity possible has been achieved with the equipment in place and given the constraints of the material chosen for scanning. By the time the Project finished, in March 1996, over 21 gigabytes of images had been produced, with a productivity rate of approximately 6000 frames per month. Unfortunately we were not able to test readers' opinions on the use of digital surrogates, but it is hoped that at some time in the future the data generated by the Project will be made available, both in the Library's reading rooms and elsewhere.

# St Pancras Treasures digitisation project

**Leona Carpenter with Clive Izard**

The Treasures Gallery at St Pancras will permanently display many major items from The British Library's collections. A proposal to digitise a selection of these items for security purposes, research, commercial exploitation, and improved access through electronic delivery, was accepted in May 1993, and a provisional budget allocated. The objective was to determine the best method, or methods, for the digitisation of existing surrogate colour images of these rare and valuable items in order that the security and conservation of the originals would not be compromised. The project was regarded as a pilot for the possible digitisation of all items on permanent or semi-permanent display. A representative sample of digitised images would be obtained, methods for manipulating the images (post-capture) examined, and subsequent storage of and access to the images explored. The project would also assess the security implications of using first-generation archival photographic material. Recommendations and cost estimates could then be made for the extension of the Treasures digitisation programme in 1994/95.

The number of images to be digitised in this preliminary project was limited to 50 representative images selected to test the scanning and digitisation processes across full colour and tonal ranges and format ratios. The images captured were to be indexed, stored off-line as an image library, and also stored in an archival format. An evaluation of the technical activities as well as staffing skills and training requirements would be included in the project report.

Clive Izard, Head of Audio Visual Services, was appointed Project Manager. He and Richard Masters, Senior Systems Analyst in the Document and Image Processing team, produced a project plan, setting out the resources required and associated risks. It was recognised that the project could not succeed without absorbing a significant amount of staff time. A Project Board was set up to oversee progress of the project, and a Project Panel to provide quality assurance. The Project Board were: Graham Shaw, Deputy Director of Oriental and India Office Collections (Executive and Chair), Jane Carr, Director of Public Services (Senior User), Michael Alexander, Head of Document and Image Processing (Senior Technical). The Project Panel were: Christine Hall, Western Manuscripts (Business Assurance), Anne Young, Publications (User Assurance), and Lawrence Pordes, Photographic Department and Peter James, Software Development (Technical Assurance). A Technical Stage Manager, Leona Carpenter (Software Development), was assigned to manage the scanning and indexing stage of the project. The project plan was approved by the Digital and Network Services Steering Committee in September and the project began officially 1 October 1993, with completion scheduled for 31 March 1994.

A consultant, Martin Ellis, was contracted to evaluate current technologies and procedures for image capture, processing, storage and access. Very experienced in these areas, he was involved in the National Gallery Micro Gallery project, and in a Microsoft-sponsored project involving the capture, storage and retrieval of thousands of digital images of works of art. His report facilitated the choice of suitable scanning, storage and image-processing methods and equipment for St Pancras Treasures images, taking into account the use of first-generation surrogates of original items. These surrogates (photographic transparencies of varying formats, 35mm to 10x8 inches) are themselves considered to be rare and valuable materials.

## System specification

An image capture and storage system was specified based on the recommendations of the consultant's report, subsequent investigation, and the following additional factors: the possibility of future upgrades (e.g., the computer could be upgraded for multimedia development) and the adaptability to broader requirements (e.g., the scanner could support other programmes of digital image capture from transparencies or opaque materials). Equipment costs were greater than had been anticipated when the project budget was set, so additional funds had to be found and the additional expenditure approved by the Project Board and the Digital and Network Services Steering Committee. The specified system consisted of the following image capture and image storage workstations.

### 1. Image capture hardware and software

| COMPONENT | MANUFACTURER | MODEL |
|---|---|---|
| 1. scanner | Scitex | Smart 340 PS |
| 2. imaging computer | Apple | Quadra 800 72/500CD |
| 3. magnetic disk drive chassis | Mountain Gate | IncreMeg Drive Chassis |
| 4. removable disk drive | Mountain Gate | IncreMeg 1200Mb |
| 5. display monitor (colour) | SuperMatch | 20.T XL |
| 6. Photoshop/graphics boosting | SuperMatch | Thunder II Light Card |
| 7. monitor colour calibration | SuperMatch | SuperMatch Calibrator |
| 8. image editing software | Adobe | Photoshop 2.5 |

The scanner[1], computer[2], removable hard disk[3, 4] and software[8] procured for the image capture part of the system were as recommended by the consultant. However, he had recommended a Radius display monitor, calibrator and Photoshop booster. Both the chosen supplier and Technical Stage Manager had reservations about the Radius monitor. The supplier's reservations were based on experience with monitors which they had supplied to clients which had proved troublesome and had not attracted what the supplier felt to be adequate support from the manufacturer when problems arose. The Technical Stage

Manager's reservations were based on having read in the computing press about similar difficulties with the Radius monitor. The impression gained from the computer press was that people had been willing to put up with a lower level of reliability for the sake of the sophistication of the related Radius products.

The Project Manager discussed these concerns with the consultant, whose view was that one of the two monitors[5] suggested as a substitute by the supplier would be a good choice for our purpose, along with a related accelerator[6] as a substitute for Radius Photobooster. The consultant also pointed out that his experience of Radius monitors was that they have proved very reliable in high-use public access installations.

A SuperMatch Calibrator colour calibration system[7] was substituted for the Radius Calibrator for compatibility. The photographers, Lawrence Pordes and Annie Gilbert, quickly mastered use of this equipment and are satisfied with the on-screen colour consistency/matching it allows them. Further evaluation will be possible when they can compare the screen output with print output produced from the digitised images.

All mainstream personal computer platforms were considered in the consultant's report, and the recommended Scitex scanner is compatible with each of these platforms. The Apple Macintosh platform was recommended because of its performance advantages over the MS-DOS / Windows platform, its cost benefits over the UNIX platform and the consultant's perception that there was no background of UNIX experience in The British Library.

Peter James, performing the Technical Assurance (Computing) role, pointed out that there is now significant experience of and support for the UNIX platform among Library staff, and that it is possible that much of the Library's core computing will migrate to the UNIX platform in the future. The consultant was asked to provide more detailed information on the costing of a UNIX-based system. The information provided made it clear that while migration to UNIX in some future phase might be considered, it was not financially feasible for this project.

Further weight was added to the choice of Apple Macintosh for the system by the use which might be made of the kit should the Treasures project not proceed beyond the first phase. The kit would be used in an area where Macintosh is the already the chosen platform for its graphics handling and multimedia superiority and for its compatibility with kit used by external partners.

Although neither had used Apple Macintosh computers before, both photographers acting as scanner operators quickly became confident in their manipulation of the hardware and common interface features such as drop-and-drag and the use of cropping tools.

The model of Macintosh chosen varied from that recommended by the consultant. The supplier advised that some fine tuning still needed to be done to the AV models before they could run certain software reliably, including Photoshop. We were assured that the substituted model could be upgraded to an AV when that platform became stable. The Quadra also provided the choice of upgrading to a Power PC, which would have very significant performance advantages. This upgrade was made for later phases of the project.

Adobe's Photoshop software for image handling has met with approval by Lawrence Pordes performing the Technical Assurance (Photographic) role. In fact, he had independently arranged introductory Photoshop training for himself, which took place just before he carried out the bulk of the Treasures scanning.

On the basis of experience using the scanner, he has also been satisfied with the performance and functionality of the Scitex Smart 340 PS hardware and software, with certain exceptions. One drawback is the absence of transparency mounts for the now superseded half-plate and full-plate formats of transparencies. Scitex have been approached about this problem. They can create a makeshift mask for us, and are also considering introducing new mask formats for these transparency formats. The latter would depend on their judgement as to whether the requirement is unique to The British Library, or if there might be a broader customer base in similar organisations with historic transparency collections to be digitised.

In addition, display of the large, high-resolution images on the monitor was noticeably slow. Further boosting of graphics acceleration would increase the speed of production. It would also reduce operator stress, which can affect both quality and quantity of work over the course of a working day. It is possible to do this relatively easily and inexpensively by adding a memory chip to the Thunder II Light Card, which was one of the factors considered in its choice. This was done prior to the next phase of the project.

## 2. Image storage hardware and software

| COMPONENT | MANUFACTURER | MODEL |
| --- | --- | --- |
| 1. storage computer | Apple | Quadra 800 72/500CD |
| 2. monitor | Apple | 14" Colour Display |
| 3. magnetic disk chassis | Mountain Gate | IncreMeg Drive Chassis |
| 4. removable disk drive [for data transfer] | Mountain Gate | IncreMeg 1200Mb |
| 5. optical disk drive [for image library] | Data Peripherals | Optistore 1300 |
| 6. 4mm tape drive [for archive and backup] | | D2 |
| 7. file database software | Claris | FileMaker Pro |
| 8. file processing software | Equilibrium | DeBabelizer |
| 9. image database software | Aldus | Fetch |
| 10.back-up software | Danz | Retrospect 2.0 |

The hardware and software for the data storage/archiving part of the system are as recommended by the consultant, with the following exceptions. A second Apple Macintosh computer with a small black-and-white display monitor was recommended to handle the data storage/archiving processes. However, the possibility of future upgrades, the desire for adaptability to broader requirements, and Peter James's recommendations based on his experience of image-file-handling applications, were factors in the decision to procure a computer[1] identical to that used for the image-capture part of the system and a 14" colour monitor[2]. In later stages of the project, a monitor with a larger screen size was added to this workstation.

The 4mm (DAT) tape drive[6], used for data archiving to tape, is from a different manufacturer than that initially recommended. This change was made on the advice of the supplier in order to ensure a high standard of service. From discussion with the consultant, project management was assured that the D2 is one of a number of brands of tape drive equally suited to project requirements, so the advice of the supplier, which was based on existing service agreements with the manufacturer, was readily accepted.

The installed storage computer and associated peripherals were checked by Peter James to ensure that all items specified (including hardware, software, system configuration, and documentation) were present. He also made a DAT back-up tape of the configured storage-system software. Identified major functions were tested by processing, storing, cataloguing and making security back-ups of a sample set of photographic transparencies. This was carried out by Leona Carpenter, Peter James, Alan Routley and Annette Cooper.

## Acquiring the system

The identification of suppliers of integrated digitisation systems was based on the suppliers' involvement in one or more of the following areas: image scanning, high-resolution image output, supply of installed and integrated systems, supply to public organisations such as research or educational bodies, supply and support of scanning equipment, supply of Apple computers, and involvement in the broad area of multimedia applications. The invitation to bid for the supply of the system outlined the purpose and function of the system, the required components and their basic configuration, and installation and documentation and training requirements. The chosen supplier would have to be able to supply and install all equipment by 23 December 1993, if a firm order from the Library was placed by 30 November 1993. This timetable was constructed in order that work could begin in the new year according to the original project schedule.

On the basis of total cost, Albion Computers plc was the clear winner. They also made the strongest case for themselves as a sound company with the resources and experience to supply the level of service required for this project. In addition, it emerged that Albion Computers was already far down the road to becoming the distributor within the M25 area for the company producing the chosen scanner. This was thought to be significant in terms of likely quality of support and timeliness of supply.

All equipment with the exception of the Scitex scanner arrived to schedule and was installed to the satisfaction of the Technical Stage Manager, and to the established Technical Assurance (Computing) criteria. Two days of initial training were supplied as part of the contract with Albion. This training programme proved invaluable in the setting up of the system and in familiarising Library staff with the equipment and software, although three days' training would have been more appropriate as there was still a large amount of self-learning involved in the early stages of image gathering and indexing.

The failure to deliver the scanner was revealed, on investigation, to be the responsibility of the manufacturer (Scitex of Belgium) who had made assurances to Albion Computers that the delivery date could be met. Albion provided a loan scanner, in order that initial system training could be carried out. This scanner was not regarded as being of sufficiently high quality to have any use to the project beyond the training sessions and subsequently it was removed from the installation. Albion meanwhile endeavoured to put pressure on Scitex to honour the deadline. Scitex in return undertook to supply a loan scanner, of a type superior to the machine ordered by the Library, within seven days of the original deadline.

Unfortunately the freighting company used by Scitex delivered, without appointment, and on separate days, *two* scanners packed for air freighting, plus a printer and two proofers packed similarly, none of which had been ordered by the Library. The equipment was of a size to require unloading with fork-lift trucks, and without the goodwill of staff in the British Museum Goods Section would never have been removed from the lorries. The goods were unloaded because it was assumed that the delivery included the ordered scanner or the loan scanner.

This began a long and complex exchange between British Library staff, Scitex, Albion and the freighting company and the time involved in solving the situation took up a significant proportion of staff time and without question delayed the project yet further. When eventually the correct loan scanner was delivered and installed, it proved not to work with the system without an intermediate PC which had not been supplied, and still further delays occurred. Even when a suitable PC was tracked down and eventually installed the system failed to be robust enough to maintain a steady platform on which to begin the project. However, some benefit was realised because, with Scitex engineers and trainers on-site, it was an adequate platform for training. Two and a half days' training were provided by Scitex. This training was monitored by the Technical Stage Manager and was felt to be effective and essential.

Although some scans were successfully completed during training, the Project Manager took the decision to delay the scanning stage of the project until the scanner originally ordered was delivered. With continued pressure from project management and Albion Computers, Scitex 'queue jumped' the order list and the scanner was delivered and successfully installed on 10 February 1994. The end result of the above complications was the delay of the scanning stage of the operation by six weeks.

When finally the scanner was installed, no further operator training in the use of the scanner and accompanying software was provided, but the installing Scitex engineer provided about an hour of familiarisation with the new equipment for one of the operators. This was found to be adequate, although some difficulty was later experienced in adjusting to slightly different scanner software from the loan scanner which was used for scanning training.

It is important to note that both Albion Computers and Scitex undertook a high-level management investigation into the problems caused to the Library and this has resulted in major structural changes within Scitex. It should also be noted that the help and goodwill provided to the project from both Albion and Scitex subsequent to the above events have given the project management renewed confidence in the quality of service of both organisations. The goodwill continues and the project management would support the involvement of both organisations in further developments.

In addition to system training, a Procedures Manual was collated between Albion Computers and project staff. This manual provides a reference for staff working on the project, records all processes involved, and assists staff new to the project in their training. The Procedures Manual can be revised as equipment and software are updated and new techniques are developed.

### Security issues

The major security issue of transporting the transparencies outside of the building was resolved at project proposal stage, by taking the decision to scan the images in-house. During project planning, the following security issues were addressed: 1] protection against loss and damage during transparency handling; 2] a secure environment for both equipment and transparencies; and 3] the security of media on which the scanned images are stored. For preservation reasons there is limited access to original manuscripts for photography. This increases the need to preserve master transparencies under the best possible conditions, to limit handling to trained staff, and to protect against loss or theft. Therefore, handling of these photographic materials was the prime security issue within the project.

The involvement of the photographers, Department of Manuscripts staff, and Publications staff on the project panel solved many of the security problems which may have occurred in transparency acquisition and handling. Because of the existing relationship between these parties, master transparencies and duplicates could be ordered, collected, and delivered to the scanning room for the single purpose of scanning and then returned immediately. A set of rules for handling transparencies was drawn up by the photographers, Annie Gilbert and Lawrence Pordes. If staff unfamiliar with the practice of ordering photographic material had been involved in the project, more time would have been spent agreeing formal ordering, delivery, and collection rules.

A room identified as suitable for scanning was made secure by the addition of a high-quality lock to the door, and procedures for issuing keys to a limited list of named key-holders were followed. Security grilles already existed on the windows. Electrical sockets which were not deemed adequate were upgraded. It was not possible to control temperature levels in the room as desired. Ideally, an air-conditioned, dust-free environment should be provided for archival photographs and it was recommended that this be provided for the next stage.

As recommended in the consultant's report, 4mm DAT tape is used to archive the scanned images. Each image is copied to two tapes, which are stored at separate storage locations.

### Scanning – procedures and productivity

A total of 93 scans were made from the 50 transparencies selected by the project team. In the early stages of the scanning phase, transparencies were scanned at three different resolutions in order that the most appropriate for each format could be determined. The scanned images, whether used for print or electronic output, would need to be increased in size, either as a whole, or smaller areas cropped and enlarged. This required capturing each image at a higher resolution than is normally required for current printing practices. In order that pixelation appeared only after a relatively high degree of magnification, transparencies were scanned at 400, 800, and 1600 Dots Per Inch (DPI). These images were carefully examined by the scanning team who determined that larger transparencies could be scanned at a proportionately lower resolution than smaller transparencies and continue to produce excellent results. Ten by eight inch transparencies scanned at 1600 and 800 DPI also produced unmanageably large computer files, and it was therefore decided, for the first stage of the project, to scan transparencies at the following resolutions for each format.

| FORMAT | SCAN AT |
| --- | --- |
| 35mm | 1600 DPI |
| 5 x 4 inch | 800 DPI |
| 10 x 8 inch | 400 DPI |

In addition to master transparencies, duplicates in all formats were also scanned in order that comparison could be made. The duplicates were also scanned according to the above table.

The size of transparency, the resolution at which it has been captured and whether it is a master or duplicate, are recorded in the scan log using identifiers specified in the procedures manual. The size of transparency and its resolution are also captured automatically as part of the image file, and this information is automatically added as part of the catalogue record when the image file is catalogued.

Initially it was very difficult to estimate the time required to scan a single image. This varied among the operators, according to each individual's time taken to adapt to the technology and/or the requirements for handling photographic materials. Also, because of the problems already mentioned, the process was slowed down in the earliest stages by the unreliability of the kit. The scan log entry for each scan recorded the operator's name and how long each step of the process took. By examining these records and in discussion with the operators it could be seen that after training and familiarisation with the robust system, a skilled operator could produce a successful scan in 12 to 20 minutes. Less time is required per scan if images of the same manuscript, photographed under identical conditions, are scanned in sequence. Scan times can be further reduced for these images by the use of batch masks so that, for instance, four 5 x 4 inch transparencies can be scanned at the same time. More time is required if a transparency requires colour correction or manipulation in the image-processing software.

## Quality of image
Everyone involved with the project who has seen the captured images on

screen on the image-capture system display monitor has been impressed with their quality. These are mostly subjective judgements, but this does not make them invalid. In some cases the judgements are made in comparison with other systems they have seen displaying similar images. Most impressive is the extent to which the images can be enlarged before there is a perceived degradation of the image. In addition to project staff, the system has been viewed by staff involved in other *Initiatives for Access* projects, curators from Publications, Education, and the Department of Manuscripts, as well as visitors from Kodak and Digital, the Educational Television Association and the Mary Rose Trust. The reaction from all those who have viewed the images on-screen is enthusiastic.

The photographers, who performed much of the image capture, based their judgements on their depth of knowledge of the material being digitised, the content of the images and their colour. They are impressed with the amount of detail which is made available from the photographic transparencies, which in ordinary viewing of the transparencies or of smaller-scale print output from the transparencies, is not able to be seen. For example, the closely packed lines of the Diamond Sutra open out to reveal numerous characterful figures. They are pleased with the colour-matching of the display.

The transparencies selected for scanning allowed a comparison to be made of the quality of image captured from different sizes and from originals and duplicates. In the judgement of the photographers, a 5 x 4 original transparency results in the highest-quality digital image as displayed on the image-capture display screen. The factors involved are the amount of detail available from the transparencies and the practical file size determining the DPI possible for a given size of transparency.

Four-colour separations are being produced from a selection of the captured images, and printers with whose work the Library is familiar will be asked to print from these. The resulting printed images will be compared with past printing to evaluate the quality of print from the digital images. Comparisons will also be made between print from images captured at various resolutions and from different-size transparencies. The expectation is that the print quality will be high, because we had sample prints made from Sforza Hours transparencies scanned on the same model scanner as the one we purchased. These were informally judged by Anne Young of the Publishing Office and by Annie Gilbert of Reprographics (who have great familiarity with the transparencies, previous print output from them, and with the manuscripts themselves) to be very good.

It was discovered early in the image-capturing process that special skills are required of the operator in order that accurate scans can be obtained, most notably the ability to accurately compare the colour, contrast, hues and tones of the transparency against the image on-screen and then manipulate the image, via the relevant software, to achieve exact replication of these properties. The photographers involved in the project proved to have these skills as did Paula Lonergan, a multimedia designer on temporary contract with the Library, and Annette Cooper from Software Development who has a background in textile design. Colour comparison ability is based on a combination of aptitude, training and experience. While image manipulation skills can be acquired through training and experience, no amount of training and experience will compensate for a lack of basic aptitude. The bulk of the scanning for the Treasures project was performed by the photographers, and their knowledge of the original manuscripts and transparencies proved to be of great advantage in producing accurate digitised images.

It should be noted that intense visual concentration is necessary to produce consistently high-quality results. This can prove extremely tiring for the operator and correct practices for observing rest breaks are therefore essential. It has been observed through interviews with the operators that it is preferable to combine scanning with other duties in order to relieve fatigue and to vary the somewhat repetitive nature of the work and thereby ensure the quality of the digital images.

### Image library, tape archive and back-up

An off-line digital image library was created by storing the image files on optical disks and indexing them using image database management software. Although it had proved possible to capture the images as quickly as the best estimates made prior to experience, storing and accessing the captured images proved more time-consuming than had been expected. Moving the larger image files to and from the optical disks and back-up tapes took about 15-20 minutes per file. In addition, and even taking this into account, the amount of machine-time required to add an item to the Fetch catalogue seemed excessive. The slowness of these processes was serious enough to be considered a bottleneck in the system and to require corrective action. There are a number of ways of improving the rate at which image files are transferred from one medium to another and displayed on screens. All require expenditure on hardware, software or memory. Little progress was possible during the first phase of the project, but further improvements were made in the second phase.

The SCSI cables linking the parts of the system only allowed data transfer at a rate which is perceived as very slow when the files to be transferred are as large as the average files in this project. Replacing these links with optical fibre links would greatly improve file transfer rates. The cost of doing this was explored for two alternative approaches: simple replacement of existing links or replacement of existing links along with linking the capture and storage parts of the system. Optical disk drive technology was rapidly developing, and since the optical drive in use here was specified, faster drives had been developed. Replacement of the drive with a faster drive in the second phase improved transfer rates substantially.

The image database management software chosen for the project is Aldus Fetch. It enables the cataloguing, locating and accessing of many thousands of digital images. It automatically creates a visual index of thumbnail-size images, and also captures the file name of each image and the name of the file folder in which each image is stored as index keywords. To each catalogued item can be added: an unlimited number of keywords (each up to 31 characters long) that can be searched when using the catalogue to find images, and a description (up to 32,000 characters long).

When searching for images, it is possible to search for a keyword or file name which matches, contains, begins with, or ends with the input search term. Complex searching is possible. Browsable keyword indexes can be created, and these can be printed as alphabetically arranged lists. In addition, each catalogue record contains several non-searchable items of information which are automatically captured, such as the file format, creation date and time, and date and time of any alterations to the image file. A catalogue-reading version of this software can be added to published collections of digital images.

The Fetch v.1.2 upgrade was installed as soon as it became available, and is faster in machine-time terms at adding items to the catalogue. In addition, it was discovered that if an image file is opened and saved in Photoshop (rather than simply opened for viewing and then closed without saving), a thumbnail is created and attached to the image file. This thumbnail can be used by Fetch. When Fetch does not have to create its own thumbnail, the machine-time for adding a record to the catalogue is so greatly reduced that it could no longer be considered a bottleneck. Since each image must be opened in Photoshop for a quality check after scanning, there is no significant increase in production time involved in saving the image in Photoshop at that stage. Saving each image in Photoshop became part of the standard scanning procedures.

Clerical and technical staff performed some archive and backup tasks to free operators' time for core scanning tasks. Trial indexing of selected images using descriptions captured from the Department of Manuscripts photograph card catalogue was carried out by David Tranter, an Information Systems Administrative Officer, with instruction and supervision from the Technical Stage Manager. This trial confirmed that such work could successfully be carried out in this way. While it is useful for such support to be provided, it should also be kept in mind that these tasks could be alternate duties to relieve operator fatigue, as recommended above.

It was not possible to fully evaluate the use of DeBabelizer for file processing. The reasons for this are that the system and staff-time resources which would have been required to do so were not available. To process files the average size of those created in this project requires more memory in order to hold an original and an altered copy in memory simultaneously. If DeBabelizer is to be used efficiently, graphics acceleration is needed. Additional memory needed for DeBabelizer would also improve the efficiency of graphics handling generally. No graphics acceleration had been provided for the storage computer, so the rate at which images could be displayed on the screen, moved around the screen or scaled up to view details was disappointing. It had not been planned to use this part of the system as a display system, but at times project staff or people who were seeing the system demonstrated wished to do so.

Staff time which might have been used to explore more fully the use of DeBabelizer with some of the smaller files created was absorbed in the difficulties described above over the delivery and installation of the system. In making up lost time, the production of cut-downs from large files and file-format conversions was seen as less central than the capture and evaluation of the complete set of master images to the successful completion of the project. Nevertheless, DeBabelizer was tried and shows promise. Training would be required if DeBabelizer were to be used by scanner operators.

FileMaker Pro was demonstrated during system training, but has not otherwise been used. It was decided that the limited staff-time available was better used maintaining a paper-based scan log. This allowed the log to be refined as experience early in the image-capture stage changed the view of the information that should be recorded and the best form in which to record it. A paper log was wholly adequate for the number of images captured in this phase of the project. The experience gained would enable the design of a FileMaker Pro database for a scaled-up second phase. The training demonstration had proved that this software is sufficiently flexible and powerful to meet production control and reporting requirements.

Peter James and other project staff who used Retrospect backup software judged it most suitable to its purpose, and easy to use. The project report recommended that it be considered for use as a standard with Mackintosh systems in The British Library, and that its availability/suitability for use with other platforms be investigated.

It was recommended in the consultant's report that image data compression should not be applied at this stage of the project. The Research and Development Division of Scitex are heavily involved in solving the compression issue as most of their existing clients have vast image libraries. We were advised both by Martin Ellis and by Scitex representatives that current compression techniques could not be applied without compromise to image fidelity and that uncompressed files should continue to be produced until such time as true lossless compression techniques have been developed. Files would then be compressed retrospectively. Uncompressed archive files stored on DAT tape do not present a storage problem, but the current principle of storing an off-line library of uncompressed files on optical disks is an issue that should be addressed both in terms of storage as well as media costs.

# PIX project

**Peter Carey**

In addition to The British Library's familiar role as one of the world's largest archives of written works, it also possesses one of the biggest collections of images. Its visual records range in scope from illuminated manuscripts to postage stamps, from the earliest 'book' around 200 BC on mulberry bark to yesterday's newspapers. The remit of the Library's Collections and Preservation Directorate is to care for the national collections, while supporting access by the provision of surrogate copies. The surrogate images for which this Directorate is responsible themselves form an enormous and important image archive. This unique archive suffers through a lack of indexing and the very considerable access problems posed by the number of sites across which the various collections are housed. The physical constraints of image storage make it practically impossible for anyone to browse the collections in search of a particular image. The British Library Electronic Photo Viewing system, or PIX for short, is an image database written and developed for the Library by iBase Image Systems Ltd of Ilkley in West Yorkshire, which allows users easy and instant access to thousands of the images held by the Library.

At the close of the *Initiatives for Access* programme, the system held 10,000 rare images from the Library's collections. In addition to other surrogate images, the images include two major collections of early photographs. The Canadian Copyright collection is an archive of photographs showing life in Canada at the turn of the century, with advertisements, scenes of pioneer life, and portraits of Canadian Indians. The Barlow Collection of Victorian psychic photographs features ghostly images and seances, mediums and ectoplasm. Other images are taken from the Library's unique treasures – the Lindisfarne Gospels, the Magna Carta and a Leonardo da Vinci notebook. Photographs of these major items are frequently requested by researchers, and the system makes it as simple as possible for them to view and order prints.

The Library holds one of the finest collections of 17th-century Indian miniature paintings, all of which have been digitised for the system, along with photographs of rare stamps, illuminated manuscripts and printed book illustrations by, for example, Edmund Dulac, William Blake, Aubrey Beardsley and Arthur Rackham. Bound albums of sheet music have yielded many decorative Victorian music covers. The albums are rarely searched for their covers, because the pictorial material is uncatalogued, so the photo viewing system is bringing to light much hidden material. The system proved very popular with readers during trials in the Library's reading rooms. 'All I wanted was more of everything' was a typical comment.

When the project was established in 1993 the most important initial decision was obviously the method of image capture. It was decided to use the Kodak PhotoCD process and the PIX software has several special features to facilitate this method of image acquisition. The system is, however, capable of importing image data from any source. The PhotoCD standard was selected for a number of reasons. It was felt that, from the point of view of a professional photographer, the process surpassed in terms of both quality and speed anything that had been seen before. The efficiency of the process means that in terms of labour costs alone it offers a cheaper solution for conversion of existing photographic archives than direct scanning with the additional benefit of providing a portable high-resolution secondary digital archive.

Images already held as transparencies or on negative film were transferred directly to PhotoCD. Other images were photographed on to either 35mm or five by four inch film depending on the particular nature of the material. For simple economic reasons, the majority of the material was mastered on to Standard PhotoCD from 35mm film at a maximum resolution of 3072 x 2048 pixels, an 18 megabyte file, and this was felt to be perfectly adequate for electronic display and most purposes of reproduction. A few special images were mastered from five by four inch film on to Professional PhotoCD with a sixth resolution of 6144 x 4096 pixels, a 72 megabyte file. Although the system cannot currently handle the highest-resolution image stored on the Professional PhotoCD, the 3072 x 2048 pixel scan is perceived to be of significantly higher quality than the equivalent Standard PhotoCD scan and can be justified where it is important to display and reproduce the very finest detail, as on very large and complex maps for example. A few hundred five by four inch transparencies from the archive and 300 new items were scanned on Professional PhotoCD, giving around 100 images per disk at the nominal 35mm resolution of 3072 x 2048 pixels. This enabled qualitative evaluation of both on-screen and hard-copy images and allowed an exhaustive trial of all the PhotoCD options over a wide range of material. The range of origination samples was increased by the inclusion of a batch of ten by eight inch monochrome glass plates (c. 1910) of illuminated manuscripts.

On-screen evaluation of 35mm and five by four inch transparencies produced some surprises, with the former giving a larger screen image, scan level-for-level. In photography, not all of the five by four inch image is used, with very generous margins allowing for scale, grey-scale, identification and colour patch. The 35mm format only includes identification, so is virtually full-frame, giving a very satisfactory display of 16.7cm x 10.8cm at the same level. It is worth noting when scanning five by four inch transparencies 100-up on to Professional PhotoCD, the top file of 3072 x 2048 pixels does not have the detail of the equivalent file produced from 35mm. This is due to the relative sizes – both approximately 18 megabyte scans, one over a four inch as against a one and a half inch scale, so that the scan of the 35mm slide produces more pixels per inch of original image.

As at least three different scanning devices would be required, the task of transfer to PhotoCD was contracted to bureaux. The very high quality of the transfers was due to the imposition of strict quality, cost, time and security parameters. Another important reason for the success of the transfer to PhotoCD was the close cooperation between the Library's project manager and the bureaux involved. The batches of 100 scanned images were periodically loaded onto the PIX workstations with basic information (mostly just the shelfmark) and cropped. The current practice is to load three images of each, a thumbnail, a display image and a x2 zoom.

As with any new product, it is not surprising that PhotoCD scanning prices vary widely: over 100% variation for a similar service in the same geographical area is common. Unexpected variations occur with continuous strips of 35mm film and mounted 35mm slides. The latter costs 300% more because of the film gate on the Kodak 2000 scanner. This means that the mounted slides require individual treatment, whereas the strip is on auto-feed. For full range Professional PhotoCD, the higher cost of a mounted slide can be multiplied by 12 times. It is clear that evaluation of precisely what is required of the images, and how they are delivered for digitising, will impinge profoundly on the costs of a large-scale programme.

The PhotoCD is a remarkable storage medium, and it is a pity that so little hard technical information about it is available. As it was designed for the amateur market, a lack of data can be excused in the short-term, but several years on, the professional questions must be answered. As a preservation and access aid in The British Library, using the disk as an archive medium would seem an excellent idea. Written technical data was requested from Kodak in 1993 as to the medium's expected life, accelerated ageing test results, recommended re-write times, and optimum storage conditions. The same important questions remained unanswered during the time of the project, but more information is now available from Kodak. (In addition to the up-to-date permanence information on Kodak's own Web site, http://www.kodak.com/daiHome/tech-Info/permanence.shtml, the paper 'Lifetime of KODAK Writable CD and Photo CD Media' (Stinson *et al.* 1995) is useful.) Current knowledge suggests that continuing availability of superseded hardware and software to read the disks is a more pressing issue than the shelf-life of the medium.

The System runs under Windows on standard PC hardware. Initially PIX was run on a 486-DX66 machine with 16MB of RAM, later upgraded to a Pentium 90MhZ machine with 32MB of RAM. Images were stored on a 3.5 gigabyte hard disk drive, to which was later added an additional 9 gigabyte drive. This machine was used for trials in the Bloomsbury reading room. Later this was upgraded to a 45 gigabyte RAID hard drive to accommodate the growing number of images and for increased data security. Two other similarly configured workstations were also acquired for use in other reading rooms of the Library, including one at Boston Spa. Hardware was provided by Evolution of Raynes Park, Surrey, and ADC of Coventry.

**User interfaces**

When your potential users are a mixture of 'tyros' and non-computer users, then issues of interface design are problematic, and it has taken a great deal of thought and development work to arrive at a functionally elegant system which

98% of those testing it in a library reading room rated easy to use. It is, after all, only too easy in developing such a system to slip in icons that seem appropriate, simple and 'right' ...only to find they are meaningless to the uninitiated.

The system developed by iBase was provided with two user interfaces. The View interface is the reader's interface to the system and, although running under the Windows operating system, this interface is stripped of the usual Windows features. This decision was made with the intention of making the system approachable and easy to use for those people coming to it with no Windows experience or even no computer experience at all. All operations are launched with the click of a mouse from labelled on-screen buttons. Context-sensitive help information is displayed in a dedicated window for constant reference. This interface is designed for the semi-public environment of the various reading rooms of the Library.

The Edit interface is a standard Windows interface where functions are performed via the usual menu and tool bars with online assistance available in the Windows help format. The Edit interface provides access to all the additional editing features of the system which are not available from the View interface.

The program can be set to run in either view or edit mode. Additionally, with the use of a specially designated key combination and a pre-set password, it is possible for privileged users to enter edit mode from the View interface and to exit the program for system maintenance. Ordinarily, the PC is configured to start in the view mode directly it is turned on. If the PC is left untouched for a pre-set period of time, the system will return to its idle state which consists of an iconic view of the various available collections (see Plate 5).

### Image quality and display options

It was decided at an early stage of the project that the quality of image presentation should not be compromised in favour of performance or storage cost. Although the system supports image compression to the popular standards such as FIF (Fractal Image Format) and JPEG, it was held that FIF Compression did not provide sufficient quality, while, without additional dedicated hardware, JPEG was too slow in decompression to be considered. Optimised palette reduction has been used for many monochromatic images and certain colour images. This technique reduces the storage requirement by a factor of three with little discernible loss of image quality. It also has the advantage over the other compression methods of reducing the access time to the image since no decompression algorithms have to be invoked. Most colour images, however, are currently held on the system in an uncompressed state as full colour bitmaps with a palette of 16.8 million colours. Most of the images are currently stored in Windows native BMP format, although the system does support other file formats such as TIFF.

A screen resolution of 800 x 600 pixels was chosen to provide the optimum viewing area for the image sets provided on PhotoCD. The other possibilities (640 x 480 and 1024 x 768) provided either not enough screen space for the images or too much space, therefore making the displayed image smaller than need be.

In its basic image display mode, the system presents images in a window occupying approximately half of the screen area. This window is designed to accommodate both landscape and portrait images at the PhotoCD resolution of 256 x 384 pixels. The rest of the screen display is devoted to data, button controls, and a 'film strip' preview of thumbnails which is used for browsing and imagebase navigation. This size of image for the main reference is chosen as offering the best compromise between quality and performance. A smaller image would not offer sufficient detail, whereas a larger image would probably be too slow to access for browsing purposes. Using this size of image the response in this mode is just about instantaneous.

From the reference page the user can choose to view the image at working resolution. This corresponds to the PhotoCD base resolution of 512 x 768 pixels. This image is displayed against a plain, customisable background to avoid clutter, with or without a simple caption. Landscape format images fit to fill almost the entire screen area; portrait format images are scrollable so that the entire image can be viewed with ease. Entire collections or any selected image set can be browsed backwards and forwards at this working resolution.

For the majority of images, the working resolution provides sufficient detail for display purposes, but in certain cases, particularly manuscripts, higher-resolution copies of the image have also been stored. These can be viewed either in an overlaid window or against a plain mask as just described. At these higher resolutions the window on the image will often be considerably smaller than the image itself, so, in addition to scrolling controls, the software also allows the image to be 'dragged' around the display with the mouse, enabling any portion of the image to be brought into immediate view.

To allow images from a collection to be compared against each other, it was decided to introduce a window called the photodesk. Images can be copied to the photodesk when browsing at either reference or working resolution. When viewing the photodesk images can be viewed at any resolution for which there exists a scan for each selected image. These are displayed in windows sized and positioned on the screen in the most sensible way for the number of images being compared. The user has full freedom, however, to move and resize these windows in any way desired. At the moment, a maximum of four images can be viewed on the photodesk at any one time.

A thumbnail representation of each image is also held on the system, displayed in two ways. As previously mentioned, in its basic display mode, the system presents a 'film-strip' preview of the entire imagebase showing four images at a time. Thumbnails can also be more conveniently viewed in what is termed the gallery where 24 images are displayed to a page. Here the user can easily browse entire collections, looking through thousands of images in a matter of minutes. This quick browse facility can also be applied to any selection of images made as a result of a search.

Images can also be collated by simple selection. As the user browses in any mode, images can be selected by marking. The ability to mark images for review was considered to be an important and very useful feature so the right

| | |
|---|---|
| Shelfmark: | HS 85/10 Vol. |
| | Canadian Deposit |
| Copyright No: | 14628 |
| Title: | |
| Floating Cloud a Yorkton Indian | |
| Place of Copyright: | |
| North West Territories | |
| Copyright registered to: | |
| Thomas Veitch Simpson | |
| Year: | 1904 |
| Mounted: | Yes |
| Dimensions: | 125 x 105 mm |
| PhotoCD: | 2339.1032.0933.75 |
| Notes: | |

Keyword Search    Build Keyword Query    Data Match Search    Global Search    Reset

Copy to Photodesk    View Photodesk    Clear Photodesk    Print    About    Gallery

**1326 records on file**
**Record 9 of 62 selected**

Click on a thumbnail to go directly to that image. Click in the slidebar control to preview any part of the collection or drag the pointer to go to a specific point.

Images 6-9

Basic image display screen for the Photo Viewing system

mouse button has been dedicated for this purpose. A right mouse click on any image – thumbnail, reference or working – will mark the image with a tick. Subsequently, all ticked images can be viewed as a set. In edit mode, this set can be saved under a given user name and reselected at any time.

The most important consideration in the design of the image editing system (available only in edit mode) has been the need to facilitate the most rapid processing of scanned images. Here, the use of PhotoCD has made possible the introduction of a number of special productivity features. Batch operations can be performed whereby all images at any specified resolution are streamed off the PhotoCD in one operation. Similarly, image colour balance, brightness/contrast adjustment and transformation can also be undertaken in batches, so the same change can be made across a large number of images. Once loaded from the PhotoCD, the unique PhotoCD number is automatically written to the database. Images can be cropped within the database with the cropping automatically applied across each image in the image set for a particular record.

All image editing changes are recorded by the system so there exists a precise audit path from the PhotoCD to the image actually stored by the system. If a mistake has been made during any image processing operation it is possible to recover the original images from the PhotoCD in a batch operation using the

Detail from the medieval illuminated manuscript The Sforza Hours, showing the high quality that can be obtained from a PhotoCD.

unique PhotoCD number to pick up the required image. As an option, it is possible to reapply any of the image processing operations previously performed on a selected set of images.

It was obvious at an early stage of the project that all images were in need of a certain amount of colour balance and brightness/contrast adjustment. This was particularly important in the case of the Johnson Collection where images were scanned directly from transparencies which had been produced over an extended period of time, but was also true for images photographed on the same media at similar times, probably because of the use of slightly different settings in the scanning process. It was imperative, therefore, that a dynamic means of adjustment be provided so that there is instant feedback to reflect the result of the changes made. To this end, an interface has been designed which shows the original image alongside a palette-reduced representation of that image which can then be used to reflect instantaneously the results of any brightness/contrast/colour changes made. Samples can be taken at any stage so that more detailed comparisons can be made and a choice as to the optimum settings clearly taken. This image editing interface also provides the opportunity to sharpen the image by the application of a confirmation filter. As indicated before, these setting changes can be simply applied across a whole set of images – even the entire imagebase – in a single operation. This facility has been extensively used in the present system to balance material drawn from different photographic archives. Density, contrast, and red/green/blue files were manipulated to make them usable. Despite the special facilities offered by the system, these changes could take as long as 10 minutes per scanned image to implement. In these circumstances, it might be more economic to undertake new photography instead of trying to correct the existing images.

**Searching and indexing**

The system has to allow fast and flexible access to image collections for all kinds of user. It therefore contains two search engines: a keyword search engine and a textual search engine. The keyword search engine represents a very powerful implementation of the simple and familiar concept of keyword association. Any number of keywords can be associated with an image, each of these keywords being categorised by a group name. This keyword/group structure forms the basis of any search, where terms are listed from a thesaurus from which the user makes their selection. In its simplest implementation the user just selects a key group in order to select keywords relevant to the subject matter in which they are interested. Clicking on a keyword will immediately select all the images which contain that reference. In a more sophisticated implementation, keywords can be combined with a number of logical operators so that quite complex queries can be made very easily. These two implementations were provided in order to fulfil the needs of both the casual user who wants to look at images as quickly and easily as possible, and the more serious researcher who wishes to search for images based on very specific criteria.

It was appreciated at the outset that keyword searching can only be as good as the indexing allows. It was therefore deemed essential to provide the tools to make it as easy as possible to build and maintain the keyword thesaurus and ensure that it forms a consistent and coherent classification system. A number of different cataloguing philosophies can be catered for. A particular keyword classification, possibly imported from an existing database, can be imposed in advance such that each keyword entry is required to fit a pre-set scheme. Alternatively, a classification scheme can be allowed to evolve during the cataloguing process. In this latter case, facilities are provided to find and remove the redundancies and ambiguities that inevitably occur, especially when more than one person has been involved in the indexing. Keywords which have no reference can be found and deleted. Duplicate keywords can be found and resolved in a number of ways. If a particular group grows too large, keywords can easily be recategorised to form a number of smaller logical groupings.

The textual search engine allows for retrieval based on any of the text fields associated with the image, matching the input data string against each record in the imagebase. Additional to this data match search, there is a global text search where all data fields are searched. Any image containing any kind of reference to the input data string will be selected.

In a similar way to image editing, all database text editing is performed 'in place' with a number of features available to speed the data entry process. The principal data set is displayed alongside the image, with any additional data displayed in separate windows which can be moved anywhere on the screen. The current keyword set is displayed in a dedicated window together with the keyword thesaurus. Keywords can be entered at the click of the mouse from the thesaurus, or new keywords can be typed directly in, the thesaurus being immediately updated to reflect any new additions. Alternatively, text can be highlighted in the database and instantly selected as a keyword. It is also possible to make links with specified database fields to create automatically keywords based on the data already entered.

Indexing information can be keyed directly at the PIX workstation or remotely. A small programme was written by iBase to allow remote data entry. A substantial amount of remote indexing was undertaken for the project by Mrs Somalatha Somadasa. Where photographic orders were identified pre-photography as being suitable for addition to PIX, extra data was extracted from the order form to be written on the identification slip. For example, author, title, date and sometimes publisher would be added to the normal shelfmark, page number and job number. In other cases, catalogue entries for items on the PhotoCD disk were identified on BLAISE, edited and then keyed in. Information for the manuscript collections (not on BLAISE) was drawn from existing manual finding aids. Books published by the Library were also drawn on to gather more information on individual illustrations.

The essential tools for searching the imagebase are now available, with powerful search engines proven. But the costs of cataloguing, identifying, then keying the information are considerable. The difficulty of acquiring resources which would allow all the images to be catalogued at a suitable level proved to be one of the major stumbling blocks for the project. Much can be done on a purely visual front, and images can be loaded on to the system with just basic identifiers, in this case a shelfmark, and automatically a unique PhotoCD number. On searching a screenful at a time, it is possible to search around 17,000 frames per hour, marking for review likely images.

### Print and other outputs, PIX project and beyond

Provision of hard copy from the system has been problematic. Users will find it disappointing that, having searched and found material almost instantaneously, printing may then take six to ten minutes. Currently the system will only allow the online output of reference prints. Where images are held on the system at a maximum resolution of 512 x 768 pixels it will not be possible to produce prints online that would compare with a photographic print. Postcard-sized prints at this resolution are certainly of good, even marketable quality, but there will probably be some discernible pixelation within the image. To produce true photographic-quality prints it is necessary to retrieve the highest-resolution image from the master PhotoCD. Although this process could ultimately be achieved by the use of a large CD Jukebox system, it can only be achieved at the moment by the manual insertion of the appropriate PhotoCD. Once in place, the system can print from the PhotoCD, streaming off the highest possible resolution image and, optionally, checking for any editing operations that may have been performed on the original scanned image, such as any cropping or brightness/contrast change, and applying these before printing so that the final print matches exactly that viewed on the display system. Standard rights information can be overlaid if necessary.

Various printing devices have been tested and a good basic machine is the Primera Pro. Cheap but flexible, producing either dye-sublimation or wax thermal, with the advantage of both A4 and, as an extra, a spacer kit to produce A5 prints. Printing A5 prints at a low resolution produces satisfactory images for reference. Ageing tests with prints from the Kodak Color Ease PS have been disturbing. Material stored in the dark in plastic file sleeves has seriously deteriorated in under three months. The normal life expectancy of six months for a dye-sublimation print is not really suitable for library usage. The Fujix Pictography 3000 is presently being evaluated, and it has proved possible to produce a reproduction-quality print with a reasonable life expectancy.

Excellent results have been produced by creating duplicate film negatives from PhotoCD. This is potentially a useful feature for the more traditional customer who likes a large piece of film in an envelope. However, the cost of providing these was affected by the cost of cutting-edge equipment used and came out at 20 pounds an image. This is too costly. A more forward-looking approach is to investigate the provision of digital files for customers. The provision of photographic negatives from digital images is only a stop-gap measure as people are weaned off bits of plastic with heavy metal particles stuck on them. There is very little future in film, but for now the Library will strive to provide an affordable film service.

The Library has for a long time aspired to use its vast photographic collections as the basis of a commercial picture library operation. It has recently begun to turn that vision into a reality. The experience of developing PIX will obviously be of great importance in the development of the Picture Library. PIX at one level could be seen as the lightbox for the Picture Library; at another as an electronic filing cabinet. Indeed, it could become its shop window and incorporate an entire Picture Library management engine as well.

The commercial possibilities of PIX were demonstrated during the trials in the Bloomsbury reading room. Antonia Fraser looked at the system and found the perfect image for the cover of the new edition of her book *The Warrior Queens*, a picture of the Roman goddess of war, Bellona. The illustration was the cover of a piece of sheet music, bound within a mid-19th-century album and therefore not catalogued separately, so it would have been almost impossible to find using traditional methods of picture research. An appointment was made for Antonia Fraser's publishers, Weidenfeld and Nicolson, to see the picture. When they had agreed it as the cover image, the system rapidly produced a print for their designer to work with.

In building on the PIX experience, there are obviously many other issues to be investigated: those involved in making the PIX imagebase available over the Library's internal network; the use of a digital back or camera to acquire digital images directly (the Library is now using digital photography to provide digital images directly for internal and commercial use); the need to transfer the system to the NT platform (which was the platform for the original iBase application) if support for the platform becomes feasible within the Library, in order to improve performance; and, of course, the development of a stable and easily accessible digital archive for the huge number of images which, as PIX showed, can be readily and inexpensively created.

The Library's ambition is to have a viewing station in every reading room, to make the images available on the World Wide Web, and to extend coverage to include much other appropriate material such as the Philatelic collection and digitised microfilm. It has welcomed the interest of external organisations in the Electronic Photo Viewing system, which has led to fruitful collaborations, including the use of the system to digitise glass plate images from the collection of St Andrews University.

PIX has been widely demonstrated at many exhibitions and conferences. In February 1995, it was among just 20 UK projects chosen for exhibition at the exclusive Showcase accompanying the G7 Ministerial Conference on the Information Society at Brussels. The summit was organised to raise awareness of the information society and its benefits. Among the hundred plus visitors to the Library's stand was US Vice President Al Gore's advisor on IT. As Brian Lang commented at the time, this honour provided recognition that The British Library is 'a key player in the international revolution in the electronic processing, storage and retrieval of information'.

# Gallery applications and educational multimedia

**Karen Brookfield, Andrew Prescott and Simon Shaw**

As part of its aim to widen access to its collection, The British Library undertakes a wide-ranging exhibition and education programme for adults and children, including teachers in schools and colleges and their pupils. The Library's present galleries in the British Museum building not only house a large permanent display including such treasures as the Lindisfarne Gospels, Magna Carta and the Gutenberg Bible, but have also been the venue for a long series of spectacular and imaginative temporary exhibitions. Recent highlights have included *The Earth and the Heavens: the art of the mapmaker* in 1995, which illustrated the variety and beauty of the Library's cartographic collections, and an exhibition exploring the literature associated with *The Mythical Quest* in 1996. The new exhibition galleries opening at St Pancras in 1998 will allow the Library to stage much larger temporary exhibitions, create a more integrated permanent display, and also permit the use of multimedia and other techniques to convey more information about the items on display.

The Library's Education Service offers a programme of activities specially designed for teachers and schools which encourages them to investigate the Library and its collections. These include special events, programmes and resource packs linked to the exhibition programme, 'hands-on' workshops for primary schools such as Chinese calligraphy and bookmaking, sessions for GCSE and A-level students in English Literature, History and other subjects, and an Adult Education Programme. However, as the national library, the Library is conscious that its audiences extend far beyond those that can visit in person. The recognition that technology can assist the Library in reaching the widest possible audience predates the arrival of digital technology. The Audio-Visual Service with the Education Service, for example, have produced a series of award-winning videos on a variety of subjects including Alice in Wonderland, the Lindisfarne Gospels and Magna Carta.

These various activities are all undertaken by the Library's Public Affairs Directorate, which recognised some years ago the potential of multimedia to enhance the outreach of its work. The provision of multimedia components for the new displays at St Pancras has, for example, been an important part of planning for the new galleries since an early stage. Public Affairs had become involved in multimedia development before the *Initiatives for Access* programme was launched, but there has been useful cross-fertilisation of work in Public Affairs with *Initiatives for Access*, particularly through the Treasures project. Over the past few years, Public Affairs has built up an impressive range of multimedia products. This article will describe some of these and illustrate the different development issues they have raised.

## Turning the Pages

In 1871, the Victorian connoisseur J. C. Robinson travelled to Madrid. Shortly after his arrival in the town, he heard rumours of a fabulous illuminated manuscript being offered for sale by a priest. Robinson's host had tried to buy the manuscript, but the money he had taken to make the purchase had been stolen. Robinson persuaded the Spaniard to arrange for the priest to bring the manuscript to him: 'The very same evening he brought the priest to my room, when with much ceremony the little corpulent velvet-covered volume was put into my hands. The very first page was opened, disclosing two glorious illuminations, blazing with colours and gold, but when every page of the book, and there were more than two hundred of them, was revealed equally enriched, the only thought was that it should not again for an instant leave my hands'. Robinson purchased the manuscript and brought it back to England. It was acquired from him by another collector, John Malcolm, who presented it in 1893 to the British Museum.

This volume was the Sforza Hours, one of the most beautiful surviving Renaissance manuscripts. It was originally commissioned by Bona of Savoy, widow of Galeazzo Sforza, Duke of Milan, in about 1490. The illuminator was the Milanese priest Giovan Pietro Birago. Before Birago had finished work on the manuscript, however, some of the folios were stolen by a friar, and it seems that the manuscript languished unfinished until 1517, when Bona's heir Margaret of Austria commissioned the Flemish painter Gerard Horenbout to execute 16 additional miniatures to complement Birago's. As a result, the manuscript juxtaposes the art of the Italian Renaissance with that of the Renaissance in northern Europe. The completed manuscript was probably then presented to Margaret's nephew, the Emperor Charles V.

The visitor to The British Library's galleries may perhaps find it difficult to recapture Robinson's excitement at the rediscovery of this stunning manuscript, since only a single opening can be displayed at a time and it is impossible to convey the wealth of illumination which so enthralled Robinson. Moreover, it is difficult to convey to the visitor the contrast between Birago's work and that of the Flemish master Horenbout.

The availability of digital images offers the possibility of allowing the visitor to explore the manuscript as if he had the volume itself in his hands. The concept has been explained by Jane Carr, the Library's Director of Public Affairs, as follows: 'As we began to plan for the exhibition galleries in the Library's new building at St Pancras, we developed the very simple concept of allowing the visitor to turn a surrogate but facsimile page. Digital technology combined with animation and televisual techniques provide the perfect medium since neither the original nor the facsimile is damaged or degraded by the process and yet the visitor can have a real sense of what it might be like to turn the pages of the real thing'.

A prototype was developed to explore the viability of this concept. Five by four inch colour transparencies of the manuscript were scanned using the Scitex 340 scanner acquired for the Treasures project at a variety of resolutions up to 800 DPI. For the prototype, photographs of 16 pages of the manuscript were scanned. Adobe Photoshop was used to process the digitised images of the manuscripts and to create the frames used in the page turning sequence. Sebastian Airy then animated these frames using Director 4, a software package produced by Macromedia.

The animation sequence allows visitors using a touch-screen display to 'turn the pages' by touching the corner of the screen and dragging their finger across, so that the page moves across, just as it would in a real book. The animation sequence allows the user to see the difference between the way vellum and paper moves. A zoom tool also allows users to see magnified details of the illumination.

Another of the Library's great treasures is the Codex Arundel, an autograph notebook of Leonardo da Vinci, which contains a wealth of scientific diagrams and notes in Leonardo's characteristic mirror writing, running from right to left. (Another of Leonardo's notebooks, the Codex Leicester, is owned by Bill Gates, and Microsoft have recently produced a facsimile of this manuscript on CD-ROM, which allows the user not only to investigate the notebook itself but provides a wealth of contextual information.) A long-term project to produce a conventional facsimile of the Codex Arundel meant that new colour transparencies of the manuscript were available and offered the Library the opportunity to use new technology to make its own Leonardo notebook more accessible to visitors. Sixteen images from the Codex Arundel were therefore also included in the 'Turning the Pages' prototype. In this case, an additional feature was a button which enabled the viewer to flip over Leonardo's mirror writing, so that it reads in the normal direction, from left to right.

The prototypes of both the Sforza Hours and the Leonardo notebook were on display for three weeks during the summer of 1996 for public evaluation. The prototype display operated on a PowerMac working at 80 Mz and storing the 16 images from both manuscripts in 136 MB of RAM. This configuration allowed the prototype to process the images at the speed necessary for successful animation. In order to expand the system further, it would be necessary to animate the images direct from the hard drive, allowing more exhibited volumes, as well as additional information, to be made available. (See Plates 6 and 7.)

The reaction to the prototype during the evaluation exercise was very encouraging. Not only were visitors to the gallery very excited by this imaginative use of new technology, but there was a great deal of television and press interest. During the three-week evaluation, 239 people used the system, with 189 completing detailed questionnaires. Of these, only three found the system at all difficult to use; the vast majority rated it very easy or easy, although 69 required a brief demonstration first. Almost all visitors made use of the zoom facility (in the case of the Sforza Hours) or the mirror facility (in the case of the Leonardo notebook). Comments were uniformly enthusiastic: 'An excellent facility, very exciting!'; 'An absolutely marvellous display. I saw it on TV last week and I never imagined that a week later I would be interacting with it myself'; 'You should have every book like this, it is a safe way of looking at them – it is just like reading a book!'.

Discussions of the impact of new technology on perceptions of text have tended to emphasise the way in which the multilinearity of hypertextual media breaks down the conventional narrative and logical structures of the book. A characteristic comment is that of George Landow: 'Hypertext, which challenges narrative and all literary form based on linearity, calls into question ideas of plot and story current since Aristotle'. However, such views perhaps oversimplify the way in which different types of people perceive different types of text. When illuminated manuscripts are only seen as objects lying open in cases or as photographs of selected pages, it is difficult to understand how they function as books. This can be the case not only with the casual visitor or school-children, but even with quite advanced students. An American medievalist has recently observed how difficult it is to understand the nature of medieval sources when one is a long way from Europe. 'My hands had held my Ph.D. before they ever held a medieval manuscript', he pointed out.

In this context, a simple presentational idea such as Turning the Pages can make an important contribution to textual perceptions. In an application such as this, the codex can be reintegrated and rescued from being a disembodied artefact in a case or a disconnected photograph in a book. Rather than breaking up the codex, new technology can help bring the codex to life.

**The Young Person's Guide to the British Library**

A huge and complex organisation such as The British Library can be bewildering to those who work for it, let alone for users and visitors. The range of the collections is flabbergasting: ancient papyri, books in oriental languages, scientific patents, sound recordings, and modern literary manuscripts, to name but a few. It is difficult to convey this range of material through even the most imaginative gallery display. At the same time as the Turning the Pages prototype was displayed in the galleries, *The Young Person's Guide to the British Library* was also made available for evaluation. This is a prototype multimedia introduction to the Library aimed at young people aged 10-16 years, created by a team in The British Library. The team included a multimedia designer Paula Lonergan, who spent a year here working on various multimedia projects, initially on a student placement following a course in multimedia design at ARTEC (Arts Technology Education Centre), where for her final project she developed a prototype interactive guide to the treasures of The British Library.

The concept behind the *Young Person's Guide* has been explained by Kate Barnes of the Library's Education Service as follows: 'We want to encourage young people, specifically the 10-16 year olds who have little contact with the Library through our schools/Further Education programme, to learn more about what the Library is and what it can offer them. We need to think carefully about how we target this age group, not just in the galleries but through the use of IT to schools/colleges and via the Internet. In developing the prototype for the galleries it was vital that we presented the basic information about the institution in an accessible and 'fun' way, to engage the user from the start. We tried out our initial ideas on content and design on groups of local students who were sophisticated IT users and said they did not want a database approach. We incorporated many of the students' own suggestions as to what to include in the prototype, such as using 'talking heads' to convey basic facts and figures and to prompt the user where appropriate. It was harder to persuade them to volunteer to be "scanned in and manipulated", but a couple of them braved it and they now introduce the main sections of the guide.'

The Library is well placed to develop multimedia packages which are genuinely media-rich, not only because of the varied nature of its collections, but also because of the wide range of materials which have been built up as a result of its educational and publications activities in the past. The award-winning series of videos produced by the Library's Audio-Visual Service under Clive Izard, for example, provides an extensive video archive on which multimedia designers can draw.

In developing *The Young Person's Guide*, Paula Lonergan used Adobe Photoshop and Illustrator to design the screens. The video action (such as a Chinese calligraphy workshop) that is incorporated into the system was digitised using a Kingfisher card and edited and compressed using Adobe Premiere. The images, video and sound to be found on the system are all drawn from the Library's collections. For example, an excerpt from a recording of Florence Nightingale is a treasure of the National Sound Archive and was incorporated into the system using soundEdit pro.

The prototype was put together using Macromedia Director. Paula Lonergan has explained this preference as follows: 'Director was used as it is one of the best ways to create single- or cross-platform applications for presentations of full-scale CD-ROM projects. Director 5 is highly optimised for simple and rapid integration of media from other environments such as Adobe Photoshop and Premiere. This is important as there were many changes to be made during the development of *The Young Person's Guide*. Director enables one to create simple presentations quickly and effectively with minimal programming requirement and so was ideal for the prototype system. To add a high-level use of programming interactivity, the programming environment Lingo can be used'.

The prototype *Young Person's Guide* is divided into four sections:

- *Behind the Bookcase.* This opens up the varied collections, many of which are not books at all. For example, by selecting SOUND, users can listen to an extract from the personal testimony of a Holocaust survivor (from the Oral History collections at the National Sound Archive), pick a favourite stamp from the Philatelic Collections or dip into the varied patent collections from the science collections.
- *Between the Covers.* Highlights of the Library's manuscript collection are shown here, along with a Manuscript Mysteries quiz to explore some of the myths about manuscripts.
- *People in Our Past.* A collage of famous and infamous individuals whose histories are told through the collections, including such varied personalities as William Tyndale, Jane Austen, John Lennon, Florence Nightingale, Leonardo da Vinci, 'Alice' and Rabindranath Tagore. (Only a few of these were 'live'

in the prototype but it turned out to be the section of the *Guide* most used by visitors in the gallery, a useful pointer for future development.)

- *The Living Library*. This section features events and activities to show how young people can get involved in workshops or family sessions in the Library's galleries and even how they can add to the Library's holdings through schemes like the National Life Story Collection or by having their own work published.

One of the most striking features of *The Young Person's Guide* prototype was the very strong emphasis on screen design. This showed the value of using a trained designer in developing the programme. As with Turning the Pages, comments received from the public evaluation during 1996 will be helpful in developing the programme further. Many of the young visitors who used the prototype system said they had very little prior knowledge of the Library and were surprised to find out how large and varied its collections are. They particularly appreciated having information about parts of the collections not on display in the galleries, which they would otherwise have not known about.

## The Image of the World

*The Image of the World* was developed for an exhibition in the Library's galleries in the summer of 1995 entitled *The Earth and the Heavens: the art of the map-maker*, which showed over 150 terrestrial and celestial maps. Again, the aim of the project was to use new technology to allow the visitor to explore some of the exhibits in greater detail. It is important to emphasise that the Library sees such displays as a means of complementing and enhancing the visitor's appreciation of the original object. The interactive display should, as far as possible, avoid upstaging the original, instead enabling the visitor to appreciate more fully the original artefact.

Ten maps were selected for inclusion in the project. These ranged from the Psalter World Map, a miniature medieval world map measuring just 10 by 15 centimetres, which forms the frontispiece of a 13th-century Psalter, to contemporary satellite images. One of the most striking visual features of maps is their intricate and often beautifully rendered detail. One of the chief aims of *The Image of the World* was to allow the user to appreciate this detail by offering access to highly magnified images. The display allowed users to view full-screen shots of each map and up to six close-ups of each. Apart from the satellite images, which were already in digital format, the maps were scanned from photographic transparencies, again using the Scitex scanner acquired for the Treasures project. The transparencies were scanned at the maximum resolution, because of the need for very high-level magnification, producing image files of approximately 80 MB. The interactive display was developed for the Library by Republic, who used Macromedia Director.

The multimedia display formed an integral part of the exhibition. In a survey of exhibition visitors using the system 97% rated it 'Very easy to use' or 'Quite easy to use' and 88% said that it had increased their overall enjoyment of the exhibition. An enhanced version of the display was also made available for sale on CD-ROM in Mac/Windows dual format. The CD version included on-screen text of the audio commentaries, an introduction to the history of cartography and a bibliography. During the exhibition itself over 1000 CDs were sold in the Library's Bookshop. The gallery version was awarded the Silver Award for Interactive Displays in the 1995 BIMA awards.

*The Image of the World* represented the most extensive use to date by the Library of computer displays as part of a public exhibition. It is encouraging that a survey across all age groups revealed that 95% would like to see similar systems in future exhibitions.

### Medieval Realms

The British Library's involvement with multimedia predates the *Initiatives for Access* programme. The Library's Directorate of Public Affairs, headed by Jane Carr, includes British Library Publications, the Education Service, the Exhibition Service and Audio-Visual Services. As soon as multimedia began to appear, the Public Affairs team recognised its potential to help users gain access to the collection in different ways. In 1993, the Library produced, in association with the Royal Society for the Protection of Birds and Yorkshire International Thomson Multimedia, a CD-ROM on *British Birds*. This contained over 500 full and quarter-screen images of birds normally found in Great Britain, over 25 full-motion clips of the birds and over 170 bird calls and sounds drawn from the British Library of Wildlife Sounds, part of the National Sound Archive. This CD won the BIMA Gold Award for Education in 1993.

In 1992, staff from Public Affairs began work on two CD-ROMs intended specifically for use in schools. The first was *Sources in History: Medieval Realms: Britain 1066 to 1500*. This was developed with the aid of a grant from the National Council for Educational Technology (NCET), and was designed to be used in Key Stage 3 of the History National Curriculum. The second was *Inventors and Inventions*, containing a wide range of photographs, video clips, animated drawings and illustrations from patent applications, designed for cross-curricular use in History, Science and Technology at Key Stages 2 and 3. It enables pupils to carry out a wide range of investigations in topics such as power, communication, flight, textiles and land transport from the invention of the wheel to the present day. *Inventors and Inventions* was produced in association with Yorkshire International Thomson Multimedia and developed by Interactive Learning Productions. These CD-ROMs were both published in 1994. The compilation of these disks helped the Library identify many issues of importance for the development of future products, some of which will be outlined here, with particular reference to *Medieval Realms*.

The *Medieval Realms* CD-ROM is a unique and comprehensive collection of original source material for the study of the Middle Ages. It contains 852 images of illuminated manuscripts, documents, objects and buildings (75% of which are from The British Library), 623 transcriptions of documents in modern and/or Middle English; and 28 sound clips comprising music, spoken Middle English and modern English narratives. The database format means that the material can be searched in a number of different ways: by topic (e.g. Government, Society, Culture, Feudalism, Food, Women); by type of evidence (e.g.

books, private papers, chronicles); date (either single dates or ranges); word (with a wild card facility); or any combination of these four methods.

In early 1992, nobody (inside or outside The British Library) had any experience of developing a multimedia project on this scale for use in schools. With hindsight everyone involved underestimated the task in hand in almost every aspect of the project.

The project was managed by Karen Brookfield, the Library's Head of Education and Roger Watson, a freelance with wide experience of educational publishing. The scope of the disk was defined with the help of curators from the Library and educational advisers, including practising teachers and teacher trainers. The actual selection of material and compilation of the database records for 1500 sources was a vast – and in many respects a specialist – undertaking, too vast for Library curators alone. It was also recognised that writing for 11 year olds is a skill that needs to be learnt, as is writing for multimedia as opposed to a linear book. The project therefore employed a number of freelance researchers and writers, together with specialists in areas outside The British Library's collections, such as arms and armour, artefacts and buildings. The project managers also worked as the editors of the material and of the database as a whole and as administrators of the lengthy process of assembling, digitising and testing. The software for the CD-ROM was developed by the External Services Department of the Open University under Mike Peterson. Although it was based on programming for an existing CD-ROM product, as the project concept developed it became necessary to make significant changes, especially to the user interface. The project was seen through to actual publication by staff in British Library Publishing.

Since CD-ROM was a completely new medium for educational publishing, it was not clear at the outset exactly how the disk would be used in a classroom. The project constantly had to return to the question 'What do teachers want and need?' Nevertheless, at that stage very few people – teachers, advisers, developers or publishers – actually knew the answer to this question. One significant lesson learnt from *Medieval Realms* was that it is a mistake to try to be too comprehensive. It is easy to get carried away by the ability of the CD-ROM to store very large amounts of information (even now the disk is not full), and to keep increasing the range of material to be included. Moreover, the team developing the project naturally wanted to give access to the vast wealth of The British Library and to provide teachers and pupils with a wide range of evidence, much of which was not otherwise available to schools. In retrospect, the project might have been more manageable if the quantity of material included on the CD-ROM had been restricted.

To give an idea of the scale of the project the task list might be summarised as follows:

- *Project Initiation:* define how the product will be used in National Curriculum; define ways in which the Library's collections will be used in it; establish budget; write project proposal.
- *Establish project structure:* define roles of project team (project director, project managers/co-ordinators, software developer, researchers, writers,

advisers); establish procedures and systems for data collection, data input (text and images), data transfer, data validation, data output.

- *System development:* establish system specification and design; modify and solve problems with developer.
- *Data collection*: research overall structure, picture research, text research, photocopying of printed sources, collect 35mm slides, scan images, convert images, edit images, identify sound recordings/ record sound clips, note writing, editing, keyboarding of records, checking of keyboarding, obtain rights for material not in The British Library.

After this initial stage, it was necessary to integrate the batches of data, check data, transfer it to the software developer, recheck the data, and test the output on disk. This leads to a further cycle of data collection and input to the system, modification of software and procedures, and revision of scope and content of data.

- *Evaluation*: conduct school trials and other evaluation.
- *Development of support features*: create information for support features of the software such as the glossary and help files.
- *Final production stages*: edit the final data set; proof-read all the text in the system; check final gold disk; mastering and production of CD-ROM.

At the time that the grant application was submitted to NCET, Windows was only just becoming available, and a Windows product was not envisaged. At an early stage of project development, however, it became evident that the user interface for the CD-ROM should be Windows-based and substantial Windows programming had to be undertaken. This work emphasised the need to integrate the work of software development fully into that of the editorial team. Ideally, there would also have been a stronger design input from the outset of the project to enhance the screen design and ensure that images and graphics were of the best possible quality.

In planning a multimedia CD-ROM project of this scale, careful thought needs to be given in advance to the respective roles of the editorial team. The experience of this project emphasises the need for one person to give it an intellectual shape. Ideally, this would have been an academic medievalist with a close involvement in the teaching of history, an understanding of technology (so that the CD-ROM is not viewed as a giant book), and a willingness to look at the data at each stage and give direction. Such a person would also have brought a network of contacts who could research and possibly even write for the project. Without such an adviser, the project team often struggled to give the disk coherence and to exploit the resources of the Library to the full.

An academic director would not, however, act as day-to-day editor or compiler. Experience on *Medieval Realms* emphasises the need for a single person acting as the compiler/editor working with the academic director and a number of other researchers/authors each working on a well-defined area. Developing an effective editorial team to realise a project such as this can be difficult. Ideally, curators in the Library should be able to guide the editorial team towards the best material, but they are not necessarily able to interpret the collections in a way suitable for school use or to write at an appropriate level. Although curators can act as gatekeepers to the collections, actual selection and

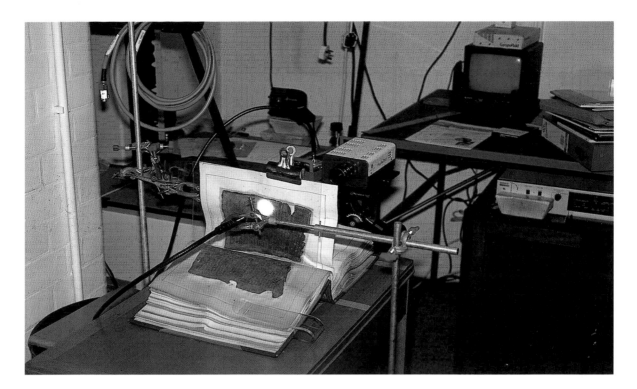

**Plate 1:** Fibre-optic cables are clamped into position behind letters or groups of letters, in order to conduct light from a remote source, producing a very intense light, but not enough heat to damage the manuscript.

**Plate 2:** The camera had to focus on a very small area of a very powerful light, but produced very readable images. Subsequent image processing made the lost letters even more legible.

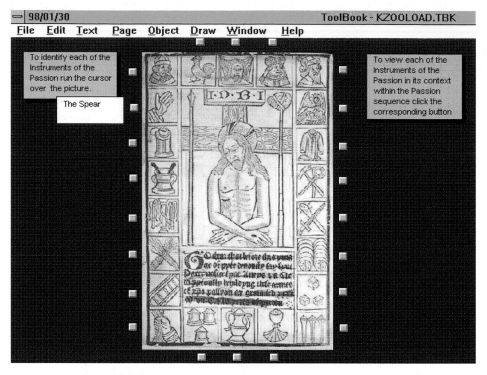

To identify each of the Instruments of the Passion run the cursor over the picture.

The Spear

To view each of the Instruments of the Passion in its context within the Passion sequence click the corresponding button

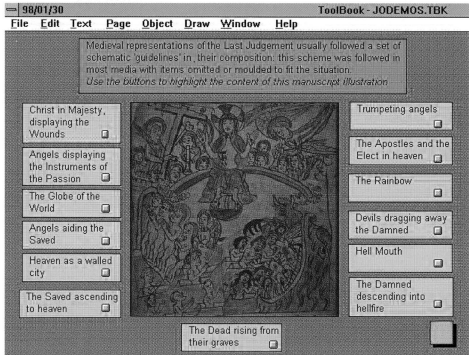

Medieval representations of the Last Judgement usually followed a set of schematic 'guidelines' in their composition: this scheme was followed in most media with items omitted or moulded to fit the situation.
*Use the buttons to highlight the content of this manuscript illustration*

Christ in Majesty, displaying the Wounds

Angels displaying the Instruments of the Passion

The Globe of the World

Angels aiding the Saved

Heaven as a walled city

The Saved ascending to heaven

Trumpeting angels

The Apostles and the Elect in heaven

The Rainbow

Devils dragging away the Damned

Hell Mouth

The Damned descending into hellfire

The Dead rising from their graves

**Plate 3:** As well as allowing for the easy comparison of pictorial and written material, through a multimedia package, different aspects of the play can be explored: the route of the pageant wagons can be mapped out on the city streets; video of a modern performance can be added to the package, and the iconography of the play can be explored in sources ranging from wallpaintings to prints.

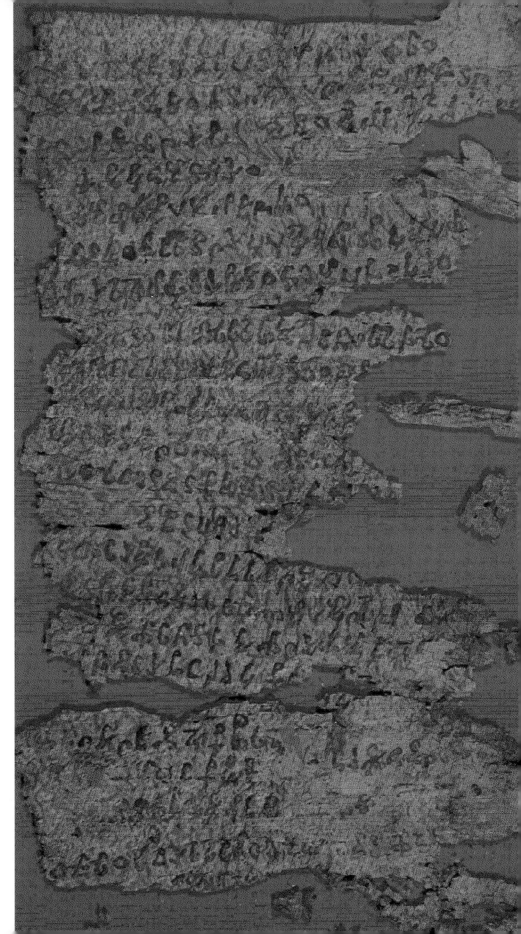

**Plate 4:** A high-resolution 24-bit colur image of one of the fragile Gandharan fragments, made with the Kontron ProgRes 3012 digital camera and viewed in Adobe PhotoShop.

# THE BRITISH LIBRARY

The world's leading resource for scholarship, research and innovation

*i*NITIATIVES *for access:* **PIX**project

iBase

| | |
|---|---|
| Johnson  | Manuscripts  |
| Barlow  | Philatelic  |
| Canadian  | Miscellaneous  |
| Music  | OIOC  |
| Printed Books | Colindale   |

Use the mouse to move the pointer around the screen and choose the collection you wish to view. Click the left mouse button to select. This window will display further help as the pointer is positioned over the various on-screen controls.

**Plate 5:** Introductory screen to PIX Project's Photo Viewer display.

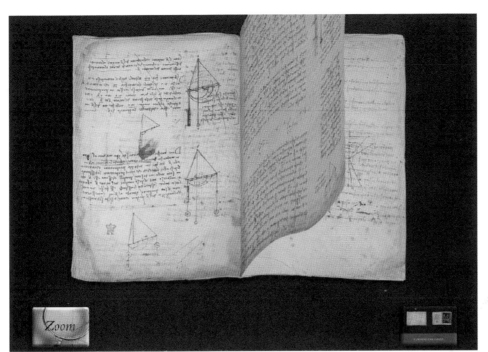

**Plate 6:** An animation sequence allows visitors to use a touch-screen display to 'turn the pages' of a Leonardo da Vinci notebook.

**Plate 7:** A detail of the Sforza Hours, one of the most beautiful surviving Renaissance manuscripts, as shown in the *Turning the Pages* display.

**Question:** How successful were the English monarchs in trying to control Ireland in the 16th and 17th centuries?

You are going to study the methods used by English rulers to control Ireland.

Siege engines

**Plate 8:** Screen from the educational CD-ROM, *The Making of the United Kingdom: Crowns, Parliaments and Peoples 1500–1750*, showing a manuscript illustration of the siege of Enniskillen Castle.

**Plate 9:** A machine for reproducing the sounds from ancient cylinder records with a high degree of fidelity. Different sized cylinders may be accommodated, and styli changed to minimise surface-noise.

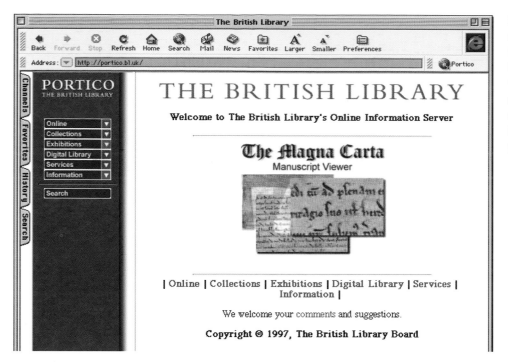

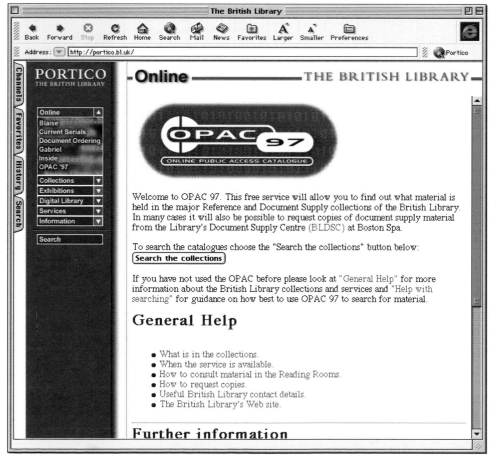

writing should be done by the editorial team. An important requirement is that selection of material should be closely integrated with writing the supporting teacher's material, upon which the successful use of a CD-ROM in the classroom often depends.

In the *Medieval Realms* project the scanning of images was done from 35 mm transparencies by external bureaux using PhotoCD. Keyboarding of text sources and of the specially written notes for each source was undertaken within The British Library. Nevertheless controlling the large quantities of data required for the project was a demanding, though routine, task, familiar now to any multimedia project editor but without precedent in the Library in 1992.

In essence the process involved: checking photographic indexes to see if 35 mm transparencies already existed; ordering new photography if necessary; adding slide numbers to record input sheets created by researchers and sending sheets for keyboarding; assembling groups of slides for scanning with lists of their record numbers and returning/filing slides; arranging scanning and dispatching slides to bureau; checking PhotoCD print outs for errors; converting PhotoCD images to Windows bitmap format; cropping and editing pictures as necessary; backing up images to tape; locating printed editions and finding relevant passages; photocopying texts from printed editions; marking up passages on photocopies of texts; assembling batches of texts with their records for keyboarding; importing keyed records into databases; solving queries with records; backing up databases; filing hard copy for later use in proof-reading; creating export formats for transfer of data to OU; assembling batches of data for transfer; transferring data to OU.

The process created not only a lot of digital data but also a large quantity of hard-copy documentation. All this data needed to be carefully organised and stored.

It will be evident that undertaking this complex series of tasks with a relatively small team is very difficult. As a result, there was a tendency for the editors to become completely overwhelmed, rushing about doing research when other researchers were not available, collecting images and texts, testing versions of the software, helping resolve bugs as well as demonstrating and publicising the project. This syndrome is one that will be familiar to anyone who has been involved in a digital project. Again, it stresses the importance of having a dedicated team working on a project such as this and clearly defining the roles of all those involved in the project. In a project like this it is also easy to underestimate the amount of time required to test the system at each stage. Schedules were revised several times to take account of the changing technology and user needs and to reflect the fact that the project had no dedicated members of staff; it was but a small part of the job descriptions of all the team members.

Karen Brookfield's reflection on the project will certainly be endorsed by anyone who has ever been engaged on creating a resource of this kind: 'Working on *Medieval Realms* was tremendously stimulating and satisfying, but also exhausting, and at times when there were not enough hours in an ordinary week almost too much for us. I think everyone involved found it much the same. We certainly all learned a great deal and are finding it rewarding to receive positive feedback from teachers'.

*Medieval Realms* was published in September 1994, two and a half years after the start of the project. It would seem that it is now in use in over 25% of the secondary schools in the UK and it has been selected by NCET for inclusion in their schemes which support the provision of IT resources for schools.

## The Making of the United Kingdom

The success of *Medieval Realms* has encouraged the Library to embark on another CD-ROM for use in teaching History in schools, this time covering the next National Curriculum study unit: *The Making of the United Kingdom: Crowns, Parliaments and Peoples 1500-1750.* Working under the guidance of Karen Brookfield as Project Manager, the editor of this new CD is Ben Walsh, Project Officer for the NCET/Historical Association History and IT Project, and the author of a number of GCSE textbooks.

The new disk uses the same database software as *Medieval Realms*, with enhancements to take account of teacher comments and to improve some elements of functionality, but also has one entirely new element. This is a set of guided investigations into key questions of religious and political change in the period 1500-1750. The investigations are being written in Macromedia Director by Footmark, a small multimedia production company. They will sit alongside the database giving teachers and pupils two different but complementary routes into a large collection of original source material, once again drawn chiefly from The British Library's collection.

In a recent issue of *Sources*, the newsletter of the Library's Education Service, Ben Walsh described *The Making of the UK*:

The new CD-ROM is designed to develop the potential of multimedia in History by including a series of interactive investigations as well as a database of source material. We shall be focusing on three key questions:

- Was Britain a United Kingdom by 1750?
- Why and how did the power of the monarchy change in the period 1500-1750?
- Why was the Reformation such an important event?

The investigation for each question is broken into manageable chunks which should not prove daunting to pupils. For example, Investigation 2 on the power of the monarchy has five parts, each of which looks at a possible turning point:

- Was there a Tudor Revolution in government?
- Was Elizabeth's reign stable and prosperous – a golden age?
- Why was there Civil War between Crown and Parliament in the 1640s?
- Why did the English Republic not survive?
- Why did King James II flee the country in 1688 and what effects did this have on the monarchy?

In the investigation on Tudor government, pupils work through a specially written illustrated narrative about how Henry VII and Henry VIII changed the way England was ruled. The narrative contains some controversial statements and some sweeping judgements. The pupils' task is to see how far the narrative stands up to the evidence from a selection of original sources including chronicles, proclamations, proceedings in the Privy Council, portraits, letters and royal warrants. They can then form their own answer to the question posed.

We hope that our piece-by-piece approach to the main themes and developments covered by the unit will give teachers the flexibility to mix and match different features and aspects of the disk to their particular needs and the time available. In theory teachers could use the disk as *the* resource for the Making of the UK study unit, with pupils working their way through the investigations. On the other hand, they may wish to use just elements of the investigations and the wide range of sources from the database. (See Plate 8.)

One of our aims with this disk is to make the latest academic thinking on the period accessible to Key Stage 3 pupils. We are therefore very pleased to have Dr Barry Coward of Birkbeck College, a recognised authority on the period, advising the project. Barry is helping us to formulate the questions and find source material which is not widely available in schools. Our other authors are all practising teachers and writers.

As well as writing the investigations, we are starting to amass the sources for the database. This will be very similar to the *Medieval Realms* database, but some refinements have been made, responding to feedback on the original. The most obvious change will be that the Introduction, which occasionally became rather long and involved, will be split into two smaller sections to make the background information about the sources a little more accessible. Teachers will also be able to set for themselves the default font and size for displaying documents and the notes on the screen.

Any CD-ROM is only a successful resource if people can use it and can find a variety of ways to use it. With this in mind we have already started thinking about how the disk might be used in the classroom and how we can help hard-pressed teachers with suggested ideas and activities which have been tried and tested. This will be a major feature of the teachers' support materials, along with the usual technical help.

The project team for this disk is working hard to put into practice the lessons of *Medieval Realms*. *The Making of the UK* will be published late in 1997 and the Library is already planning a third disk in the series for 1998 on the History study unit for the period 1750-1900.

# Document Management and Descriptive Data

Collections of digital documents in either image or text format require catalogue data or finding aids to identify and retrieve them from within cyberspace. The projects in this section examined different ways in which that catalogue data could be defined and produced. Patent Express (**Access to Patents**) represents the use of a bespoke index provided as part of a patent database. The **CD Demonstrator Project** produced catalogue records for digital material using the normal catalogue rules of AACR2. **Project Digitise** tested collection management methodology for the provision of service and conservation versions of early recorded material, such as wax cylinder and tapes, and converted analogue sounds to digital form.

Both the **British National Corpus** and **Survey of Illuminated Manuscripts** project have used the strengths of SGML to provide flexible structures for the production of catalogue records and indexes. The **International Dunhuang Project** adapted an off-the-shelf relational database in order to minimise costs while still providing the capacity to include images and non-Roman scripts. The **Excalibur** project used the techniques of OCR (Optical Character Recognition) software to produce machine-readable text from which indexes could be automatically created while the advanced technology of Adaptive Pattern Recognition is used to compensate for the deficiencies of OCR.

The experimental work undertaken at the University of Kentucky (**Image – the future of text?**) not only looks forward to the possibility of different scholars being able to interactively interrogate and manipulate images of text and other multimedia objects but also accommodates the way in which different users have varying perceptions of the same object.

All these projects illustrate the importance of having mechanisms to allow detailed and accurate searches of digital documents, but also show that the overhead in allowing this can be very considerable.

# Access to Patents

**David Newton**

At its inception, The British Library took over the former functions of the Patent Office Library in providing reading room access to patents and offering a patent copy service. These two activities are among the Library's most important services to the scientific and business community, the copy service being now called Patent Express. In the late 1980s, the various national patent offices decided that copies of their documentation should be in electronic form to enable faster access for their own staff. The three large patent offices, that is the US Patent Office, the European Patent Office and the Japanese Patent Office, began to scan and capture in electronic form a huge back-file of patent documentation. In 1987, The British Library started to explore with ScanEurope, a company which was scanning documents on behalf of the European Patent Office, a programme to develop CD-ROM products containing patent specifications from a number of countries arranged by subject classification. Funding was obtained from the European Community to set up a market research study assessing the viability of such a product. A test disk was developed to assist with this project, but the conclusions of the market research indicated that it would be difficult to produce a product with sufficient sales to make it commercially attractive.

At about the same time the European Patent Office started to put current patent material onto CD-ROM disks. Each disk held about 800 patent specifications in a compressed image format. In 1990, The British Library started offering access to these CD-ROMs in the patent reading rooms of its Science and Reference Information Service as an alternative to using the patents on paper. The number of disks produced increased rapidly from this point and many other countries, including the United Kingdom, began to publish their patents in both CD-ROM and hard-copy format. Back-files of earlier material also started to be produced from the files of scanned images which had been created in earlier exercises. There are now many thousands of CD-ROM disks containing patent images available in the reading rooms at The British Library. Here the patents are available on workstations, and readers are able to select the CD-ROMs that they require from a store of disks in caddies and insert them in the drive of the workstation that they are using. It soon became apparent that this method of mounting individual disks when required was a very cumbersome procedure, and it is not surprising that readers preferred to use the paper versions, which were readily available in a highly organised sequence. In 1990 it was not clear how we could, for a modest cost, set up a system to enable users of patents in our reading rooms to undertake a subject search and then have access to a large number of patents on CD-ROM.

At the same time that CD-ROMs started to be issued by the patent offices, CD-ROM jukeboxes first appeared. One particular model, produced by Incom, a company based in Germany, was reasonably priced and was also quite widely supported. It became apparent that we might be able to serve our remote Patent Express customers from a jukebox system in which they would enter their order by a telephone touch-tone keypad system and have the document delivered by fax to their office. After much consultation and gathering of information, a study was commissioned towards the end of 1991 to look at the technical possibilities of establishing a system of digitised images for Patent Express. As a result of this study it was decided that we should proceed in a step-by-step fashion to realise the ultimate vision of a complete paperless document requesting system. The first step was to be able to develop a jukebox system containing a large number of patents which would print out the correct patent on request. Towards the end of 1992 we discussed with a number of interested companies and consultants the setting up of a system to offer a service of printing from CD-ROM. In the end we decided to work with consultants Middletreat Ltd to develop a system to meet our requirements for printing on demand. In 1993 a system was set up to produce copies of British, European, US and international patents documents from disk. It was not until May 1994 that the Library formally launched its service. The system now comprises some 27 jukeboxes, each containing 100 disks, and providing access to about two million patent documents.

Over the last year we have been working steadily to develop other aspects of the originally envisaged system. An order management system is being planned which will enable customers to place orders for patent documents electronically, by e-mail or touch-tone telephone for example, and for these orders to be dispatched directly by fax from the jukebox system. Because a large number of patents which are requested are still not available electronically, and will not be for some time, our order management system has to cope with directing orders not only to the jukebox system but also to staff who retrieve printed documents directly from the shelves to provide photocopies. It is envisaged that the order management system will offer customers flexibility in the way they place orders, allowing them to use e-mail and ARTtel (the Library's Document Supply Centre system for ordering journal articles etc.), as well as the traditional ordering methods of fax and post. The system will also allow for eventual delivery of files across the Internet.

Meanwhile, users in the patent reading rooms still have access to the patents on disk by taking a disk and inserting it in a drive. With the growing number of disks, this is proving less and less satisfactory and therefore we have started a process of reviewing how reading room access can be delivered from a jukebox-type system. This has a number of difficulties compared to the delivery of a document to a remote site, such as the requirement for immediate delivery of images. We are starting this review process by surveying our users through questionnaires and interviews before determining what technical options might be most suitable. While the Library has been receiving each copy of patent documents both on paper and on CD-ROM there has not been much impetus to develop a system for online access, but when, as seems likely from the start of the next millennium, patents will only be made available in our reading rooms electronically, there will be a need to provide a robust and user-friendly system for readers.

The systems that we have employed have all been developed on PC-based architecture which has been preferred principally because of our wish to keep costs as low as possible. The use of PCs has enabled us to develop the systems in a modular way, particularly as PCs have developed in power and size since the early days of this project. There a number of potential bottlenecks in the system, but to date these have not presented any major problems. The central server and print servers have been upgraded from time to time as the need arose and printers, originally Hewlett Packard Laserjet 3Si models, have been progressively upgraded and supplemented with a 45 page per minute OCE 6845 printer. The number of 100 disk jukeboxes has expanded along with their servers (one server per six jukeboxes). Our Ethernet LAN is still viable although running at 40% of its theoretical capacity. There remains a limitation that the system does not allow such rapid response as we would like and is not as fast as, say, delivery over the Internet, but we are making changes on a rolling basis to overcome these problems.

Our software has had to be adaptable, in part because of our own changing requirements, but also because we are reliant on the data that we receive on CD-ROM from the patent offices and we have little influence over the way that this data is presented. Another requirement has been to emulate as much as possible the service that our customers have expected to be provided from the original paper document. As one example of a software change, we found as the system grew that at times of peak demand documents could not be produced sufficiently quickly to meet the demand of our fax service, so we introduced several levels of priority in order to ensure that all of our service targets could be met. Although there is some standardisation among patent offices in their CD-ROM products, these standards are not universally observed. In addition there is a move away from disks containing files of facsimile images of the pages towards 'mixed-mode' SGML-type files in which pages are held as character-coded text along with images of non-text information. Our software has already been adapted to take account of some non-standard variations and we are currently investigating changing it so as to be able to accept Japanese mixed-mode disks. As we use the disks in the format in which they are supplied, we anticipate changes to the software will be continually needed. In supplying copies from our paper files, we are easily able to supply the original document as issued along with any errata or other additional information subsequently issued, since all related documentation is filed together. Our software has been adapted to follow this approach in the jukebox system. The system will automatically print out errata and subsequently published search reports or provide a note to our staff that they must retrieve such information from the paper file where this is not available electronically.

# The CD Demonstrator Project – a case study in cataloguing CD-ROMs

**Sandie Beaney with Stephen Bagley, Richard Moore, Sue Skelton and Anne Sykes**

Legal deposit of print material, and of course, the overwhelming numerical significance of books in the Library's collections, means that the increase in publication of electronic material has not seen a proportionate increase in the amount of time and energy invested in newer material types – until recently, when the importance of preserving electronic publications was set down in a document proposing the legal deposit of non-print materials. In support of this application, several areas of the Library, from the Legal Deposit Office through to the reading rooms, were involved in a project which aimed to demonstrate the Library's ability to deal with non-print material. Responding to the increasing probability of legal deposit of non-print items, The British Library began to investigate the impact this would have on current processing and access requirements. As an example of the media identified as 'non-print', CD-ROMs were selected as the trial material type. The British Library is unusual amongst research libraries in that until now, comparatively few CD-ROMs have been made available to its users. The case study which follows examines one aspect of the CD Demonstrator Project – cataloguing – without which none of this material would be readily accessible by British Library users.

Essentially, the Project aimed to test the ease of practical cataloguing within current procedures, and prove or disprove that the absorption of CDs into the existing processing stream would be possible. CDs would be received by the Acquisitions section of the Library's Acquisitions, Processing and Cataloguing Directorate, and passed to Cataloguing with as few changes from the normal procedure as was possible. Attention was also given to the cataloguer resource and the equipment which would be required for the addition of CD-ROM cataloguing to the Library's traditional cataloguing responsibilities.

The official start date for the cataloguing stage of the Project was 1 December 1996. Initially, a period of three months was allocated for processing the material; it was anticipated that during this time enough material would be handled to make it possible for general conclusions to be drawn about the cataloguing of CD-ROMs on a large scale. Two days a week each were dedicated to the descriptive cataloguing of monographs and serials, plus whatever proved necessary for authority control work. This time was covered by the Electronic Media Group (EMG), involving two cataloguers from the Monographs section, one from the Serials team and a member of the Authority Control section who carried out authority control work on both name, subject and uniform title headings. In cataloguing these items, various standards and schedules were applied, including the most recent edition of the Anglo-American Cataloguing Rules (AACR2), UKMARC coding and Library of Congress Subject Headings (LCSH). Addition of a Dewey Decimal Classification (DDC) number was not one of the original project requirements, although this DDC was added at a later stage.

The equipment used for the project did not have a higher specification than the PCs normally used for cataloguing, with the exception of CD-ROM drives, and in three cases, soundcards. Three members of the EMG used 486 PCs with CD-ROM drive, Soundblaster 16, and 16MB RAM. The other team member used a 486 PC with CD-ROM drive and 8MB RAM. All PCs were equipped with CleanSweep, a package for deinstalling applications, and a virus checker, and all were networked. The team also had access to a Macintosh Power PC for cataloguing CD-ROMs for Macintosh. No facilities were available for accessing Atari or Acorn CD-ROMs. Technical support was provided by a member of the Library's Information Systems (IS) Directorate. All material was assessed for suitability for installation – this meant that with the time and expertise available, and the limitations of the deinstallation package, only Windows-based applications were installed (this accounted for most of the CDs which were processed as part of the project). DOS-based applications proved particularly unfriendly and it was acknowledged that our level of expertise would have to improve for us to feel comfortable installing and deinstalling some of the less accommodating material.

Detailed evaluation of the cataloguing process was given for each item by means of an evaluation form which involved giving information on time taken, technical difficulties, system inadequacies, and problems with applying cataloguing and classification rules. The expectation from the very beginning was that all would not necessarily go smoothly, as there was plenty of unfamiliarity with equipment and there had been no changes made to the cataloguing system to accommodate new MARC fields required for computer files. The normal processes carried out by the ISSNUK Centre for assigning ISSNs were integrated into the treatment of electronic serials in the project, as this would normally happen for any serial catalogued. Regular EMG meetings were planned for the duration of the project to address any queries that may arise, and to provide regular feedback. As a result of the first three-quarters of the project, 60 fully catalogued and authority controlled CD-ROMs were passed to Bibliographic Services for an experimental British National Bibliography-type publication. There were an equal number of serial and monograph publications in this sample.

**Cataloguing**

The evaluation form provided the cataloguer with several places to mark the amount of time required by various aspects of the procedure. The departmental targets suggest that the cataloguing of a print item takes on average 39 minutes if the item needs authority control work. One of the aims of the Project was to determine how much longer (or shorter) the cataloguing of CD-ROMs would take, and which elements of the procedure recorded the greatest increase of time. Before starting the Project, the estimate was that it would take at least twice as long to catalogue a CD-ROM as it would a book, with a more realistic view of three or four times as long (depending on the item) replacing the original estimate before the Project had been under way for too long. In practice, installation and deinstallation had the greatest effect on cataloguing time, sometimes doubling the time required to actually retrieve the necessary bibliographic information.

Having started with the tools normally used, it became clear that whilst we may not like some of the terms used in AACR2, which seemed outdated and on occasions not very helpful, the rules do work, as there is an item to be described with access points needed as for any print item. The challenges faced were more to do with finding our way around bits of AACR2 never ventured into before. We encountered situations where we were dealing with items with credits as long and as involved as film credits, with video excerpts, and music often playing an important role. Exploring past the first two chapters of AACR2 – general rules and printed books – to find out what to do with orchestral performances was something of a new experience, and we are more familiar with the whole of AACR2 as a result, which can only be a good thing for cataloguers. There were no real problems in applying the rules – more frustration that so many more explanatory notes were required, and some duplication of information in different fields which did not always seem necessary. The bane of everybody's cataloguing life was when a CD-ROM could be used on several platforms, and copious system requirements notes were required for each platform. Questions we had not anticipated were raised – wondering whether to describe a database as having an index seems foolish, particularly when it has been designed around indexed fields, but as the index did not exist in the conventional print form, it was a valid question.

Preferred sources of information for different types of material are listed in AACR2. These sources of information provide most of the information which forms the bibliographic record. Where books may have a title page, CD-ROMs may have a title screen, although it is rarely as simple to find bibliographically necessary information in a CD-ROM as it is in a book. The title page of a book is usually reassuringly present exactly where you would expect to find it. Not so with the latest interactive multimedia, and there are often many more places a cataloguer needs to search to find essential information. Familiarity with CD-ROMs means that cataloguers are increasingly able to judge where the desired information might be. 'About' files, 'Readme' files, icons and hotlinks of all kinds reveal authors, publishers, dates and titles which in books can be found in the space of two pages. This inevitably means that more time is taken if the cataloguers thoroughly check all internal sources, which the cataloguing rules deem preferable to packaging and labels. Differences aside, there are many parallels between books and CD-ROMs, not least of which is the fact that they are clearly defined, finite packages of information. In terms of description, this is one of the major obstacles the team did not have to face, as it might if the time comes for The British Library to catalogue parts of the World Wide Web.

Having one serials cataloguer working on the Project seems a little unkind with hindsight, as many of the awkward questions arose in the serials area. Problems of complete and incomplete duplication of information from print serials, and particularly expansion of information from print serials taxed our knowledge of linking fields, uniform titles and deciding whether an item was actually related to another. Sometimes it was even difficult to decide if an item was a serial or a monograph, as many had several dates on the labels, and if they were not installed and had limited documentation, their frequency was difficult to ascertain. It was often the case that annual CDs and backfiles arrived as separate items, and it became difficult to know what to take as a first issue which would hopefully be representative of issues to come. The packaging with the first issue of a serial appeared to be better than with follow-up issues, which highlighted once again the importance of installation. In relation to the work of the ISSNUK centre, prior to the Project, a CD had arrived containing several periodicals, all with different ISSNs, an issue which had been particularly difficult to resolve at the time, and we were prepared for more, although another one like that has not yet arrived. The Project was particularly important as a pilot in the Serials area as much periodical publishing seems set to become electronic in some form.

The correct application of Library of Congress Subject Headings (LCSH) is an exact science, and the CDs were given as much attention as anything entering the Library's main collections. Before many items had been processed it soon became apparent that subject indexing was not going as smoothly as for print material. LCSH guidelines indicate that for any one aspect of a work to be indexed, it must occupy at least 20% of the item. With the book, this is straightforward as pagination, chapter headings, indices and even something as basic as the thickness of sections of the book can aid the process of checking this; in a work of 100 pages, a topic which occupies 20 of those pages will merit an entry. Not so, we discovered with the CD-ROM. Many, in fact, were clearly designed to be as exciting and unpredictable to navigate around as possible, clearly an asset in an entertainment package, but not particularly helpful for having a quick look round, and because of the abstract nature of 'space' on a CD-ROM, it meant that what was seen at any one moment could quite well have been 90% or 1% of the intellectual content of the disk. To complicate things a little further, if, as we supposed, the rule of 20% was designed to highlight a significant quantity of information, it becomes so much more difficult to decide if the subject is important when 5% of the information on a CD-ROM may well have the breadth and detail of twice the volume of information in 20% of a book. Ultimately, this meant that the cataloguers spent what they felt to be a reasonable amount of time on the item and did not provide comprehensive subject indexing, or spent too long navigating around the CD-ROM to comply with the guidelines. With some CDs of course, this was more enjoyable than others, which was a temptation in itself. Conversely, subject analysis was difficult if installation was not possible and the documentation was limited. As The

British Library works alongside Library of Congress in candidating new subject headings, new headings and rule applications were proposed throughout the Project – and it turns out that Library of Congress has a few problems with its subject indexing for CD-ROMs too.

The wealth of credits on many of the items handled meant that the Authority Control section had plenty of involvement in the Project. The various functions of those who put together a CD-ROM makes the identification of book author, editor and compiler roles pleasantly simple to determine. Functions of production, viewing, software provision and design have unknown intellectual weight and overlap, and the place of the publisher is increasingly taken over by individuals claiming an intellectual role. It was rare to find a single statement of responsibility, as is common in books. This meant that decisions had to be taken on who in these lists of people were actually intellectually important, for the purpose of name entries, and no doubt a few of those listed would be offended if they knew they had been left out – but that's cataloguing.

## Technical issues

Here we come to the crux of many of the challenges faced as part of this Project. It is worth mentioning at this point that none of the team members laid any claim to being highly IT literate, although all had used Windows and two had PCs at home. For most, creating files in Microsoft Office and some Internet navigation is as far as it went. The learning curve was quite steep, particularly for installation and deinstallation, and we saw more of the internal workings of directories than we had anticipated. Although the Library's IT Help Desk provided support, much of what occurred had to be managed ourselves.

Our first task, as part of installation, was virus checking. Despite the fact that CD-ROMs are one of the most virus-free media, the obligation we carried to the other Library staff using the network meant that virus checking had to happen, even if it did add 10 minutes to cataloguing time – predictably, we never encountered a virus. This done, we then came to installation, where we soon discovered that many of the CD-ROMs required several stages of installation, the first often being one of three or four types of viewer. In an attempt to cut down on the time it was taking to catalogue, we investigated using the viewers which were available over the network. This worked on occasions, but the lack of standardisation meant that for some, the installation of the viewer also affected the decompression of other necessary files, and without the installation process the item was inaccessible even with the correct viewer. Adobe's Acrobat would normally work, but Quicktime caused a few problems as it seemed to provide an integral part of the software to run the CD, not just functioning as a viewer. If we were able to find a way round this problem, installed viewers for Read-only access would help a great deal. This does not remove the fact that because of the lack of standardisation in the installation procedures, time spent extending technical expertise would still be very necessary or cataloguers would have to have higher levels of technical expertise initially. The cataloguing system, which is not Windows-based, took up valuable memory, and it was usually necessary to be logged out of the cataloguing system for installation of the CD-ROM to be possible – not terribly practical when the motivation behind installing the CD-ROM is to catalogue it. For the moment this meant a return to the days of manual cataloguing. The new corporate system which has been commissioned, will, it is hoped, alter this situation, the alternative being the use of two PCs per cataloguer, one for cataloguing and one for installing the item to be catalogued.

The idea of installing CleanSweep had been to remove and restore everything which installation had added or changed, without too much trouble. As with many good ideas, this had its flaws. We discovered that some set-up files are not recognised by CleanSweep, and unfortunately we discovered this after the items had been installed. Manual deinstallation was not always successful, as occasionally a file would not delete, particularly if it had ended up in a directory requiring further changes which we could not make. For maximum efficiency, CleanSweep could be set up to deal with a particular sort of material at a time (i.e. to recognise particular installation file names), but this would still be time-consuming. When items required more than one application to be installed before they would run, this doubled the time taken, and usually the problems too. Some .DLL files were left behind, and are still on the PCs. Sometimes items installed by-passing CleanSweep and at other times a double go at deinstallation was necessary, as CleanSweep saw certain files as protected and would not delete them, yet the next time it would quite happily delete these same files! At times, PC logic was quite beyond us, and not only us but the Help Desk staff as well.

Now of course, with the speed that PCs become obsolete, any replacement machines at the Library would be Pentiums, which we would hope would speed up everything except the process of cataloguing itself. As it was, the PCs we were using were capable of most things we wanted to do, albeit slowly on occasions. It was discovered that knowing the technical limitations of the PC in use is necessary as many CD installation procedures ask technical specification questions. In particular, knowing how much RAM is available, what kind of screen resolution is necessary and whether the machine has the correct kind of soundcard will affect how long a cataloguer might attempt the impossible. Some software only ran on Windows 95, which the Library does not have on networked PCs, and as this is now the standard for recently purchased home PCs, it is probable that more and more material aimed at the home market will use Windows 95. As mentioned, Acorn and Atari material could not be installed. In the long term, this of course would not need to be a problem, as long as the Cataloguing department had a choice of platforms amongst the computers in use.

**Procedural issues**

Although technical issues were a significant part of the project, procedures and workflow were also under investigation. One suggestion that came from the team is that before the items reach the cataloguer they could be batched according to viewer type, or according to the type of installation required (or even batched according to the possibility of installation). One of the main time problems was caused by the vast quantities of documentation with many of the CDs, which all needed to be read before installation – sometimes only to find out that installation would not be possible. This was one of the areas where a higher level of technological expertise would have been helpful. Information overload was mentioned as a distinct problem, as everything had to be read to find out anything, particularly at the beginning of the Project when the team were less used to dealing with this type of documentation.

At the moment, work in the Cataloguing section is divided into several areas, two of which are Record Creation and Authority Control. Books which need authority control headings are passed to the relevant staff after they have been catalogued, where the items are looked at carefully. This process caused a few problems with CD-ROMs as every installation or deinstallation problem then had to happen twice, not to mention exploring the item for information about the authors. The amount of duplicated effort has reinforced the idea that multiskilling in these two areas would be of real benefit. Installation and deinstallation take at best over five minutes and some closer to 20 minutes. Extensive notes in the message field of the record are necessary so that Authority Control staff know where cataloguers found the information about headings they have included. This would not be necessary if one person completed the work on the whole item. Double handling becomes an expensive option in terms of staff resource when dealing with CD-ROMs.

In using records derived from other sources, the Library aims to make the most of work that has been completed elsewhere and edit the record for Library use. For this Project, derived sources had not been explored, and it is possible that with access to other records, savings could be made on the time needed for inputting certain parts of the catalogue record, particularly if fields like system requirements notes were already present in the record. This Project was one of the few areas when all items were dealt with via original cataloguing, and this does carry a significant time overhead.

**Staff response**

It is not by chance that the regular team meetings which occurred throughout the Project were referred to as therapy sessions. A consensus amongst the team identified stress as the main staff-related issue, rather than some of the other computer-use problems which we had anticipated. There seemed to be very little perceived discomfort in working more with a VDU, apart from the occasions when items installed had rather violently coloured or rapidly flashing screens. Particularly at first, the constant and changing installation problems led to high levels of apprehension and dismay, which only began to resolve themselves as the Project went into its third month. Often encountered was the demoralising feeling of time wasted when a high proportion of the CDs did not install properly and the PC would crash. At other times, there was the false hope that the package had installed and then an error message would appear, or only a very limited part of the CD would be accessible, or it would freeze. The advantage of it freezing (and there was one) was that screens which might scroll through far too quickly to take down bibliographic information would be readable. The disadvantage was that once frozen, the CD could not be explored for other information, so the documentation or packaging had to be consulted anyway, which was equally frustrating. These problems might be overcome if a dedicated team of cataloguers dealt with this type of material, although it was suggested that this might be asking for a sudden increase in stress-related sick leave! The situation is not ideal at the moment because of the problems with having to exit the cataloguing system before an item can be installed, and again, it can be felt a real waste of time, even if there is no other way to go about it at the moment. The writing down of all information needed and the deinstallation of the item before cataloguing is soul-destroying if the cataloguer discovers they need information from the internal sources of the CD-ROM again. Support and backup would be needed for cataloguers to operate in healthy fashion, and a focus for technical assistance, advice and training is necessary for the well-being of the team. One of the other questions raised has concerned the Cataloguing section's use of targets which relate to departmental performance and therefore performance pay. The frustrations mentioned would take on a more serious perspective if staff felt that technical problems beyond their control were affecting their targets, so some kind of resolution would need to be reached to prevent cataloguers choosing not to be involved in this kind of work. That said, comments have been made about the rewards of being challenged by new technology, and there have been expressions of interest by members of the team in being involved in CD-ROM cataloguing when it becomes part of the regular duties of the Library. Clearly in some measure the interest outweighs the trauma!

## Conclusions

We are now at the point where the Project has finished and we need to assess the experience of the past three months. The cataloguing rules have been proved adequate for this type of material, although terminology updates for AACR2 would be very welcome. The fundamental principles still appear to be appropriate, and the professional challenge of wider use of AACR2 chapters means that cataloguers cannot be complacent about their current knowledge of the rules. Technical issues remain less resolved, and there are still areas which need investigating, like the use of stand-alone PCs for installing items, and cataloguing on a separate computer. This has been suggested by our IT support as far less stressful, because deinstallation becomes unimportant – the hard disk can be wiped and the image reinstalled at the end of the day. This will also prevent problems which occur when other applications on the networked PCs become affected by file changes on installation. In theory this would mean each cataloguer needed two PCs, not to mention all the other platforms to be catered for. Somewhere between the two extremes of networked and stand-alone, we are looking for a workable compromise.

There are still areas which need ironing out and the cataloguing system needs changing so all the necessary fields can be added to the records. Although at present output is low compared to cataloguing print material (averaging four serials a day and six monographs), with refinement of the process and increasing familiarity, routine cataloguing will be a practical proposition. The possibility of having a dedicated technician (i.e. to virus check, print screens, look for derivable records etc.), would save cataloguer time. However, one of the greatest efficiency gains for the immediate future would be use of multiskilling, and long-term, the Corporate Bibliographic System (CBS) has the potential to make an enormous difference, simply through allowing cataloguers to cut and paste and move about the screen more easily. If networked PCs proved to be the way forward, the CBS would also allow simultaneous access to the cataloguing system and the item to be catalogued. Either way, the need for manual cataloguing is removed.

There have been some fraught moments, particularly when it seems that installation of something has caused apparently irreparable damage to the workings of the computer. One of the conclusions we have been able to draw from this has been that the IT support staff have always managed to undo that damage, therefore we can be far less afraid of doing something wrong than at the beginning, which makes the work less stressful. This may be of little consolation to the Help Desk, who may reap the rewards of our fearlessness! IT training for staff involved in cataloguing, or the recruitment of cataloguers who already have good IT skills would increase the self-sufficiency of the cataloguers, which would make for a pleasanter work style. From the cataloguer point of view, confidence and broader experience have been the main gains from this project, so that while CD-ROM cataloguing has been demanding, on the whole, the experience has been rewarding, and the learning curve has been successfully taken in our stride. From the corporate point of view, it provides the confirmation that not only is it theoretically possible to catalogue this material according to the needs of the Library, but with some fine-tuning and some further investigation into equipment, we will be well able to handle any CD-ROM-based material that comes our way.

# Project Digitise

**Peter Copeland**

Project Digitise was a pilot project set up by the National Sound Archive of The British Library (NSA) to explore issues arising from the conversion of analogue sounds to digital. The Project ran from October 1993 to June 1995. Its aims were as follows:

- To test collection management methodology regarding the provision of service and conservation versions and back-up copies.
- To develop the skills of NSA technical staff in analogue/digital transfer procedures including (where appropriate) segmentation and data reduction.
- To gain experience which would enable the accurate sizing of a large-scale digitisation project, and propose a costed programme of further work.
- To gain 'hands-on' experience of working with a wide range of digital carriers in order to assess their potential suitability for a large-scale programme.

These four objectives formed the main thrust of the Project and there were significant achievements under each heading which are covered in detail later. An additional objective was to establish a set of digitised recordings and develop an experimental online playback service. A set of digitised recordings was produced, some ground-breaking and of considerable interest to NSA users; but the online playback service was not developed, partly because a similar aim was being successfully pursued by the separate Project Jukebox, a project supported by the European Commission's Libraries Programme in which the NSA was also heavily involved. Project Jukebox tested the market and the technology for a service of remote access to the holdings of a sound archive from public and academic libraries.

In the course of Project Digitise, subsets of the NSA collections were transferred from analogue to digital format. These subsets were chosen to meet the overall objectives. The choice of subsets was made by the end of the first financial year, and was not altered. Most of the subsets were completed, but much slower progress was achieved on the wax cylinders than had been hoped, owing to technical difficulties.

As a result of the Project, there should be proven hardware and software for use if a larger-scale project should follow. Much hardware was acquired which worked well, but many difficulties were encountered with computer hard- and software. Ultimately the debugging of the computerised elements in the digitisation system and the experience thus gained may be seen as the main achievements of the Project.

There will be a system providing access for users to the digitised recordings. This was interpreted as the provision of digitised recordings on a convenient and accessible format which could be easily controlled by users, and took the form of compilations on CD-R. It was also hoped that a prototype system providing access to both high-quality digitised sound and related visual material (e.g. record sleeve images and notes) could be developed, and the Project pursued a number of aspects of this.

The Project produced a report containing analyses of the comparative processing costs of different media done in different ways. As part of the project, a complete discographical study of the NSA collection of ethnographic wax cylinders was prepared. One thousand one hundred and seven cylinders were documented, but only 166 digitised. The documentation in itself was a major achievement, greatly improving the accessibility of much of the collection following detailed research. The disappointing progress on digitisation resulted from numerous problems with new equipment and serious unforeseen difficulties with the initial cylinders selected for processing, which proved to be untypical but very time consuming. (See Plate 9.)

### Recordings selected for digitisation

In the early stages it was assumed that a sizeable quantity of recordings would be processed during the Project, which could reduce the backlog of vulnerable NSA recordings in urgent need of copying. There were three main categories to choose from. The first were the so-called 'acetate' discs. This is an inaccurate term for a grooved disc record made from cellulose nitrate lacquer coated onto a base (usually sheet aluminium). Various effects, such as delamination, evaporation of solvents, etc., make such records vulnerable even if they are never played. However, these discs were ruled out, since they were already being tackled with support from operational budgets, but the other two categories, wax cylinders and acetate-based magnetic tape, were considered very suitable. Acetate-based magnetic tape was suitable for digitisation because it suffers geometrical distortions and tends to go brittle. The wax cylinder is a form of sound-recording in which the sound is cut into a groove on the curved surface of a cylinder. It differs from the 'moulded cylinder', essentially a mass-produced medium in which the groove was formed by a moulding process. Wax cylinders may either be 'originals' or one of a limited number of mechanically produced 'copies', but the format was the only practicable form of location sound-recording before electrical methods in the mid-1930s.

Wax cylinders are made from organic waxes which tend to dry out and/or go mouldy. Detailed work by the project discographer indicated that there were almost exactly 3,000 wax cylinders in total, of which about half had previously been copied onto tape using analogue techniques. With high hopes of digitising the whole lot during the Project, an initial subset (cylinders recorded by Alice Werner in Kenya, 1912–3) was embarked on because they had better accompanying documentation than most of the rest. Unfortunately Alice Werner proved to have been one of the world's worst recording engineers, and technical problems resulting from this and other teething troubles slowed the work down drastically. This was a disappointment, but did not prevent the gathering of sufficient data to enable average throughput times to be extrapolated, particularly once further more straightforward cylinders, from those recorded by Edgar Thurston in India before 1909, had been added to the sample.

Most tape recordings made in the 1950s are on acetate-backed tape which is now at risk. The Project therefore identified a collection of such recordings in order to gain experience of the medium and contribute to reducing the conservation backlog. It comprised about 900 reels of tape, emanating originally from the 'Voice of America' (VOA) radio station in the USA, which were used by the BBC for broadcasting to eastern Europe whenever reception conditions made it impossible to relay the VOA's news bulletins. Twenty-one reels likely to have archivally important recordings of live orchestral music performances and jazz were chosen as a sample.

To enable sizing data to be produced for the more common, less vulnerable media held at the NSA, samples of vinyl LPs, audio cassettes (i.e. the type introduced by Philips in 1963), and modern polyester-backed quarter-inch tape were identified. The choice of LPs was not determined by any urgent preservation need, but by public demand. When a LP belonging to the NSA has been played to listeners three times, a copy is then made and the original is not subjected to further wear. A small selection of LPs was made from those awaiting copying, picked to represent each decade in which LPs were manufactured. After much deliberation the collection of tape recordings assembled by the eminent folk music writer and broadcaster A.L. Lloyd were chosen as an example of modern tape with sufficient documentation problems. A quantity of cassettes entered for the 1987 Sony-Radio Awards was selected for digitisation. Higher priority was given to cassettes where the discographer found that the original recordings had been destroyed by the radio stations concerned (more than half).

## Collection management methodology

At present, where copies of analogue recordings are made for preservation purposes it is NSA policy to make two copies, both containing sounds which have been through identical processes and referred to as the 'archive copy' and the 'playback copy'. The latter is used for general playback purposes and takes the wear-and-tear. The archive copy is never used, except in the rare event that the playback copy becomes irreparably damaged.

Engineering and subjective compromises must be made if all copies are produced through identical processes. A 'quadruple conservation' strategy would be more satisfactory. This would mean the archive might hold four versions of a recording, although two or more might sometimes be combined in one:

- The original, kept for as long as it lasts.
- A copy with 'warts-and-all' sounding as much like the original artefact as possible (referred to below as the 'archive copy').
- A copy with all known objective parameters compensated (the 'objective copy'). 'Objective parameters' are the deliberate (but usually undocumented) distortions made by analogue recording engineers.
- A copy with all known subjective and cultural parameters compensated (the 'service copy'). Subjective and cultural factors are features which would have been preferred by the performers and/or present-day listeners.

The first objective of Project Digitise was to gain practical experience of making four versions. Below is a summary of the results.

With 'vulnerable' media the principal objective must be to recover the sound in a way which allows future processing if better technology becomes available. (In other words, 'don't do anything which can't be undone'.) Analogue copies are known to corrupt 'clicks' and 'pops' from grooved media, making it difficult to apply de-clicking at a later stage. But it was found that this did not apply to digital copies, which could be processed with the same results as if the original record were being played.

On the other hand, there are several processes which cannot be applied in the digital domain with present-day technology (or at sensible costs) such as equalisation and groove wall selection. These are therefore better carried out in the analogue domain wherever necessary, especially in cases where this may be the only opportunity to replay vulnerable media.

There is less hurry for non-vulnerable media, but future technology may improve on ours, although we can define the limits of what is possible from the 'power-bandwidth principle' and from measurements. (The Power-Bandwidth Product is one method of estimating 'the quality' of an analogue recording. The principle depends on the fact that frequency-range can always be traded against the power of the background noise, and vice-versa.) However, the craftsmanship aspects of recovering recorded sound – especially the undocumented features – may become lost or misunderstood. When this Project digitised non-vulnerable analogue media, rigorous alignment procedures were followed (to much higher standards than normal NSA practice).

New systems for numbering individual wax cylinders prior to digitisation, and for marking these numbers indelibly on the cylinders themselves, had to be devised, thus providing solutions to long-standing problems in the NSA. This was done at the time of 'pre-digitisation documentation', and for any given set of recordings comprised a simple serial number starting from 1, which was called 'the running-number'. After much experiment, we adopted the method used by the Science Museum for labelling their cylinders. The numbers were painted in enamel paint within the cylinder, between the ridges which grip the mandrel (part of the player upon which a cylinder record fits during recording or reproduction).

The implications of the foregoing for the management of preservation and access copies are that:

- The production of one 'archive copy' meets the sound preservation requirement, but will not necessarily meet the needs of listeners.
- The processes needed to produce a copy for listeners vary with the source-media afforded.
- In the latter case, consideration should always be given to generating a second version for listeners using whatever technology is appropriate, as it may be more difficult after the sound has been digitised.

### Analogue/digital transfer procedures

It was decided that the production of digital copies should be governed by the following general principles. The balance between objective and subjective techniques should be as follows:

- The ear should remain the final arbiter, but only the final arbiter. All procedures before this point should be subject to objective verification by measurements.
- The aim should be to recover the original sound with as much faithfulness as possible.
- But where the recording engineer (or producer) has made deliberate distortions to the sound as part of the creative process of making his recording, the aim should be to reproduce the sound the way the original engineer (or producer) would have wished it to be reproduced.
- Some consideration also needs to be given to the role of others in the creation of the recording, such as the performers (and their supporters), contemporary listeners, present-day listeners, and users of sound-recordings in other media such as broadcasters. It so happened that this project did not encounter such issues, and they are of comparatively minor importance anyway.

The Project involved developing the skills of NSA technical staff in segmentation. With the vast majority of the material transferred to CD, individual tracks were labelled as on commercially published CDs. This is particularly beneficial for the NSA Playback Service when LPs and reel-to-reel tapes (neither of which are straightforward to cue) are transferred to CD.

Two problems should be noted. The transfer operator was asked to record a spoken announcement before each item. This has been normal NSA practice for decades and seems to be appreciated by Listening Service users. Another advantage is that as long as they remain playable the sounds can be identified independently of the documentation. Unfortunately, when LPs were transferred to CD the announcement formed an extra 'item'. The CD recorder automatically incremented the track-numbers when the PAUSE button was pressed. As a result, photocopies of the LP sleeve made for inclusion with the CD gave track-numbers which were wrong. (The CD format does not allow a 'Track Zero'.) The quickest solution found was to assemble the announcement and the first track on a digital editor such as SADiE, and then the remaining tracks can be done direct from the LP.

Therefore, in order to obtain the benefits of segmentation, it seems inevitable that the sounds often have to be transferred twice. However, subsequent to our tests, the makers of SADiE have introduced new software in which the track labels can be edited as part of the sound recording, and then transferred at high speed onto the destination CD-R. This option should be researched by any successor to Project Digitise.

**Theory and practice**

In order to achieve the aims of the Project a system was set up in which all the main elements of an archival audio digitisation process could be tried out and quantified. It consisted of four processes: pre-digitisation documentation, the actual digitisation, post-digitisation documentation, and processing and transfer of the digitised recordings to the final destination medium. Not all recordings needed to go through all four stages, e.g. the first stage could be omitted for items with reasonable documentation.

The purpose of pre-digitisation documentation was essentially to check that the recording was what it was supposed to be, to check engineering details and prepare for potential difficulties. The documentation would also help in the selection of material by curatorial staff and to establish the existence and technical quality of other copies of the material held elsewhere.

The first recordings tackled by the project were the cylinders recorded by Alice Werner in Africa in 1912–3; the existing documentation was more complete, since Alice Werner's diaries had survived. Since the Werner collection was disappointing from the point of view of sonic quality, the discographer prepared a 'Best of Werner' CD, suitable for non-specialist listeners. This in fact comprised a good cross-section of the subject-matter, therefore serving both the needs of the casual listener, and of most serious inquirers.

As far as vinyl LPs were concerned, we found spoken word LPs needed extra attention when digitised, because the start IDs could not be done automatically. (The machines are designed to recognise gaps between music tracks, but not between poems or acts of plays.) So careful editing (moving, adding, or deleting the IDs) was found essential. We also found that, when digitising to R-DAT, we would often get audible breaks in the surface-noise when we interrupted a transfer in the middle of a LP side. This was not thought significant when it occurred between tracks; but occasionally there was a change of LP side in the middle of an item (a scene in a play, for example), and in these cases the item was edited to eliminate the audible interruption. Thus we learned to go straight to the SADiE in these cases

Open-reel tapes presented different problems. Both the A.L. Lloyd and VOA tapes were originally recorded to obsolete standards. A set of calibration tapes was acquired. Some of the Lloyd collection antedated the European change from CCIR (The *Comité Consultatif International des Radiocommunications* which set European standards for interchange of magnetic recording tapes in 1953) to IEC (International Electrotechnical Commission Authority which revised and extended the CCIR standards in 1966) characteristics, and we had to commission a special test-tape for this. The VOA tapes were recorded to NAB (National Association of Broadcasters) characteristics. (The NAB standardised analogue magnetic tape-recording characteristics in North America in 1955, using the practices of the leading tape recorder manufacturer implemented the previous year.) In each case, the frequency response was correct within half a decibel at all frequencies up to 16kHz (20kHz from 15ips tapes). This is much more accurate than normal NSA work, and was achieved at little extra cost, because it was possible to plan the work and avoid the need for piecemeal realignment.

The VOA tapes had been professionally recorded in America in the mid-1950s on acetate tape. It proved surprisingly difficult to get a modern (European) tape reproducer to work to 1950s American standards, but this was eventually achieved. It proved necessary to increase the back-tension of the feed spool.

As anticipated, technical documentation of the Sony Awards cassettes was difficult. Virtually none of those selected had any indication whether they were mono or stereo, or Dolby or non-Dolby. They came in both ferric and chrome formulations. (Ferric tape is magnetic recording tape in which the magnetism is stored in particles of ferric oxide. Chrome tape is magnetic recording tape in which the magnetism is stored in particles of chromium dioxide. For cassettes, different equalisation from ferric tape is implied.)

There was thus a fairly long 'learning curve' for some of the source-media. When the learning curve had been navigated, reasonable measurements of the time taken to digitise a medium could be made. (This was an additional point in favour of not changing unnecessarily from one source-medium to another.)

The digitisation process had three main components: recovering the maximum power-bandwidth product from the source media; digitising the analogue signal without degradation; generating 'archive' and 'service' copies, as decided by the Project Manager. For most of the media, post-digitisation documentation was confined to updating the original database records. However, the LPs and VOA tapes were the last to be done, and the resulting CD-R discs were eventually entered on the new NSA catalogue database.

The CD-Rs themselves were marked with hand-written short titles in spirit-based ink. The idea of self-adhesive labels was explored and rejected, but if a full-scale programme using thousands of discs were to be pursued, blank discs with a pre-printed NSA ownership mark and running shelf mark could be ordered.

For the other source-media inset-cards were generated using Microsoft Word for Windows, which was also used for making spine labels for all the CD-Rs, so the subject matter could be seen on the shelf.

A Meridian CD recorder was used throughout the project to make the final CD-Rs, although we also investigated several alternatives. We were unable to detect any difference in sound-quality between the Analogue-to-Digital converters on board the Meridian, and the ones on the Sony 2700 R-DAT recorder. Thus we were free to send analogue or digital signals to the Meridian, depending on operational convenience.

The actual making of the CD-Rs was very straightforward. The principal difficulty was the segmentation. After the disc was recorded it took about four minutes to write the permanent table of contents, thereby preventing rerecording. This was a surprisingly long time, which might become significant in a major project.

### Digital destination media

Since analogue sounds were being converted to digital, it was necessary to decide upon a digital storage format. All digital media have the advantage that they can be monitored for degradation using objective and (largely) automatic processes requiring no skilled labour. They also offer the advantage that when degradation reaches a certain level (within the error-correction capability of the system), the recording can be 'cloned' without loss of quality. (When a digital recording is replayed with successful error-correction throughout and a digital copy made, the recording is said to be 'cloned'.)

Considerations affecting the choice of destination medium can be stated in the following order of priority:

- A long shelf life, i.e. greater than one human working life (say 50 years).
- High quality. The 'power-bandwidth product' is an objective way of measuring quality. All the digital media we considered had a power-bandwidth product far exceeding that of all but a few very specialised analogue originals (usually those designed for ultrasonic sounds).
- Wide acceptance and distribution. This would give four advantages: wide familiarity with the medium, its virtues and vices, and its accessibility and documentation; survival of playback equipment in working order for the expected shelf-life; lower costs; less likelihood of minor 'upgrades' defeating the other three advantages.
- Flexibility. The medium should still be capable of being 'stretched' to allow it to carry specific archival requirements.
- Robustness. Should be capable of repeated playback without failure.
- Reasonable cost.
- Long uninterrupted playing-time, ideally about four hours.

The audio compact disc was selected as the destination medium for the Project. The Philips Compact Disc Interactive (CD-I) version of the CD was the most flexible and therefore initially seemed the most suitable for the project. This is a compact digital disc made to the Philips CD-I specification, which may incorporate still pictures, moving pictures, and text as well as sound. However, CD-I did not 'take off' to the extent of PhotoCD, and by the time the issues of image digitisation had been addressed, PhotoCD seemed preferable.

Two makes of CD-R blank were available when the choice had to be made, Taiyo Uden and Kodak, although others appeared later. As with magnetic tape, close inspection may be needed to decide the true provenance when repackaged. Kodak discs were used wherever possible, but when it was necessary to make separate 'archive' and 'service' copies, Taiyo Uden were used for the latter so we would gain experience of these.

Philips 'Red-Book' CD-R discs were used, with Kodak blanks being used for the 'archive copies'. Time will tell if this strategy was correct, but the only disadvantage found so far is the comparatively short playing-time of the format. It will be essential to monitor the recorded CD-R discs for longevity. Unfortunately, an adequate tester for CD-Rs does not appear to exist; a search for such a device should continue.

**Summary**

The project set up a working prototype system for digitising sound recordings. Several digital destination media were assessed. CD-R was selected as an archivally satisfactory medium which was convenient and accessible and could be easily controlled by users. In order to provide a variety of experience and sizing data, samples of fragile and other vulnerable recordings, and also of more robust recordings not in immediate danger, were digitised. Among vulnerable material held by the NSA, the 'acetate' discs were already being tackled by an existing project so were not included, but the other two categories, wax cylinders and acetate-based magnetic tape, were considered very suitable. Samples of vinyl LPs, conventional audio cassettes, and modern polyester-backed quarter-inch tape were identified as examples of less vulnerable media. The project examined the methodology of archival digitisation, concluding that three digitised copies, each engineered to a different specification and serving a different purpose, may be required. This would be preferable to the NSA's current policy of producing two copies with identical engineering.

With 'vulnerable' media the principal objective must be to recover the sound in a way which allows future processing if better technology becomes available. Digitisation procedures were established in response to methodological requirements and therefore procedures for segmentation were introduced. The unsuitability of both 'lossy' and 'loss-less' data reduction as part of archival digitisation procedures was confirmed.

# The Survey of Illuminated Manuscripts

**Andrew Prescott, Michelle Brown and Richard Masters**

The British Library's collection of illuminated manuscripts is unmatched in its range and quality. Insofar as the Library is able to justify its claim to be the world's leading library against larger collections such as that of the Library of Congress, it is partly because of the great variety of its collections of early manuscripts. Sir Frederic Madden's claim to a Royal Commission in 1847 that it is to these manuscript collections that the British Museum Library chiefly owes its international celebrity still holds true 150 years later.

However, there is no detailed listing of the illuminated manuscripts in the Library comparable to, say, Pächt and Alexander's three-volume catalogue of the illuminated manuscripts in the Bodleian Library. The Library's collections remain, in Michelle Brown's words, 'an unexcavated treasure house'. Many illuminated manuscripts are identified in the indexes to the *Catalogues of Additions to the Manuscripts* for acquisitions since about 1880, but the bulk of the illuminated manuscripts are found in collections acquired before this date, such as the Cotton, Harley, Royal, Sloane, Arundel, Burney and Stowe manuscripts, as well as in the early Additional and Egerton sequences. The catalogues for these collections were mostly published at the beginning of the 19th century, and in some cases the entries were compiled much earlier than that. They frequently do not identify illuminated manuscripts in the descriptions and did not attempt to index them.

Some special catalogues can help in identifying illuminated material in the Library. Volume 92 of the Class Catalogue, a subject catalogue for the manuscript collections, draws together descriptions of illuminated manuscripts in the Library, but this was compiled in the 1870s and suffers from the deficiencies of the published catalogues on which it was based. Moreover, it ceased being maintained in the 1950s. Birch and Jenner's *Early Drawings and Illuminations* is a useful basic index to the contents of illustrations, but is based on only a selection of manuscripts and, having been published in 1879, is now very old. A complete iconographic index compatible with the needs of modern scholarship is still required. Recent general and selective surveys, such as the Harvey Miller *Survey of Manuscripts Illuminated in the British Isles* edited by J.J.G. Alexander, are of great assistance for specific categories of manuscripts, but no such guidance is yet available for large swathes of material, such as the French or Italian manuscripts (although Cahn's volumes on Romanesque manuscripts have just appeared as the first offering in a companion survey of French illumination).

It might be expected that the illuminated manuscripts would be stored separately, and could be readily identified in this way. However, because the physical arrangement of the Library's manuscript collections has developed over more than two centuries, this is not the case. In the British Museum's original home, the 17th-century mansion Montagu House, each collection was kept in separate rooms on the first floor of the house, with the Harley manuscripts in rooms five and six, the Cotton and Royal manuscripts in room seven, and so on. Room three contained the Sloane, Birch and Hastead collections, together with a very small group of select manuscripts, comprising the most precious volumes, which were not generally available in the reading room. The Harley and Sloane manuscripts were arranged according to very cumbersome subject classifications. The Royal and Cotton manuscripts were placed on the shelves according to the pressmarks borne by the manuscripts when they entered the Museum – the 1808 *Synopsis of the Contents of the British Museum* apologised for the fact that 'These two libraries are not classed in a strict scientific order'.

During the Easter week of 1827, the manuscript collections were transferred from Montagu House to the accommodation in the new Museum building which (until the opening of the St Pancras building) they still occupy. The motley mixture of placing systems used at Montagu House was abandoned and the manuscripts were ranked on the shelf in collection groups according to size, regardless of previous numeration. The bulk of the manuscripts were placed in the present Manuscript Saloon and Middle Room and no attempt was made to place together particular types of manuscripts. The only exception was the select manuscripts, whose character was succinctly described by Sir Frederic Madden shortly after he became Keeper of Manuscripts in 1837: 'the MSS. termed Select are such as from their general value, interest or curiosity have been chosen from the general collection of MSS. and placed in a case in the Keeper's room such as the Alexandrian Codex, Royal Letters, Pope's autograph of Homer, the Durham copy of the Gospels & c... With regard to these Select MSS. the utmost care is taken to preserve them, united with every proper facility of access' (Additional MS 62002, f. 15v). Some were read only under supervision in the offices of the Manuscripts Department; others were read at a desk close to the Superintendent of the Reading Room. These select manuscripts were a very small and heterogeneous collection. As Madden goes on to remark, they 'by no means include all or even the larger portion of the more valuable and curious MSS. many of which, equally entitled to consideration, are included in the General Collection of MSS.' *(ibid.)*

At that time, manuscripts were consulted in the general reading room, and the fact that the majority of the manuscripts were freely available to anyone with an ordinary reader's ticket was a constant cause of concern to Madden. The Trustees turned down his proposal for a supplementary ticket for readers wishing to consult manuscripts. To protect the collections, Madden therefore designated more and more manuscripts as select, particularly after the opening of the Round Reading Room, which was ill-suited for the invigilation of readers using precious manuscripts. Two categories of restricted manuscripts emerged, the select manuscripts, which were issued in the reading room but subject to special restrictions, and reserve manuscripts, which had to be consulted in the departmental offices. In 1857, Madden notes that he 'Continued the list of Select MSS & made alterations in regard to the selection; returning to the general presses about two dozen Horae of no artistic merit' (Additional MS 62011, f. 70v).

Madden helped lay the foundations of the present classification of the manuscript collections. They assumed their present form as a result of preparations made for the evacuation of the collections in war time. As Bertram Schofield, Keeper of Manuscripts from 1956 to 1961, noted. 'The general principle in the evacuation of the collections of manuscripts has always been to list the manuscripts in various categories according to their value, so that the most precious may be given priority in an emergency. Such lists were first made during the First World War, and they were revised and brought up to date, first in 1933, then again in 1937–8' (Memorandum in Departmental Archives). In February 1918, as the risk of damage to the Museum from Zeppelin raids increased, 47 cases of the 'best' manuscripts were sent for safekeeping to the National Library of Wales, returning between December 1918 and March 1919. As alarm about the possibility of another war with Germany grew in the 1930s, more elaborate classifications of the manuscripts were made. By the time the Second World War broke out, the manuscripts had been graded in four categories, A*, A, B and C, in descending order of value. A further category, D, was established not on individual selection but on a block basis, including, for example, manuscripts from foundation collections not already in higher categories. The first two classes represented the cream of the collection, about 100 manuscripts, while category B was an attempt to identify the remainder of the most important manuscripts. These manuscripts were identified by a team led by the three most senior curators of the Department, the Keeper of Manuscripts, Idris Bell, his deputy, Eric Millar, and Arthur Collins.

The graded manuscripts had been dispersed throughout the collections, and they were assembled together in newly constructed presses to prepare them for removal. As soon as the German-Soviet pact was signed in August 1939, they were packed up and dispatched once more to the National Library of Wales at Aberystwyth. By the time war broke out, all manuscripts in the first three categories, and many of those in the D category, had safely reached Aberystwyth. When the manuscripts were returned after the war, it was decided to place all manuscripts in the A*, A and B categories together (with the exception of a few of the most precious, kept in a special safe). The war-time evacuation thus laid the basis of the present category of select manuscripts. These are subject to special handling restrictions and were the first part of the collections to be stored in environmentally controlled conditions. They are also the only part of the collections in which an attempt is made to store together manuscripts of a particular type (whether they are literary, musical, historical, and so on). In the case of the illuminated select manuscripts, an attempt is made to group manuscripts according to schools of illumination.

It will be seen, then, that the physical arrangement of the manuscript collections, particularly the designation of select manuscripts, does not reflect any sophisticated analysis of the structure of the collections, but rather the practical demands of collection management, whether the problems of issuing manuscripts in a general reading room in the 19th century or the demands of wartime emergencies in the 20th. The select manuscripts do not simply comprise illuminated medieval manuscripts, but the most valuable manuscripts of all types, ranging from early wax tablets to modern literary autographs. Moreover, the identification of select manuscripts was made very hurriedly while the first air-raid practices were starting and was concerned simply to identify the most precious manuscripts, a highly subjective process.

Under these circumstances, it is not surprising to find that some manuscripts which would undoubtedly now be regarded as of artistic importance were not included in the select manuscripts. For example, Lansdowne MS 204, a copy of the chronicle of John Hardyng probably prepared for presentation to Henry VI, containing a famous map of Scotland and an imposing pedigree illustrating Edward III's claim to the throne of France, is not a select manuscript. Similarly, the celebrated Additional MS 37049, a 15th-century Carthusian miscellany enlivened by vigorous pen-and-wash illustrations, which the famous art historian Francis Wormald declared to be his favourite manuscript, is stored with the general manuscript collections, presumably because its crude drawing style was not considered worthy of ranking with the outstanding works of art in the select manuscripts. As anomalies like this are identified, individual manuscripts are upgraded, but, given the importance of the Library's collection of illuminated manuscripts, the need for a systematic approach is pressing.

This need became more urgent as the next great move of the Manuscript Collections, the move to St Pancras, was contemplated. Illuminated manuscripts are prone to environmental shock, as movement of the vellum when it is exposed to different atmospheric conditions could damage the pigment on the surface of the manuscript. Good housekeeping clearly required that all illuminated material in the collections should be identified in advance of the move. The only way of doing this was by a detailed examination at the shelf of each volume in the collection, an immense task. In the summer of 1995, it was proposed that a Survey of Illuminated Manuscripts should be undertaken. The initial conception, the organisation of the project and the examination of the volumes has been the responsibility of two curators in the Department of Manuscripts, Michelle Brown and Scot McKendrick. They have been working in consultation with Janet Backhouse, the senior curator of illuminated manuscripts, and have been assisted by two graduate trainees successively attached to the Department, John Draper and Brett Dolman. This team have already completed an enormous amount of work and have gone a long way towards filling perhaps the most significant gap in our knowledge of the Library's collections. Funding has been obtained from the Getty Grant Program to appoint an assistant to the Survey for a three-year period (commencing summer 1997) to help with data capture and record management and to free more specialist curatorial time for the project.

It is estimated that about 75% of medieval manuscripts in the Library (excluding single-sheet documents) will fall within the scope of the Survey. All pre-1200 materials will be recorded, as well as all illuminated manuscripts dating before 1600, any important later materials relating to the history of earlier manuscripts (e.g. handmade facsimiles and transcripts) and the continuing arts of calligraphy and illumination. A broad definition of an 'illuminated manuscript' has been adopted for the project – all material except that with the most basic decorated or pen-flourished initials is being recorded. Summary electronic descriptions of each of these manuscripts will be prepared. The descriptions will be linked to a limited sample of images of the manuscripts. It is intended that these will be produced by scanning Ektachromes where these exist, but it should be borne in mind that many of the manuscripts in question have not yet received scholarly attention or publication, and have no existing photography. The precise procedures for scanning and storing the very large number of images required have yet to be finalised – one possibility is the use of the Kontron ProgRes 3012 digital camera in the Manuscripts Conservation Studio.

The most urgent need was to identify all illuminated manuscripts in readiness for the move to St Pancras, currently scheduled for the autumn of 1998. This will allow volumes to be upgraded to select categories as necessary, permit conservation work and boxing to be undertaken where required, and allow handling procedures for the move to be defined. In order to allow time for these preparatory activities to be completed well in advance of the move, this initial identification needs to be completed by the summer of 1997.

A pilot project whereby a section of the collections was surveyed and 100 descriptions prepared was undertaken from November 1995 to January 1996. The bulk of the work since has concentrated on completing the initial identification of illuminated manuscripts in the collection and making house-keeping recommendations, but nevertheless descriptions have been prepared of over 500 manuscripts, and approximately 10,000 manuscripts have been identified for further description. Once the initial identification is complete, the curators will concentrate on preparing the descriptions. Very many of the illuminated manuscripts not categorised as 'Select' manuscripts do not appear to have been cited in publications, and work on the Survey to date has emphasised how the same materials are regularly consulted while many others languish owing to inaccessibility. Modern scholarship is increasingly showing that the most well-known illuminated manuscripts can only be properly understood in their broader context. The level of access and searchability provided by the Survey will greatly stimulate research into the socio-historical context of the Library's 'treasures'.

The Survey has already yielded a number of rich finds, in the form of items which could not be readily identified from the existing catalogue entries and which appear to have so far eluded published reference or photography. Many of these are fully illuminated de luxe volumes, including a book of hours which is stylistically related to the famous Hours of Joanna the Mad, one of the Library's treasures. Others include interesting images, such as Romanesque drawings of a scribe, whose headgear bears a striking resemblance to that of a spaceman, and a plan of the Temple and Tabernacle in Jerusalem (this accompanies a 12th-century copy from Kirkham Priory of Bede's commentary on the subject and is closely related to the early 8th-century symbolical diagrams in the Codex Amiatinus, a world-famous Bible made at Monkwearmouth or Jarrow during Bede's life there). Other notable discoveries include a number of fragments of early books subsequently used as parts of bindings, in the hands of Insular, Carolingian and Anglo-Saxon scribes. The post-medieval material has also revealed some surprises, including landmarks in facsimile production and manuscript studies such as a hand-written facsimile of the Textus Roffensis (a 12th-century Rochester volume containing the earliest English law code from the early 7th century) made in 1712 by William Elstob and his sister Elizabeth (a renowned blue-stocking and early Anglo-Saxonist), and an exquisitely written and illustrated early 19th-century tract on spanking. The value of the collections is being enhanced at every level by such excavations within the stacks.

The intention was always that the Survey should produce a searchable record of the Library's illuminated manuscripts. Given the range and extent of the Library's holdings, the advantages of being able, for example, to produce listings of all manuscripts of a particular date, from a particular country or in a certain script, are obvious. Moreover, the detailed work of preparing the descriptions would be expedited by being able to enter codes for hierarchical decorative features such as decorated initials, line-fillers or miniatures. However, the technical options for proceeding were by no means obvious.

An outline form of description was prepared by Michelle Brown and Scot McKendrick. This defined the elements to be described as manuscript number, a brief description of contents, place of origin, date, language, dimensions (including written space), provenance, script, hierarchical components of the illumination, codicology (comprising format and material), location, binding, quality and notes. The most common types of illumination, format, material and binding were defined in advance in order to facilitate the use of codes in describing these features. Given the very varied nature of the manuscript numbers used in the different collections, a sort code was also required to allow records to be sorted into manuscript number order. Although this is far from representing a complete description of the manuscript (details of gatherings of the manuscript are, for example, omitted, and iconographic contents of miniatures are not described in this phase of the project), this 'summary' record is still quite complex in structure, and represents a more extensive record than would be found in many library applications. Moreover, in producing these records in automated form, some provision had to be made for the possibility that they would be upgraded at some stage. In future phases of the project, the descriptions may be expanded and an electronic iconographic index may be created. It is intended that the project will ultimately feed into any recataloguing of the collections concerned.

The two available technical options were evidently either to use a relational database package or to explore methods of handling free text. The final decision was driven essentially by the limited resources available for technical development. An initial decision was taken to explore the use of Microsoft Access, which is the database package most widely used in The British Library and was being used in the development of a system to control the move of the

Manuscript Collections to St Pancras as well as in the project for retroconversion of the printed *Index to Manuscripts*. The flexibility of Access, and in particular the availability of memo fields for longer entries, seemed to make it more suitable than other packages for this purpose. An attempt was made locally to develop Access entry forms corresponding to the descriptive schema, but it became evident that, because of the large number of fields required, substantial professional programming time would be required to develop a usable and reliable system.

This prompted a decision to explore the use of SGML-tagged word-processed descriptions for the project. The initial decision to explore this route was taken because it was evident that development costs, restricted largely to the development of the Document Type Definition (DTD), would be smaller. Curatorial time was available to undertake DTD development and tagging; programming time for the development of an Access-based package was not available. However, it was also evident that the use of SGML for this project had other advantages. As noted, images of the manuscripts were always conceived as an integral part of the Survey. Cross-references and links to images are easily implemented in SGML. The hypertext capabilities of SGML also seemed to offer an interesting way of presenting relationships between manuscripts. It was intended that the Survey would support a variety of different products – possible publication on CD-ROM was envisaged perhaps in conjunction with some form of hard-copy publication; it was hoped to incorporate the Survey in any future automated catalogue of the manuscripts; and the possibility of Internet publication, perhaps linked to an image ordering service, was envisaged. The Survey would also be used for a variety of different purposes – internal housekeeping, academic research and picture research were three obvious possibilities. SGML-tagged records offered great flexibility of potential use and searchability, which could readily allow all these requirements to be addressed. Moreover, the great advantage of SGML, that it is not software dependent and that SGML-tagged text can be viewed under a number of different packages, is attractive in this context, since it is unlikely that the resources would ever again be available to undertake a Survey of this kind, and future-proofing of records is an important consideration. Finally, the archive world was beginning to take a great interest in the use of SGML as a means of both automating and standardising archive descriptions, and the use of SGML for the Survey of Illuminated Manuscripts seemed to offer an opportunity for The British Library to explore the applicability of SGML to its own records.

However, the adoption of SGML for the Survey required a great act of faith on the part of the curators responsible for the project. It was impossible to develop in advance a 'programme' which would show the curators before they started work exactly how their records would be handled. The work proceeded in a reverse fashion to that which would normally be expected in a library automation project. Detailed descriptions of about 100 manuscripts were prepared in advance of the full development of the automated system. These descriptions were provided in word-processed format. Richard Masters and Andrew Prescott began to draw up a DTD which was refined as more descriptions were provided. Eventually the pilot descriptions were tagged. This was done manually in a word-processing package so that issues requiring further development of the DTD could be more readily identified. Even then, the curators were only able to see very crudely how the tagging would work, using the Panorama Pro SGML browser, which offers very limited search capabilities. A fuller demonstration was not feasible until it was possible to mount the descriptions on a server using the more sophisticated Open Text LiveLink software.

The creation of the DTD for the Survey was not an easy task. Given that there were no 'industry standard' DTDs for the description of manuscripts as a class of documents, and certainly not specifically for illuminated manuscripts, careful thought had to be given to the structure. As the model evolved it became clear that, although the basic structure was fairly straightforward, there were some aspects which would prove to be difficult to resolve, and further problems arose as more descriptions were fed into the tagging process. Some of these detailed questions are discussed later, but an important lesson was learnt early on in the development, and it is one which is worth mentioning here – if only because it is often overlooked and yet is crucial to all projects – namely that of configuration management.

This term is more usually associated with the development of 'traditional' computer systems, but it is no less appropriate to document analysis and the subsequent design and implementation of a computer-based storage and retrieval system. Given the overhead in tagging the descriptions of manuscripts, it is important that the DTD evolves in a way that minimises the amount of re-tagging required by hand. This is best done by ensuring full backward compatibility of the DTD, and straightforward cross-translation from one version to another using an SGML-aware programming language such as Omnimark.

The elements identified in document analysis and the subsequent tags used can represent (i.e. capture or mark) format, structure, or content. In this project a model was required which would allow a combination of structure and content to be tagged. This provides the greatest opportunities for retrieval, for providing navigation aids, and for presenting the descriptions in a useful and meaningful way. Information which has been tagged in this way is also most likely to be future-proof. This, together with a prescriptive (and detailed) DTD, offers the greatest opportunity for re-purposing the data. As it had not been decided at the start of the project what software would be used for delivery, and it is impossible to know what software will be available in the future, the aim has been to capture the maximum amount of detail while trying not to impose impossible restrictions on the flexibility of the prose. It is always possible to down-translate to a simpler tagging structure such as HTML for example – but very difficult or impossible to up-translate (that is to impose a more detailed tagging structure) automatically.

A 'tight' DTD was adopted for this project as it deals with highly structured information and it appeared that there would be little difficulty in this being enforced. A prescriptive DTD leaves few options for the elements and attributes to be used and the order in which they may appear. A possible unfortunate side-effect of insisting on a prescriptive DTD is 'tag abuse syndrome', defined by Maler and El Andaloussi as 'a condition that afflicts authors who choose inappropriate markup to get a certain formatting effect or choose markup that isn't as precise or accurate as possible', or, to put it more succinctly, an activity which tries to subvert the intention of a rule. While there is always a risk of an outbreak of this highly contagious condition, it was felt that it would not be a problem in this project as the data itself is highly structured and curators of manuscripts are used to the requirements of presenting catalogue information in a rigorously controlled fashion, whether in a manual or automated environment.

It is important to note that one cannot deprecate or recommend models through a DTD, only allow or disallow them. Tagging guidelines are used to provide guidance on the 'best' models to adopt but ultimately it is only with a rigorous DTD that one can be certain about the quality of the recorded information.

There are some common pitfalls into which all unwary DTD designers fall when constructing a model from scratch. Two of the most common are ambiguous content models and mixed content models. The latter especially is difficult to avoid and often leads either to less precision or greater complexity in the markup. There were a number of parts of the model developed for describing illuminated manuscripts which had to be reconsidered as these problems were discovered.

It was necessary to increase a number of the values as supplied in the ISO standard declaration, in order, for example, to make element names more meaningful. This has implications for all aspects of SGML processing within the project and stresses the importance of configuration management – an aspect normally associated with traditional information system development.

It was decided early on that there would be no markup minimisation. The only reasons for considering such minimisation would be to cut down the amount of storage required and to minimise the amount of typing required at data capture. As neither of these were a critical factor in this project, and some of the SGML tools used in the project require normalised data anyway, full markup was chosen.

Another way of making the markup as prescriptive as possible is through the use of general entities for as much of the text as possible. A number of the main elements consist of one or more terms from a restricted vocabulary, and there was already extensive use of automatic abbreviations in Microsoft Word at the data capture stage which made use of this fact. In cataloguing it is possible to have Word expand the abbreviations automatically and in SGML authoring software these terms can be picked from a list. This means that the risk of not finding relevant information decreases significantly as the terms can be presented to the researcher in the form of a pick list at search time, and misspellings are also kept to a minimum. Examples of the elements to which this applies are: binding, in which general entities are defined for each of the major categories of binding that will be encountered; illumination, in which all decorative features which occur such as miniatures, major and minor decorated initials, line-fillers or manufacturing aids are again defined as entities; the codicological status, indicating for example whether a manuscript is on vellum or paper or whether it is a roll or codex; and the different collection names in the manuscript number, such as Cotton MS, Royal MS, and so on.

Some parts of the information analysis were fairly straightforward, and the DTD model for these was easy to design. The terminology used to describe the script and language of the manuscript was, for example, extremely consistent and standardised. Where appropriate, elements and constructs were derived from the Text Encoding Initiative (TEI), as it was clearly worth while drawing on the huge development that lay behind that work, and also to minimise the risk of not being able to translate descriptions tagged to our DTD to conform to any TEI extensions which may be proposed in the future. Cross-references (using the *<ref>* element in conjunction with *target* attributes) and the linking of images to specific places within the text (using the *<figure>* element) provide two such examples.

Other aspects of the DTD development were less straightforward. In some cases, information might be supplied by the curator, such as an extension of a personal name. In order that users are given the fullest possible indication of the status of particular information, it is important to indicate where information has been supplied by the cataloguer in this way. In a conventional description, this supplied information might be designated by the use of square brackets. Sometimes, the curator will be very confident about the accuracy of the supplied information; in others he or she will be less certain. Thus, an extension of the abbreviated form of a Christian name of the owner of a manuscript 'Edw' to Edw[ard] will have a high level of certainty. An extension of an abbreviation 'E' to E[dward] may have a much lower level of certainty. Another example of supplied information might be where an epithet identifying a person more closely is supplied, such as Edward, [Prior of St Victor?]. The DTD therefore needed to include elements indicating that the curator has supplied some words or information and extent to which this information is reliable. These elements, *<certnty>*, with the attribute *level,* and *<supplied>*, were derived from TEI equivalents. The tagged version of the epithet noted above would thus be:

<SUPPLIED><CERTNTY LEVEL="LOW">Prior of St Victor</CERTNTY> </SUPPLIED>

One problem which required the introduction of an artificial data element was a mechanism for sorting the description. As descriptions were being compiled from a survey of the manuscripts on the shelf, they were not cumulated in manuscript order. It was clearly a basic requirement that they should be capable of being sorted into manuscript order. The formats used for numbering the manuscripts vary considerably. The numbers of the Cotton manuscripts, for example, are pressmarks whose format is due to the use in the 17th century of busts of Roman emperors to designate the bookcases containing the manuscripts. Typical numbers for this collection are Cotton MS Nero D. iv or Cotton MS Otho A. xii. The pressmarks of Royal MSS are a combination of letters and both roman and arabic numerals, such as Royal MS 12 C. IV. The Additional Manuscripts bear simple registration numbers such as Additional MS 60000, but there is a complication in that the manuscripts numbered 1–4100 in this sequence are called Sloane Manuscripts. Thus, the manuscript number itself is not in a format which would allow for easy sorting, so a *<sortcode>* element was adopted. This expresses the manuscript number as a simple alphanumeric code, so that Cotton MS Nero D. iv becomes A/COTNER/D/04. The content of this can be derived from the manuscript number with a simple program so there is no additional overhead of manual tagging. This may prove to be an unnecessary inclusion but without knowing the capabilities of the software eventually to be used, it was felt best that this was built-in from the start.

Even what would at first sight appear to be relatively straightforward elements turned out to have hidden complexities. An example is the element recording the dimensions of the manuscript. Initially, it was assumed that this would simply give the overall dimensions of the manuscript in millimetres as height by width by depth in the form 208 x 134 x 43. However, it is normal in describing medieval manuscripts to also give the dimensions of the space occupied by the text block on the page (written space). This is indicated in brackets after the overall dimensions in the following form: 208 x 134 x 43 (112 x 30). But in some cases, the margins of the manuscript contain a gloss, so the dimension element needs to take account of this, and may read as follows: 208 x 134 x 43 (112 x 30. 116 x 100 with gloss). The tagged version of this would be as follows:

```
<DIMS><MSDIM><HEIGHT>208</HEIGHT><WIDTH>134</WIDTH><DEPTH>43
</DEPTH></MSDIM><TEXTDIM><HEIGHT>112</HEIGHT><WIDTH>30</WIDTH></
TEXTDIM><TEXTDIM><HEIGHT>116</HEIGHT><WIDTH>100</WIDTH></TEXTDIM
> with gloss</DIMS>
```

There have been a number of cases where the structure of the DTD has proved less predictable than first thought. This has meant that the DTD has required constant revision – but this has been far easier than having to amend traditional database structures. While it is undoubtedly true that excavating the treasure-store is exciting and fascinating from a scholarly perspective, the unexpected revelations it leads to can raise serious problems for those trying to construct automated finding aids. A number of such issues have been raised so far, some of which have necessitated major changes to the DTD and for some of which we are still seeking the best solution.

A major difficulty is dealing with composite manuscripts. Early collectors frequently bound together unrelated manuscripts into a single volume and the vagaries of early book production may also mean that a book was not produced at one place at one time. A description will need to cover the whole volume but elements in the description will differ for each part. Thus, Additional MS 22790 may contain three articles, each with a different date, language, text dimension, script, type of illumination and perhaps even codicological status (one part may be on vellum, another on paper). A single overall description is required for this volume, but, within these elements, it is necessary to distinguish which part is of a certain date, language and so on. This has been achieved by use of an attribute *mss-part* for each of these elements. This provides the required flexibility in searching, retrieval and presentation.

Another two aspects of manuscript description which present problems are dating and foliation. The main problem is with representation and the way in which this can then hinder effective searching. Some manuscripts can only be dated within a general period. In other cases, there is information which permits a firm dating. For example, one manuscript may be dated by curators as being from the second quarter of the 14th century, while another contains an inscription which dates it specifically to 1329. Devising a way in which both of these dates can be recorded accurately while also ensuring that they will both be retrieved when a scholar wishes to identify all manuscripts from the first half of the 14th century is difficult. Of course, this capability is dependent upon the facilities in the software used for retrieval, but it is never straightforward. When dates are stored in a traditional database structure, or in descriptive text, some complex programming is required to translate the inquiry and the data to correlate descriptive terms for periods of time with specific dates. This is also true to some extent when the information is tagged but the advantage of using SGML is that one has maximum control over the form in which the information is recorded. The elements chosen are *<date>*, with the attribute *value* and *<daterange>*, with attributes *from* and *to*. Thus the date of a manuscript could be recorded as *<daterange from=1325 to=1349>second quarter of the fourteenth century</daterange>*. The success of this solution has yet to be proved in practice but early indications are that with the right software we will be able to offer the flexibility of searching demanded by scholarly research.

Foliation poses a similar problem in that sometimes an element will include a reference to a range of folios, while in other cases the reference will be to a single folio. Thus, the provenance field might refer first to a depiction of a female patron on f. 21v, then to ownership inscriptions on ff. 34 and 35v, and finally to notes on land grants by a monastic owner on ff. 45–50v. In addition to this, there might be references to another manuscript – there might, say, be a reference to a similar ownership inscription in Cotton MS Otho A. xii, f. 4v. The user will want to ensure that all information about a folio within a particular range is found by a search. For example, a search for information about a particular item comprising Cotton MS Otho A. xii, ff. 2–29v will need to return the reference to Cotton MS Otho A. xii, f. 4v as well as references to the whole range. To help overcome these problems, the DTD includes a *<folio>* element with *<f>* and *<ff>* sub-elements with the only text required being the number(s) of the folio(s). Thus *<folio><f>40v</f></folio>* and *<folio><ff>23–45v</ff></folio>*.

Finally, there is an area of description which still requires further work and refinement, that of the hierarchy of illumination. Entities are currently deployed to ensure that a controlled vocabulary is used (see above), but this is a flat representation and there is a requirement to represent a more sophisticated hierarchy of illumination. For example, major initials and minor initials can be decorated and might also be zoomorphic; borders can be full or partial and decorated and might also be inhabited and with heraldic decoration and white vine ornament. By analysing this classification, devising an appropriate model group in the DTD, and applying the tags according to these rules, SGML has the capa-

Diagram showing
structure of Document
Type Definition used in
Survey of Illuminated
Manuscripts.

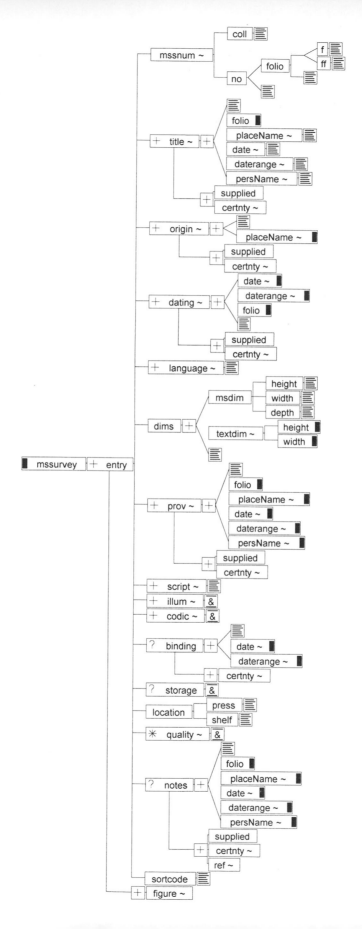

bility to represent the structure of the decorative scheme of the manuscript in a way that is difficult using any other approach. This will enable scholars to explore the information in the Survey to see the interrelationships and interconnection between manuscripts in completely new ways.

Recording all this information is not an end in itself; it has to be accessible. The Survey will be used for a wide range of inquiries. It will be used not only for scholarly research but also to provide information for planning the move of the Manuscript Collections to St Pancras and to assist in housekeeping of the collections there. Moreover, the research uses of the data will be extremely wide-ranging. The Survey will not only be useful to art historians. Since the existing catalogues of many of the most important collections of medieval manuscripts in the Library are very old and only provide limited information about the manuscript, the information about the contents, origin, date, provenance and so on of a particular manuscript will be useful to all scholars consulting it. Palaeographers will find the Survey a valuable resource for identifying manuscripts in a particular script or of a particular date. The ownership information will be useful for those interested in the history of libraries. The attraction of SGML is that complex and varied inquiries can in theory be readily addressed. However, the ability of the user to take full advantage of the potential offered by elaborate tagging of the kind undertaken in the Survey depends on the quality of the SGML browser used to view the document.

For initial access, with a simple 'find' facility, the descriptions are being made available for viewing with Softquad's SGML viewer Panorama Pro. A range of stylesheets can be defined which present the elements in the descriptions with different colours, fonts, layout depending on the view required. There is also a navigator which provides a 'table of contents' view of a set of descriptions in a window on the left of the screen while the full entries are displayed in the main window. The table of contents view is very flexible and can be customised to show any degree of the hierarchy, and can also show the contents of selected elements. Images can be displayed in-line or can be loaded into a more powerful image viewer for more detailed study. Panorama Pro also allows the user to create their own set of cross-references and as a separate layer to the descriptions file itself in the manner of 'webs'.

To overcome the limitations of Panorama (e.g. its handling of raw SGML in a single file and its restricted search capabilities) it has been decided to use the SGML-aware full-text indexing software, Livelink, from Open Text. Livelink can handle large amounts of data – the software has been used by Open Text itself to index the whole of the World Wide Web – retaining the SGML context in its indices. By doing this it allows for sophisticated searching, for example all 15th-century manuscripts in Latin script that were owned by Julian Marshall. The researcher has a choice in the format of the information to be delivered to them. The raw SGML can be sent for viewing in software such as Panorama, or it can be converted on-the-fly to HTML for viewing with a standard Web browser. It is likely that the latter will be the usual means of viewing the records, with SGML delivery being used by the few who want to study the records in greater detail.

It has already been noted that one of the attractions of using SGML for the Survey was that it would enable the Library to investigate a technical approach to manuscript cataloguing which is becoming increasingly popular among archivists and manuscript scholars. An important part of the DTD development was therefore the examination of the work of other projects to see how far their experience was relevant to the requirements of The British Library. The templates provided by the Text Encoding Initiative (TEI) were found to be of limited application. The concern of the TEI is primarily with literary texts, not with specialist records of the kind involved in the Survey. Although care was taken to ensure that headers in the DTD were TEI-compliant and TEI conventions were used wherever available (such as for date ranges and place names), the bulk of the DTD was specially developed.

Another international initiative which might at first glance seem relevant here but which turned out to have limited applicability is the work being undertaken under the direction of Daniel Pitti of the University of California at Berkeley on archival description standards, which has led to the development of the Encoded Archival Description (EAD) standard. This is now being promoted as an international standard by the Research Libraries Group. EAD is essentially designed to deal with groups of papers or records, in which the description is hierarchical. There is an overall description of the record group at a high level, then detailed descriptions of each item. However, in the case of manuscript volumes, each volume has to be considered as an entity in itself, and there is frequently no need for a high-level description of the collection as a whole. In other words, records frequently stand by themselves, and are not in a hierarchical relationship to other records. In developing the DTD for the Survey of Illuminated Manuscripts, EAD was examined at a pre-alpha stage but, for these reasons, it was felt that the tag set was not suitable for descriptions of manuscript volumes.

It quickly appeared that the development work for the Survey was applicable elsewhere. Richard Gartner, the Pearson New Technologies Librarian at the Bodleian Library, used a draft of the DTD for the Survey as the basis for a more comprehensive set of tags for full descriptions of manuscripts at a level of detail not required for the Survey. As a result of his work, it was felt that it was worth extending the TEI to provide a standard for descriptions of manuscripts. Meanwhile, in the United States, the Hill Monastic Manuscript Library at St John's University, Collegeville, Minnesota, had begun to develop EAMMS (Electronic Access to Medieval Manuscripts), a project financed by the Mellon Foundation to convert the catalogue of its massive holdings of microfilms of manuscripts. EAMMS was seeking to develop both 'first-level' and 'detailed' catalogue records for medieval manuscripts in both MARC and SGML formats. The initial experiences of this project had emphasised the need for the development of common standards of description for medieval manuscripts.

Contact between Hope Mayo, the Director of EAMMS, and Peter Robinson of De Montfort University, one of the Directors of the Canterbury Tales Project, led to the convening of a workshop at Studley Priory in November 1996 as a first step in an initiative to devise an agreed format for manuscript descriptions.

This workshop was partly financed by The British Library and attended by Michelle Brown, Richard Masters and Rachel Stockdale, the Cataloguing Manager for the Department of Manuscripts. Rachel Stockdale subsequently visited the HMML for a further meeting of EAMMS in December 1996. The Studley Priory workshop considered very extensively the issues involved in developing a common standard for manuscript descriptions and its relationship to other initiatives, such as the Dublin Core scheme, intended to provide a common metadata protocol. The workshop discussed the possible contents of a common set of elements for manuscript description as well as which elements might be mandatory in any description and which might form the basis of any 'first level' description, suitable for abbreviated catalogue records. It is intended that these discussions might form the basis for the provision of TEI standards for manuscript description of the sort primarily intended to accompany digitised images. The Studley Priory conference led to the establishment of a formal project, MASTER (Manuscripts Access through STandards for Electronic Records), which has recently bid for EU funding and in which The British Library is an associate partner.

The work on the Survey will therefore not only fill a long-felt gap in The British Library's records of its holdings. It is also enabling the Library to occupy a central place in the discussion of bibliographic standards which are of critical importance for the future of manuscript studies.

## APPENDIX 1

### Survey of Illuminated Manuscripts: Structure of Descriptions

Descriptions to be arranged as follows, with separate fields for each element. Terminology is derived from M.P. Brown, *Understanding Illuminated Manuscripts: a Guide to Technical Terms* (The J. Paul Getty Museum & The British Library, 1994) and from M.P. Brown, *A Guide to Western Historical Scripts from Antiquity to 1600* (The British Library & University of Toronto Press, 1990, 1994).

**MS no**.
Title: 1. Short or summary title    2. Articles (i.e. major textual items, if more than one text is included)

**Origin**
Date
Language
Dimensions: overall dimensions (height x width x thickness, for storage purposes) and written space (height x width, within ruling pattern) in mm.

**Provenance**
Script
Status of illumination (components arranged in hierarchy)
Codicological status (materials / form)
Binding
Storage (for in-house use, to include recommendations on preservation and storage)
Shelf
Notes (to include a qualitative grading of artistic status, any general observations, whether features such as musical notation or calendars are included, and any major bibliographical citations)

## APPENDIX 2
### Survey of Illuminated Manuscripts: List of automatic abbreviations

The normal style on the laptops used at shelf for the survey has been set up so that certain abbreviations used are automatically extended. This has been done using the Autocorrect facility in Word 6. For definitions of terms, see M.P. Brown, *Understanding Illuminated Manuscripts: a Guide to Technical Terms* (The J. Paul Getty Museum & The British Library, 1994).

*Abbreviations for use under MS no.*

| | |
|---|---|
| Ad | Additional MS. |
| Ar | Arundel MS. |
| Bur | Burney MS. |
| Cot | Cotton MS. |
| Eg | Egerton MS. |
| Harl | Harley MS |
| Lan | Lansdowne MS. |
| Roy | Royal MS. |
| Sl | Sloane MS. |
| Yt | Yates Thompson MS. |

*Abbreviations for use under Title*

| | |
|---|---|
| B | Bible |
| Bh | Book of Hours |
| Br | Breviary |
| Ch | Choirbook |
| Hb | Herbal |
| M | Missal |
| Pon | Pontifical |
| Ps | Psalter |

*Abbreviations for use under Language*

| | |
|---|---|
| Eng | English |
| Fr | French |
| Ger | German |
| Gr | Greek |
| Ital | Italian |
| Lat | Latin |

*Abbreviations for use under Provenance*

| | |
|---|---|
| Bk | Bookplate |
| Col | Colophon (may also occur under Script and Date) |
| Exl | Ex libris |

*Abbreviations used under Script*

As an interim measure numbers may be given corresponding to examples of scripts in M.P. Brown, *A Guide to Western Historical Scripts from Antiquity to 1600* (The British Library & Toronto University Press, 1990, 1994)

*Abbreviations for use under Status of Illumination*

| | |
|---|---|
| Bdp | Bas-de-page |
| Bf | Borders (full) |
| Bp | Borders (partial) |
| Ca | Cadels |
| Cd | Coloured |
| D | Drawing |
| Dec | Decorated |
| Diag | Diagrams |
| Ds | Display Script |
| Fp | Fully painted |
| G | Grisaille |
| Grot | Grotesques and/or figural decoration |
| H | Head or tailpieces |
| Her | Heraldic decoration (may also occur under Provenance) |
| Hi | Historiated |
| Inh | Inhabited |
| L | Line-fillers |
| Lf | Litterae Florissae |
| Ln | Litterae Notabiliores |
| M | Miniatures |
| Ma | Manufacturing aids (incl. quire nos/signatures, guide-letters, instructions etc) |
| Maj | Major initials |
| Marg | Marginalia |
| Min | Minor initials |
| O | Outline drawing |
| P | Printed image |
| Pp | Purple pages |
| R | Run-over symbols |
| T | Titlepieces |
| Tin | Tinted |
| U | Unfinished |

| Wv | White vine ornament | | Or | Original |
|----|---------------------|----|----|---------|
|    |                     |    | Pr | Pre-1700 |

*Abbreviations for use under Codicological Status*

| | | | *Abbreviations for use under Storage* | |
|---|---|---|---|---|
| C | Codex | | Bo | Boxed |
| Ch | Charter | | Con | Conservation needed |
| E | Ephemera | | Rb | Requires boxing |
| Gl | Glass | | Up | Upgrade (storage area / status) |
| Pa | Paper | | | |
| Ro | Roll | | *Abbreviations for use under Notes* | |
| S | Single sheet | | Po | Poor |
| Ta | Tablet | | St | Standard |
| V | Vellum / parchment | | | Standard / Good |
| | | | Go | Good |
| *Abbreviations for use under Binding* | | | | Good / Fine |
| Bib | Bibliophile | | F | Fine |
| Fc | Foundation collection | | Ex | Excellent |
| Fo | Foredge painting or tooling | | I | Interesting |
| Lv | Limp vellum binding | | Mus | Musical notation |
| Met | Metalwork | | | Calendar |

# The British National Corpus

**Lou Burnard**

The British National Corpus (BNC) is a rather large SGML (Standard Generalized Markup Language) document, comprising some 4124 samples taken from a rich variety of contemporary British English texts of every kind, written and printed, famous and obscure, learned and ignorant, spoken and written. Each of its 100 million words and six and a quarter million sentences is tagged explicitly in SGML and carries an automatically generated linguistic analysis. Each sample carries a Text Encoding Initiative (TEI) conformant header, containing detailed contextual and descriptive information, as well as more conventional SGML mark-up.

The corpus was created over a four-year period by a consortium of leading dictionary publishers and academic research centres in the UK, with substantial funding from the British Department of Trade and Industry, the Science and Engineering Research Council, and The British Library. It is currently available under licence within the European Union only, where it is increasingly used in linguistic research and lexicography, in applications ranging from the construction of state of the art language-recognition systems, to the teaching of English as a second language.

This paper begins by describing how the corpus was constructed, and gives an overview of some of the SGML encoding issues raised during the process. A description of the special purpose SGML-aware retrieval system developed to analyse the corpus is also provided.

## How to build a corpus

The building of large-scale corpora of text for use in linguistic analysis pre-dates the technical feasibility of such resources in digital form by several centuries. The *Oxford English Dictionary*, for example, may be regarded as the product of an immense corpus of citation slips, collected and collated in hand-written form over a period of decades during the last century. However, the term corpus is most typically used nowadays to refer to a collection of linguistic data gathered for some specific analytic purpose, with a strong presupposition that it will be stored, managed, and analysed in digital form. The grandfather of linguistic corpora of this type is the one-million-word Brown corpus, created at Brown University in the early 1960s using methods still relevant today. Linguists and linguistics thrive on controversy, and the dignifying of corpus-based approaches to the subject into a recognised academic discipline has had its fair share. Nevertheless, certainly in Europe, and increasingly in North America, corpus-based linguistics is widely perceived as central to many aspects of research into the nature and functioning of human language, with applications in fields as diverse as lexicography, natural language processing, machine translation, and language learning. A general introduction to corpus linguistics with particular reference to the BNC is provided in the forthcoming BNC Handbook, which cites a number of other recent introductory textbooks.

Many of the most well-known language corpora were created within an academic context, where slightly different constraints tend to affect quality control, budgets, and deadlines than those associated with commercial production environments. The BNC project was, by contrast, a joint academic-industrial project, in which both academic and industrial partners learned a little more of their colleagues' perspectives by means of an enforced collaboration. In crude terms, if the academic partners learned to cut their coat according to the cloth available, the industrial partners learned that there were more complex things in life than boilersuits.

The BNC is a collection of over 4000 different text samples, of all kinds, both written and spoken, containing in all six and a quarter million sentences, and over 100 million words of current British English. Work on building it began in 1991, and was completed in 1994.

The project was funded by the Science and Engineering Council (now EPSRC) and the Department of Trade and Industry under the Joint Framework for Information Technology (JFIT) programme. The project was carried out by a consortium led by Oxford University Press, of which the other members are major dictionary publishers Addison-Wesley Longman and Larousse Kingfisher Chambers, academic research centres at Oxford University Computing Services (OUCS), Lancaster University's Centre for Computer Research on the English Language, and The British Library's Research and Innovation Centre.

Organisationally, the tasks of designing and building the corpus were split across a number of technical work groups on which each member of the consortium was represented. Task Group A concerned itself with basic issues of corpus design – what principles should inform the selection of texts for inclusion in the corpus, what target proportions should be set for different text types, and so forth. Task Group B focused on one key issue in corpus construction, the establishment of acceptable procedures for rights clearance and permissions to include material in the corpus. This might have been the subject of a major research project in its own right: in practice, the output from the task group was a standard agreement, in some sense a precedent-setting document for other European corpus-builders.

Task Group C concerned itself with technical details of encoding and text processing; these are discussed in more detail below. Task Group D concerned itself with corpus enrichment and analysis. In practice, the distinction between the two turned out to be largely the distinction between the creation of the corpus and of specific software to make use of it. Since the latter task was not possible until the end of the project, by when there were no funds left to do it, it is unsurprising that little was actually accomplished in this group within the time of the original BNC project.

SGML played a major part in the BNC project: as an interchange medium between the various data-providers; as a target application-independent format; and as the vehicle for expression of metadata and linguistic interpretations encoded within the corpus. From the start of the project, it was recognised that SGML offered the only sure foundation for long-term storage and distribution of the data; only during its progress did the importance of using it also as an exchange medium between the various partners emerge. The importance of SGML as an application-independent encoding format is also only now becoming apparent, as a wide range of applications for it begin to be realised.

The scale and variety of data to be included meant that an industrial-style production line environment had to be defined: this was dubbed the BNC sausage machine by Jeremy Clear, the project manager at the time, and may be summarised as follows:

- Data capture. Each of the three commercial partners selected and prepared material to a different defined format, reflecting to some extent the diverse nature of materials for which they were primarily responsible.
- Primary check and conversion. OUCS checked each text against its data capture format, automatically converted it to project standard format, and made an accession record for it in the project database.
- Linguistic annotation. Valid SGML texts were passed to Lancaster for automatic addition of word class tagging and linguistic segmentation, using the CLAWS software discussed further below.
- Text cataloguing and final checking. Lexically annotated texts were run through a final conversion at OUCS; a detailed TEI header was generated from the project database and the text itself added to the corpus.

A wide literature now exists on corpus design methodologies, which this paper will not attempt to summarise, although the experience of designing and creating the BNC has contributed greatly to it.

A corpus which, like the BNC, aims to represent all the varieties of the English language cannot be assembled opportunistically, although a project with a defined budget and timescale inevitably finds design principles sometimes have to be sacrificed to pragmatic considerations. At the outset, target proportions were agreed for certain broadly agreed categories of material, and these were adhered to. In the spoken part of the corpus, 10 per cent of the whole, a balance was struck between material gathered on a statistical basis (i.e. recruited from a demographically balanced sample of language producers) and from material gathered from a pre-defined set of speech situations or contexts. A moment's reflection should show that this dual practice was necessary to ensure that the corpus included examples of both common and uncommon types of language. Equally, in the written parts of the corpus, published and unpublished material, of a wide range of topics, registers, levels, etc., were all represented. From high-brow novels and textbooks to pulp fiction and journalism, by way of school essays, office memoranda, email discussion lists, and paper-bags, our aim was to ensure that every form of written language is to be found in the corpus, to a greater or larger extent.

As noted above, data capture for the whole project was carried out by the three publishers in the BNC consortium (OUP, Longman and Chambers). Three sources of electronic data were envisaged at the start of the project: existing electronic text, Optical Character Recognition (OCR) from printed text, and keyed-in text. It soon become apparent that the first source would be less useful than anticipated since either the material was encoded in formats too difficult to unscramble consistently, or the texts available did not match the stipulated design criteria. Scanning and keying text brought lesser problems of their own, of which probably the worst was training keyboarders and scanners at different places to be consistent under tight time constraints. In the case of spoken data, keyboarding was the only option from the start, and proved to be very expensive and time-consuming, in part because of the very high standards set for data capture. Transcribing spoken language with attention to such features as overlap (where one speaker interrupts another), and enforcing consistency in the representation of non-lexical or semi-lexical phenomena are major technical problems, rarely attempted on the scale of the BNC material, which finally included 10 million words of naturally occurring speech, recorded in all sorts of environments.

For a variety of reasons, the three data suppliers all used their own internal mark-up systems for data capture which then had to be centrally converted and corrected to the project encoding standard. Had this standard, the Corpus Document Interchange Format (CDIF) been available at the start of the project, the need for conversion would have been lessened, but not that for validation. CDIF, like many other TEI-conformant Document Type Definitions (DTDs), allows for considerable variation in actual encoding practice, largely because of the very widely different text types that it has to accommodate. To help ease the burden on data suppliers, the tags available were classified according to their perceived usefulness and applicability. Some – such as headings, chapter or other division breaks, and paragraphs – were designated 'required' parts of any CDIF document; when such features occur in a text, they must be marked up. Others – such as sub-divisions within the text, lists, poems, and notes about editorial correction, were 'recommended', and should be marked up if at all possible. Finally, some tags were considered 'optional' – dates, proper names and citations which are easily identifiable. The process of format conversion and SGML validation was automated as far as possible (fortunately for us, the SGML parser became available early on during the project): these constituted the 'syntactic' check. Where time permitted, we also carried out a 'semantic' check to determine whether material which should have been tagged had in fact been marked up, though it was of course impossible to carry out a full-proof-reading exercise. Materials which fell below an agreed threshold of errors, either syntactic or semantic, were returned to the data capture agency, for correction or replacement.

Management of the many thousands of files and versions of files involved as texts passed through the production line was managed by a relational database system, which also managed routine archiving and back-up. This database also held all of the bibliographic and other metadata associated with each text, from which the TEI headers eventually added to each text were generated.

The project was funded for a total of four years, of which the first was devoted to agreeing and defining in full operational detail the procedures summarised above. By the end of the fifth quarter (March 1992), 10 per cent of the corpus had been received at OUCS and procedures for handling it were in place. A small sample (two million words) had been processed and sent on to Lancaster for the next stage of processing. The rate at which texts were received and processed at OUCS fluctuated somewhat during the course of the project, but ramped up steadily towards its end.

The following table shows the approximate number of words (in millions) received at OUCS, converted to the project standard, and received back from Lancaster in annotated form, for each quarter (parenthesised figures indicate 'bounced' texts – material which had to be returned because it did not pass the QA (Quality Assurance) procedures discussed above):

| QUARTER | RECEIVED | VALIDATED | ANNOTATED |
|---|---|---|---|
| 6 | 2 | 4 | — |
| 7 | 6 | 4 | — |
| 8 | 5(1) | 8 | 6 |
| 9 | 6(2) | 14 | 13 |
| 10 | 14(3) | 11 | 5 |
| 11 | 12(2) | 13 | 8 |
| 12 | 25 | 16 | 17 |
| 13 | 25 | 32 | 22 |
| 14 | 3 | 8 | 30 |

## How to mark up a corpus

A full description of the BNC mark-up scheme is beyond the scope of this paper, and is in any case available in the documentation supplied with the corpus and elsewhere. Instead, I would like to focus on the way in which the anticipated uses of the corpus conditioned the mark-up scheme actually applied.

It has often been said of general purpose DTDs such as the TEI (which was being developed symbiotically with the CDIF scheme used in the BNC) that they allow the user too much flexibility. In practice, we found that the richly descriptive aspects of the TEI scheme were of least interest to our potential users. For purpose of linguistic analysis, the immense variety of objects in a fully marked up text, with all their fascinating problems of rendering and interpretation, are of less importance than a reliable and regular structural breakdown, into segments and words. This was an unpalatable lesson for academics with a fondness for the rugosities of real language, but an important one. The scale of the BNC simply did not permit us to lovingly mark up every detail of the text – distinguishing sharply every list, foreign word, editorial intervention, or proper name.

Instead we had to be sure that headings, paragraphs, and major text divisions were reliably and consistently captured in an immense variety of materials. For purposes of linguistic analysis, segmentation at the sentence and word level was crucial but, fortunately, automatic. By comparison with other, more literary-oriented, TEI texts, the tagging of the BNC is thus rather sparse, despite its 150 million SGML tags.

The basic structural mark-up of both written and spoken texts may be summarised as follows. Each of the 4124 documents or text samples making up the corpus is represented by a single <bncDoc> element, containing a header, and either a <text> (for written texts) or an <stext> (for spoken texts) element. The header element contains detailed and richly structured metadata supplying a variety of contextual information about the document (its title, source, encoding, etc., as defined by the TEI). A spoken text is divided into utterances, possibly interspersed with non-linguistic elements such as events, possibly grouped into divisions to mark breaks in conversations. A written text is divided into paragraphs, possibly also grouped into hierarchically numbered divisions. Below the level of the paragraph or utterance, all texts are composed of <s> elements, marking the automatic linguistic segmentation carried out at Lancaster, and each of these is divided into <w> (word) or <c> (punctuation) elements, each bearing a POS (part of speech) annotation attribute.

Considerable discussion went on at the start of the project as to the best method of encoding this automatically generated information. There are about 60 different possible POS codes, each representing a linguistic category, for example as a singular noun, adverb of a particular type, etc. The codes are automatically allocated to each word by CLAWS, a sophisticated language-processing system developed at the University of Lancaster, and widely recognised as a mature product in the field of natural language processing.

For approximately 4.7 per cent of the words in the corpus, CLAWS was unable to decide between two possible taggings with sufficient likelihood of success. In such cases, a two-value word-class code, known as a portmanteau tag is applied. For example, the portmanteau tag VVD-VVN means that the word may be either a past tense verb (VVD), or a past participle (VVN). We did not make any attempt to represent this ambiguity in the SGML coding, though at a later stage of linguistic analysis, perhaps based on the TEI feature structure mechanism, this might be possible. Without manual intervention, the CLAWS system has an overall error-rate of approximately 1.7%, excluding punctuation marks. Given the size of the corpus, there was no opportunity to undertake post-editing to correct annotation errors before the first release of the corpus.

Since then two successor projects have been completed by the Lancaster team which should result in the availability of a much improved new version. The first step was to manually check a two per cent sample from the whole corpus, using a much richer and more delicate set of codes. This corrected sample was then used to improve and extend the CLAWS tagging procedures, essentially by expanding its knowledge of common English phrasal sequences, before re-running the automatic procedure over the whole corpus.

Further details of the CLAWS tagging procedure and the linguistic concepts underlying it are available in a number of research publications from the Lancaster team; this paper focuses on the encoding issues its use involved. Firstly, we had to decide how to represent the fact that CLAWS does not always allocate codes to single orthographic words. For example, the word 'won't' is regarded as two tokens by CLAWS: 'wo' (verbal auxiliary) and 'n't' (negation marker); similarly possessive forms such as 'Queen's' are regarded as two tokens. Further to confuse matters, some common prepositional phrases such as 'in spite of' are regarded as a single token, as are foreign phrases such as 'annus horribilis'. (This last phrase appears over 30 times in the BNC, as a consequence of the Queen's speech to Parliament in 1993.)

Secondly, we had to decide how to represent the code itself. There is some controversy amongst linguists about whether or not POS codes of this kind should be decomposable: that is, whether the encoding should make explicit that (for example) NN1 and NN2 have something in common (their noun-ness) which (say) VVX lacks. The TEI, of course, has a great deal to suggest on the subject, and proposes a very powerful SGML tagset for encoding such feature systems. To keep our options open, and also for ease of conversion from the data format output by CLAWS (which was already in existence, and had been for many years), we began by representing the code simply as an entity reference following the token to which it applied. Thus:

The&AT0 Queen&NP0's&POS annus horribilis&NN1

This option, we felt, would enable us to defer to a later stage exactly what the replacement for each entity reference should be: it might be nothing at all, for those uninterested in POS information, or a string, or a pointer indicating a more complex expansion of the TEI kind. The problem with this representation however, is that it relies on an ad hoc interpretative rule (of the kind which SGML is specifically designed to preclude the need for) to indicate, for example, that the code AT0 belongs to the word 'The', rather than to the word 'Queen'. In fact this is not encoding the truth of the situation: we have here a string of word-annotation pairs. A more truthful annotation might be:

<pair>
<form>The</form>
<code>At0</code>
</pair>

A further possibility is to use an attribute value, for either the form or the code: thus <form code=AT0>The</form> or, equivalently, <code form= The>AT0</code>

From the SGML point of view these are equivalent. From the application point of view, the notion of a text composed of strings of POS codes, with embedded forms seems somehow less appealing than the reverse, which is what we eventually chose, our example being tagged as follows:

<w AT0>The <w NP0>Queen<w POS>'s <w NN1>annus horribilis

The decision to use an often deprecated form of tag minimisation for the POS annotation was forced upon us largely by economic considerations. A fully normalised form, with attribute name and end-tags included on each of the 100 million words would have more than doubled the size of the corpus. Data storage costs continue to plummet, but the difference between 2 Gb and 4 Gb remains significant!

A second major set of encoding problems arose from the inclusion in the corpus of 10 million words of transcribed speech, half of it recorded in predefined situations (lectures, broadcasts, consultations etc.), and the other half recorded by a demographically sampled set of volunteers, willing to tape their own everyday work and leisure-time conversation.

Speech is transcribed using normal orthographic conventions, rather than attempting a full phonemic transcript, which would have been beyond the project's limited resources. Even so, the mark-up has to be very rich in order to capture the process of speaker interaction – who is speaking, and how, and where they are interrupted. Significant non-verbal events such as pauses or changes in voice quality are also marked up using appropriate empty elements, which bear descriptive attributes. Here is an example of the start of one such conversation, as encoded in CDIF:

```
<u who=D00011>
<s n=00011>
<event desc="radio on"><w PNP><pause dur=34>You
<w VVD>got<w TO0>ta <unclear><w NN1>Radio
<w CRD>Two <w PRP>with <w DT0>that <c PUN>.
<s n=00012>
<pause dur=6><w AJ0>Bloody <w NN1>pirate
<w NN1>station <w VM0>would<w XX0>n't
<w PNP>you <c PUN>?
</u>
```

The basic unit is the utterance, marked as a <u> element, with an attribute who specifying the speaker, where this is known. This attribute targets an element in the header for the text, which carries important background information about the speaker, for example their gender, age, social background, inter-relationship, etc. Where speakers interrupt each other, as they usually do, a system of alignment pointers simplified from that defined by the TEI, is used. This requires that all points of overlap are identified in a <timeLine> element prefixed to each text, component points (<when> elements) of which are then pointed to from synchronous moments within the transcribed speech, represented as <ptr> elements. Pausing is marked, using a <pause> element, with an indication of its length if this seems abnormal. Gaps in the transcription, caused either by inaudibility or the need to anonymise the material, are marked using the <unclear> or <gap> elements as appropriate. Truncated forms of words, caused by interruption or false-starts, are also marked, using the <trunc> element.

A semi-rigorous form of normalisation is applied to the spelling of non-conventional forms such as 'innit' or 'lorra'; the principle adopted was to spell such forms in the way that they typically appear in general dictionaries. Similar methods are used to normalise such features of spoken language as filled pauses, semi-lexicalised items such as 'um', 'err', etc. Some light punctuation was also added, motivated chiefly by the desire to make the transcriptions comprehensible to a reader, by marking (for example) questions, possessives, and sentence boundaries in the conventional way.

Paralinguistic features affecting particular stretches of speech, such as shouting or laughing, are marked using the <shift> element to delimit changes in voice quality. Non-verbal sounds such as coughing or yawning, and non-speech events such as traffic noise are also marked, using the <vocal> and

<event> elements respectively; in both cases, a closed list of values for the *desc* attribute is used to specify the phenomenon concerned. It should, however, be emphasised that the aim was to transcribe as clearly and economically as possible rather than to represent all the subtleties of the audio recording.

The metadata provided by the header element, mentioned above, is of particular importance in any electronic text, but especially so in a large corpus. Earlier corpora have tended to provide all such documentation (if at all) as a separate collection of reference manuals, rather than as an integral part of the corpus, with obvious concomitant problems of maintainability and consistency. In SGML, particularly the TEI header, we felt that we had a powerful mechanism for integrating data and metadata, which we used to the full: each component text of the BNC carries a full header, structured according to TEI recommendations, and containing a full bibliographic description of it, and of its source, as well as specific details of its encoding, revision status, etc. A corpus header, containing information common to all texts, is also provided: this includes full descriptions of the corpus creation methodology, and the various codes used within individual text headers, such as those for text classification.

A particular problem arises with large general-purpose corpora like the BNC, the components of which can be cross-classified in many different ways. Earlier corpora have tended to simplify this, for example, by organising the corpora into groups of texts of a particular type – all newspaper texts together, all novels together, etc. A typical BNC text, however, can be classified in many different ways (medium, level, region, etc.). The solution we adopted was to include in the header of each text a single <catRef> element carrying an IDREFS-valued attribute, which targeted each of the descriptive categories applicable to the text.

For example, the header of a text of written author type 2 (multiple authorship), written medium type 4 (miscellaneous unpublished), and written domain type 3 (applied sciences) will contain an element like the following:

<catref target="wriaty2 wrimed4 wridom3">

The values wriaty2 wrimed4 etc. here each reference a <category> element in the corpus header, containing a definition for the classification intended. The full set of descriptive categories used is thus controlled and can be guaranteed uniform across the whole corpus, while at the same time permitting us to mix and combine descriptive categories within each text as appropriate.

A similar method was used to link very detailed participant descriptions (stored in the header) with utterances attributed to them in the spoken part of the corpus.

In retrospect, had we all known as much about SGML at the start of the project as we did by the end of it, we would have made much more impressive progress, and perhaps delivered a better product. Needless effort went into converting from one format to another, which might have been better spent on gathering more reliable contextual information, for example.

**How to analyse a corpus**

Linguistic analysis, particularly of large and diversely organised corpora, is not the same as text retrieval. While some of the application needs of the BNC user community might be met by standard SGML browsers or text database systems, many are not. The typical user of the BNC is interested in its contents as raw material for analysis, not as material to be searched for particular words or references. There is a correspondingly greater emphasis on statistical output, on ways of patterning and re-ordering result sets, as well as a need to support more complex kinds of inquiry than are usual in text-retrieval products. To meet some of these needs, the BNC is now delivered with a purpose-written SGML-Aware Retrieval Application (SARA), developed at Oxford.

From the start of the BNC project in 1990, it had always tacitly been assumed that some kind of retrieval software would need to be delivered along with the corpus. The original project proposal talks of 'simple processing tools' and an informal specification for an 'information search and retrieval processor' was also drawn up by the UCREL team early on. In the event, the need to complete delivery of the corpus on time (or at least, not too late), meant that development of any such software beyond that needed for the immediate needs of the project was increasingly deferred.

It was argued that the lack of such software might be only transient, since the corpus was to be delivered in SGML form, tools for which were already becoming widely available, as a result of the widespread adoption of this standard both within the language engineering research community and elsewhere.

However, a major stated goal of the project was to make the corpus available and usable as widely as possible, that is, not just at a low cost, but also within as wide a variety of environments as possible. It seemed to us that the potential user community for large-scale corpora like the BNC extended considerably as far beyond the natural language processing research community as it did beyond the immediate needs of commercial lexicographers, although it was largely on behalf of these groups that the project had originally been funded and largely therefore these groups which had determined the manner in which it should be delivered.

It seemed to us that the software needs of some of the potential users of the BNC would be only partially met by the generic SGML software available in late 1994 (and to a large extent still today).

The choice lay amongst highly specialised, but high-performance, application development tool kits which given sufficient expertise could be customised to suit the needs of niche markets in natural language processing or lexicography, but which were somewhat beyond the needs, comprehension, or indeed purse, of the person in the street; generic SGML browse and display engines, designed originally for electronic publication or delivery over the web, often with very attractive and user-friendly interfaces but generally unable to handle the full complexity and scale of the BNC; or simple concordancing tools which were equally unable to take advantage of the added value we had so painfully put into the encoding and organisation of the corpus. Moreover, existing software was either very expensive (being aimed at large-scale electronic publishing environments), or free, but requiring considerable technical expertise for anything beyond the most trivial of applications. As discussed further below, the scale and complexity of the BNC (with its 100 million tagged words, six and a quarter million sentences, and 4124 interlinked texts) seemed likely to stretch the capacity of most simple text-based concordancers available at that time.

We were fortunate enough to obtain funding, initially from The British Library Research and Innovation Centre, and subsequently from the British Academy, to produce a software package which might go some way to fill the gaps identified. Development of the system was carried out by Tony Dodd, with valuable input from members of the original BNC Consortium, and from early users of the software. The system is called SARA, for SGML-Aware Retrieval Application, to make explicit that although aware of the SGML mark-up present in the corpus, it is not a native SGML database. In this respect, however, it is no better or worse than a number of other current software packages.

### The SARA system

The SARA system was designed for client/server mode operation, typically in a distributed computing environment, where one or more work-stations or personal computers are used to access a central server over a network. This is, of course, the kind of environment which is most widely current in academic (and other) computing milieux today. The success of the World Wide Web, which uses an identical design philosophy, is vivid testimony to the effectiveness of this approach.

The system has four chief components:

- the indexing program, which generates an index of tokens from an SGML marked-up text;
- the server program, which accepts messages in the Corpus Query Language (CQL); and returns results from the SGML text;
- the SARA protocol, a formally defined set of message types which determines legal interactions between the client and server programs; this protocol makes use of a high-level query language known as CQL;
- one or more client programs, with which a user interacts in any appropriate platform-specific way, and which communicate with the server program using the protocol.

### The SARA index

Computationally, the best-understood method of accessing a text the size and complexity of the BNC is to use an index file, in which search terms are associated with their location in the main text file, and into which rapid access can be obtained using hashing techniques. Such methods have been employed for decades in mainstream information retrieval systems, with the consequence that the advantages and disadvantages of the various ways of implementing the underlying technology are well known and very stable.

The SARA index is a conventional index of this type. Entries in the index are created by the indexing program, using the SGML markup to determine how the input text is to be tokenised. The tokens indexed include the content of every <w> or <c> element, together with the part of speech code allocated to it by the CLAWS program. For example, there will be one entry in the index for 'lead' as a noun, and another for 'lead' tagged as a verb. The index is not case-sensitive, so occurrences of 'Lead' may appear in either entry. The tokenisation is entirely dependent on that carried out by CLAWS, which accounts for the presence of a few oddities in the index where CLAWS failed to segment sentences entirely.

The SGML tags (other than those for individual tokens) themselves are also indexed, as are their attribute values. For example, there is an entry in the index for every <text> start- and end-tag, and for every <head> start- and end-tag, etc. This makes it possible to search for words appearing within the scope of a particular SGML element type. For some very frequent element-types (notably <s> and <p> ) whose locations are particularly important when delimiting the context of a hit, additional secondary indexes called accelerator files are maintained.

The index supplied with the first version of the BNC occupies 33,000 files and 2.5 gigabytes of disk space, i.e. slightly more than the size of the text itself. Building the index is a complex and computationally expensive process, requiring much larger amounts of disk space or several sort/merge intermediate phases. This was one reason for delivering the completed index together with the corpus itself on the first release of the BNC, even though development of the client software was not at that stage complete. More compact indexing might have been possible, at the expense of either a loss in performance or an increase in complexity: in practice, the indexing algorithm used provides equally good retrieval times for any kind of query, independent of the size of the corpus indexed. The index included on the published CDs necessarily assumes that the server accessing it has certain hardware characteristics (in particular, word length and byte addressing order). To cater for machines for which these assumptions are incorrect, a localisation program is now included with the software. This can either make a once-for-all modification to the index or be used by the server to make the necessary modifications 'on the fly'.

The indexer program is intended to operate on generic SGML texts, that is, not just on the particular set of tags defined for use in the BNC. However, we have not yet attempted to use it for corpora using other tag sets, and there are almost certainly some features of its behaviour which are currently specific to the BNC.

### The SARA server

The SARA server program was written originally in the ANSI C language, using BSD sockets to implement network connections, with a view to making it as portable as possible. The current version, release no 928, has been implemented on several different flavours of the UNIX operating system, including Solaris, Digital UNIX, and Linux, which appear to be the most popular variations. The software is delivered with detailed installation and localisation instructions, and can be downloaded freely from the BNC's Web site (see http://info.ox.ac.uk/bnc/sara.html), though it is not yet of much interest to anyone other than BNC licensees.

The server has several distinct functions, amongst which the following are probably the most important:

- it allows registered users to log on or off and to change their passwords;
- it implements the key functions required of the CQL, in particular: looking for tokens in the index; solving a query; supplying bibliographic information about a text; displaying some or all of a text at a given location; thinning or filtering the result set from a query.
- it handles all housekeeping, allowing concurrent access by several different users.

The server listens on a specified socket (usually 7000) for login calls from a client. When such a call is received, the server tries to create a process to accept further data packages. If it succeeds, the client is logged on and set up messages are exchanged which define, for example, the names and characteristics of SGML elements in the server's database. Following this, the client sends queries in the CQL, and receives data packets containing solutions to them. Once a connection has been established in this way, the server expects to receive regular messages from the client, and will time out if it does not. The client can also request the server to interrupt certain transactions prematurely.

## The Corpus Query Language

The CQL is a fairly typical Boolean-style retrieval language, with a number of additional features particularly useful for corpus work. It is emphatically not intended for human use. Like many other such languages, its syntax is designed for convenience of machine processing, rather than elegance or perspicuousness. A brief summary of its functionality only is given here.

A query is made up of one or more atomic queries. An atomic query may be one of the following:
- a single L-word (that is, a token as recognised by the indexer: this may or may not correspond to an orthographic word);
- a wildcard character, which will match any single L-word;
- a delimited string of L-words;
- an L-word+POS pair, e.g. CAN=NN1;
- a regular expression;
- an SGML query, that is, a search for a start- or end-tag, possibly including attribute;
- name-value pairs.

Four unary operators are allowed in CQL:
- case. The $ operator makes the query which is its operand case-sensitive;
- header. The # operator makes the query which is its operand search within headers as well as in the bodies of texts (it thus assumes that a TEI-conformant DTD is in use);
- optional. The ? operator matches zero or one solutions to the query which is its operand; it makes no sense unless the query is combined with another;
- not. The ! operator matches anything which is not a solution to the query which is its operand. It makes no sense unless the query is combined with another;

A CQL expression containing more than one query may use the following binary operators:

- sequence. One or more blanks between two queries matches cases where solutions to the first immediately precede solutions to the second.
- disjunction The [verbar] operator between two queries matches cases where either query is satisfied.
- join. The [star] operator between two queries matches cases where both queries are satisfied in the order specified; the operator between two queries matches cases where both queries are satisfied in either order.

When queries are joined, the scope of the expression may be defined in one of the following ways:

- SGML element. A join query followed by an operator and an SGML query matches cases where the joined query is satisfied within the scope of the SGML query.
- number. A join query followed by an operator and a number matches cases where the joined query is satisfied within the number of words specified.

If no scope is supplied for a join query, the default scope is a single <bncDoc> element.

## SARA client programs

The standard SARA installation includes a very rudimentary client program called solve, for UNIX. This provides a command line interface at which CQL expressions can be typed for evaluation, returning result sets on the standard UNIX output channel, for piping to a formatter of the user's choice, or display at a terminal. This client is provided mainly for debugging purposes, and also as a model of how to construct such software. The SARA client program which has been most extensively developed and used runs in the Microsoft Windows environment, and it is this which forms the subject of the remainder of this paper.

In designing the Windows client, we attempted to make sure that as much as possible of the basic functionality of the CQL protocol could be retained, while at the same time making the package easy to use for the novice. We also recognised that we could not implement all of the features which corpus specialists would require at the same time as providing a simple enough interface to attract corpus novices. In retrospect, there are several features and functions we would liked to have added (of which some are discussed below); but no doubt, had we done so, there would be several aspects of the user interface with which we would now be equally dissatisfied.

The SARA client follows standard Microsoft Windows application guidelines, and is written in Microsoft C++, using the standard object classes and libraries. It thus looks very similar to any other Windows application, with the same conventions for window management, buttons, menus, etc. It runs under any version of Windows more recent than 3.0, and there are both 16- and 32-bit versions. A TCP/IP stack (such as Winsock) to implement connection to the server is essential, and a colour screen highly desirable. The software uses only small amounts of disk or memory, except when downloading or sorting result sets containing very many (more than a few hundred) or very long (more than 1Kb) hits.

The Windows client allows the user to:

- search the word index and check what tokens it contains;
- define, save, re-use, or modify a query (effectively, a CQL expression to be evaluated);
- view, sort, save, or print all or some of the results returned by a query;
- configure and manipulate the display of results in a variety of ways;
- view contextual and bibliographic data for any one text;
- combine simple queries to form a complex one, using a visual interface.

A brief description of each of these functions is given below; more information is available from the built-in help file and from the BNC Handbook

**Types of query**

The Windows client distinguishes five types of query, and allows for their combination as a complex query. The basic query types are:

- word query. This searches the SARA word index, either by stem (right-hand truncation only is performed) or by pattern (see below). All index-entries matching the string entered are returned, and the user can then select all or some of them for dispatch to the server as CQL queries against the corpus.
- phrase query. A phrase query behaves superficially like a word query, in that it searches for occurrences of a particular word or phrase. It differs in that it can be case-sensitive, can search text headers as well as bodies, can include punctuation, and is aware of the tokenisation rules used by the CLAWS tagger. A phrase query can also include a 'wild card' character to match any word in a phrase.
- pattern query. A pattern query allows for queries using a simple subset of UNIX-style regular expressions, for example to find variant spellings of a word. Some limitations on the kind of pattern which can usefully be searched for are imposed by the nature of the index: for example, left-hand truncation of the search term always implies a scan through the entire index, and is therefore not allowed.
- POS query. A part of speech (POS) query carries out a word query, further restricted by a given POS code, for example to find occurrences of 'lead' tagged as a noun. It should be stressed that this is only feasible for a specified word, since the POS code is only a secondary key in the SARA word index – it is not possible to search for (say) all nouns with the current system.
- SGML query. An SGML query carries out a search for a given SGML tag in the corpus, optionally qualified by particular combinations of attribute values, for example to find all occurrences of <event> elements in which the desc attribute has the value 'laughing' or 'laughter'. It is particularly useful when restricting searches to texts of a particular type, since text type information is typically carried by SGML attributes in the BNC.

One or more of the above types of query may be combined to form a complex query, using the special-purpose Query Builder visual interface, in which the parts of a complex query are represented by nodes of various types. A Query Builder query always has at least two nodes: one, the scope node, defines the context within which a complex query is to be evaluated. This may be expressed either as an SGML element, or as a span of some number of words. The other nodes are known as content nodes, and correspond with the simple queries from which the complex query is built. Content nodes may be linked together horizontally, to indicate alternation, or vertically to indicate concatenation. In the latter case, different arc types are drawn, to indicate whether the terms are to be satisfied in either order, in one order only, or directly, i.e. with no intervening terms.

Query Builder thus enables one to solve queries such as 'find the word "fork" followed by the word "knife" as a noun, within the scope of a single <u> element'. It can be used to find occurrences of the words 'anyhow' or 'anyway' directly following laughter at the start of a sentence; to constrain searches to texts of particular types, or contexts, and so forth.

For completeness, the Windows client also allows the skilled (or adventurous) user to type a CQL expression directly: this is the only form of simple query which is not permitted within the Query Builder interface.

### Display and manipulation of queries

By whatever method it is posed, any SARA query returns its results in the same way. Results may be displayed in one of line or page modes, i.e. in a conventional key-word-in-context (KWIC) display, or one result at a time. The amount of context returned for each result is specified as a maximum number of characters, within which a whole sentence or paragraph will usually be displayed. Results can be displayed in one of four different formats:

- plain text-only display which effectively ignores and suppresses all mark-up.
- POS. Individual words are colour-coded according to their part of speech and a user-defined colour scheme.
- SGML. All SGML encoding in the original is displayed uninterpreted.
- custom. The SGML encoding is interpreted according to a simple user-supplied specification.

It will often be the case that the number of results found for a query is unmanageably large. To handle this, the SARA client offers the following facilities:

- A global limit is defined on the number of results to be returned. When this limit is exceeded, the user can choose to over-ride the limit temporarily for this result set, specifying how many solutions are required, discarding any surplus from the end of the result set;
- to discard all but the first solution in each text;
- to take a random sample of specified size from the available solutions.

When the last of these is repeated for a given large result set, it will return a different random sample each time.

Once downloaded to the client, a set of results may be manipulated in a number of ways. It may be sorted according to the keyword which defined the query, by varying extents of the left or right context for this keyword, or by combinations of these keys. Sorting can be carried out either by the orthographic form, in case-insensitive manner, or by the POS code of words. This enables the user to group together all occurrences of a word in which it is followed by a particular POS code, for example. It is also possible to scroll through a result set, manually identifying particular solutions for inclusion or exclusion, or to thin it automatically in the same way as when the limit on the number of solutions is exceeded.

A result set may simply be printed out, or saved to a file in SGML format, for later processing by some SGML-aware formatter or further processor. Named bookmarks may be associated with particular solutions (as in other Windows applications) to facilitate their rapid recovery. The queries generating a result set, together with any associated thinning of it, any bookmarks, and any additional documentary comment, can all be saved together as named queries on the client, which can then be reactivated as required.

### Additional features of the client

The main bibliographic information about each text from which a given concordance line has been extracted can be displayed with a single mouse click. It is also possible to browse directly the whole of the text and its associated header, which is presented as a hierarchic menu, reflecting its SGML structure. The user can either start from the position where a hit was found, expanding or contracting the elements surrounding it, or start from the root of the document tree, and move down to it.

A limited range of statistical features is provided. Word frequencies and z-scores are provided for word-form lookups, and there is a useful collocation option which enables one to calculate the absolute and relative frequencies with which a specified term co-occurs within a specified number of words of the current query focus.

### Limitations of the current system and future plans

As noted above, the current client lacks some facilities which are widely used in particular fields of corpus-based research. This is particularly true of statistical information. There is no facility for the automatic generation of collocate lists, or any of the other forms of more sophisticated forms of statistical analysis now widely used. Neither is there any form of linguistic knowledge built into the system (other than the POS tagging): there is no lemmatised index, or lemmatising component, though clearly it would be desirable to add one. For those sufficiently technically minded, or motivated, the construction of such facilities (whether using SGML-aware tools or not) is relatively straightforward; the problem is that no simple interface or hook exists to build them into the current Windows client.

Similarly, it is not possible to define, save and re-use subcorpora, except by saving and re-using the queries which define them. The SARA client can address only the whole of the SARA index, which indexes the whole of the BNC. This is a design issue, which has yet to be addressed. If queries become very complex, involving manipulation of many very large result streams, they may exceed the limits of what can be handled by the server. This has not yet arisen in practice, however.

A more common complaint about the current system is that it cannot be used to search for patterns of POS codes, independently of the particular word forms to which they are attached. This is fundamentally an indexing problem, which may be addressed in the next major release of the system.

The performance problems associated with queries containing very high frequency words are derived from the same problem, and may be addressed in the same way. And again, it is a trivial exercise for a competent programmer to write special-purpose code which will search for such patterns across the whole of the BNC.

Despite these limitations, the system has attracted great enthusiasm when tested and demonstrated, despite performance problems and difficulties of access, perhaps owing largely to the intrinsic interest of the BNC data itself. At the time of writing, October 1996, the current software system appears stable enough for general release, not only to BNC licensees for their own internal use, but also to suitably qualified users wishing to access a national online service. Plans are already well advanced for the establishment of such a service as part of The British Library's *Initiatives for Access* programme. Plans have also been mooted for the further development of the SARA system, enabling it to be used with other SGML document-type definitions, and on other platforms.

For up-to-date information on the availability of the SARA system, or the BNC in general, including full bibliographic details please see our Web site at http://info.ox.ac.uk/bnc. Development of other SARA clients, in particular for the World Wide Web, is a further exciting possibility for the system. SARA, who came late into the BNC's world, seems likely to be equally late to leave it.

# A database for cataloguing Chinese and Central Asian manuscripts: the International Dunhuang Project

Susan Whitfield

Too often libraries or other institutions do not consider *whether* to computerise but only *when*. The costs of computerisation are high, both in setting up (for equipment, technical support and man-hours) and in maintenance, and these need to be weighed against the expected benefits. For an example see N.L. Hahn (Hahn 1990) who has estimated that an average of 1.1 hours is required per manuscript for encoding, proof-reading and making corrections. Despite the fact that computer technology is not new, the skills and knowledge required to exploit its potential and the infrastructure of back-up and services are still patchy. In 1991 W.V. Egmond observed that computers were being used much as printing technology was in 15th-century Europe: to provide an alternative means of doing what was already being done. Six years later, technology is still often used unnecessarily, rarely fully exploited, and has brought new problems which are sometimes not acknowledged: it is time-consuming, expensive and, because of incompatibility, in some cases may prove to be of little long-term use. Printed catalogues have served very well and extra time may be best spent, for example, in providing a concordance and improving the index rather than on computerisation. There should be a strong argument for the additional benefits of computerisation which will counter the additional costs.

The International Dunhuang Project is a compelling example of how computer technology can be applied to make resources available in a manner previously unimaginable. The manuscripts and printed documents from Chinese Central Asia (hereafter referred to as 'the manuscripts') are scattered in collections throughout the world. In particular over 40,000 manuscripts from Cave 17 in Dunhuang, Gansu province, are now largely housed in four major institutions – the National Library of China, The British Library, the Bibliothèque Nationale de France, and the Institute of Oriental Studies, St Petersburg – with smaller holdings elsewhere. There is not an existing complete catalogue. None of these institutions can offer full access to its collection for one or more of the following reasons: the poor condition of the manuscripts; the lack of a complete finding list, let alone a catalogue; and the policy of the institutions (this especially applies to Beijing and St Petersburg, where it is not usual for readers to be given access to material). Although there are microfilms and other facsimile forms of the manuscripts, these are still incomplete and often of poor quality. Therefore, the situation is that, even if scholars travel to all the places where the manuscripts are held and buy all the catalogues, microfilms and other facsimile forms now available, they will not be able to see the greater part of the collection.

The main reason for the limited conservation and cataloguing has been – and continues to be – a combination of lack of resources coupled with lack of sufficient numbers of scholars and conservators with the necessary expertise. This situation will continue to apply nationally in the foreseeable future. In other words, working in isolation it is unlikely that any of the major collections will complete conservation and cataloguing and open their entire collection to scholars. Even if they were to do so, the preservation of the manuscripts would continue to be a limiting factor to their accessibility. Some are so frail as to make any handling inadvisable; and even though the majority are in good condition, handling should still be kept to a minimum to ensure their long-term preservation. Moreover, each collection is still only part of a whole which needs to be available in its entirety to be understood fully.

Therefore there is a compelling argument for international co-operation to create a widely available computer catalogue of all the manuscripts with images. It is the only means to provide scholars with access to the entire collection. Using images means that the manuscripts can be studied both by scholars interested in the text and those interested in the object. Moreover, despite the massive input of resources needed to achieve this end, it will save each individual institution considerable work because of the exchange of ideas and the possibility of sharing techniques, especially in conservation and catalogue design. They can also combine their energies for fund-raising and the collaborative nature of the Project should increase the chances of success in this vital area. The Project will also make the manuscripts available for research to many more scholars whose work will contribute to the maintenance and updating of the database.

Because of the differing physical locations and the age and condition of the manuscripts, it is vital that, if they are to be made accessible to more scholars, it is achieved mainly by using surrogates. Providing transcriptions of the texts would not be satisfactory for several reasons. First, the texts are often illegible or at least open to different interpretations. Second, they contain many characters and glyphs that are not found in existing Chinese character coding systems. Third, a full-text transcription does not show the context, handwriting, type of manuscript, colour of the paper, and numerous other details that could be vital for understanding and dating the text. This being said, it is planned that some transcriptions be included in the database. It is also hoped that the database will, at a later stage, be linked to full-text databases of, for example, the Buddhist Canon, so that researchers can compare the manuscript texts with other versions.

Other forms of providing a complete catalogue with images would be so unwieldy and expensive as to make them effectively inaccessible to many scholars. It is a premise of this argument that the computer catalogue will be made available in a large number of places and in a variety of forms. A truncated version, for example, will be accessible on the Internet. Egmond's argument that a computer catalogue must fulfil four basic characteristics to rival its printed form, namely completeness, flexibility, usability and portability, is accepted (with the caveat that any printed catalogue of the Dunhuang collection would be far from portable [Egmond 1990]). The International Dunhuang Project database will, at the very least, be available at major institutions in its complete form and more widely accessible in HTML/SGML format on the Internet, or on CD-ROM and other media. The database, in a partial form, will be available in The British Library reading rooms and on the Internet early in 1998. Decisions about how to make it more accessible will be taken after then in light of the current state and availability of technology, but always working towards the aim of making it accessible to as many people as possible.

### Cataloguing, character code and transliteration standards

The Project is in the enviable position of being able to co-ordinate the setting up of databases across major institutions in an area where little computer cataloguing has already been carried out. Although each institution in the Project will develop and maintain its own database these will contain, for the most part, common fields in a common format and using common software. The databases will be linked and presented to the user as a single entity. (For an example of this see the Gabriel project, as described by Graham Jefcoate [Jefcoate 1996].)

The extensive literature on manuscript computer cataloguing has been taken into account when designing the database and there are sufficient fields in common to mean that it can be mapped, at least in part, on to other systems. (See, for example, Folkerts and Kühne 1990, Faulhaber 1991, Stevens 1991 for collections of papers on this topic.) Hope Mayo has shown the gymnastics necessary to adapt catalogues of Western medieval manuscripts to this format (Mayo 1991a and 1991b), and these problems are compounded when dealing with manuscripts in non-roman scripts. The Project database is not attempting to work within a MARC format, but it is hoped that a route to connect the Project catalogue with existing MARC catalogues will be possible.

A more pressing problem is the coding of non-roman scripts and transliteration standards. The latter are now receiving more attention with the appointment in 1996 of a new chair and secretary for the International Organization for Standardization subcommittee responsible for transliteration: ISO/TC46/SC2: Conversion of Written Languages. (The new chair is John Clews and the new secretary is Evangelos Melagrakis). An electronic mailing list has been set up (for details contact John Clews). It is hoped that some agreement will be reached before the Project starts to catalogue the non-Chinese manuscripts, and original script will be used wherever possible in addition to transliteration. Of course, this also presents problems because some of the scripts used do not have fonts. The Project will use existing, widely used fonts as much as possible but will otherwise develop new fonts and provide them with the database where necessary.

The coding of characters is controversial. UNICODE, even if it does become the standard, only codes a proportion of the characters found in classical Chinese, let alone those in Buddhist texts. There is also the matter of glyphs, of which the Dunhuang manuscripts contain many variants. This continues to be the subject of much discussion. (See, for example, the discussion on the mailing list ASIANDOC [see Further Reading for URL]; the proceedings of the meetings of the Electronic Buddhist Text Initiative, and articles in *Electronic Bodhidharma* [see Further Reading for URL].) Many scholars are working towards solutions and in the next few years it is expected that larger coding sets will be available and ways of coding variants and glyphs will be largely standardised. However, the problem of interpretation will remain: in most cases the cataloguer will decide which character is represented and code it accordingly. One solution for uncertain cases or variant glyphs is for the coding to link to a graphic of the character as it appears on the manuscript, but this then omits the character from the index: ordinary text searches will not find it as it is stored as an image.

The International Dunhuang Project database circumvents the first problem, that of the lack of suitable codes, by incorporating digitised images of the manuscripts. Uncoded, unrecognisable or variant characters will be marked in the database and a graphic of the individual character brought up for the reader, who will then also have the option of seeing the manuscript itself so that the character can be seen in context.

A solution to the second problem, searching, is being explored by the Project within The British Library. A report commissioned by The British Library Research and Innovation Centre from Central Research Laboratories Ltd of Thorn EMI suggests that it is feasible to develop a method of searching the images which would obviate the need for full-text entry. This would not be an OCR system and would not have the same aims: the images would be stored as graphics and there would be no need to attempt a hit rate of 99% + which is required to make OCR programmes viable. But as digitised images are increasingly used it would be extremely useful to have some system of searching the text on them. The development of this technology is still at a preliminary stage, but given the obvious advantages to scholars of being able to view an image of the manuscript itself rather than a full-text transcription, a method whereby the images could be searched for characters which incorporated pattern recognition techniques to allow approximations as hits would be of immense use.

**Digitisation**

Apart from circumventing the problem of coding, digitisation also lessens several other pitfalls associated with manuscript cataloguing, enabling the user to ignore the interpretation of the cataloguer as, for example, to the identity of the text. It is also especially useful for the Dunhuang collection of manuscripts as many of the manuscripts are split between collections and there are numerous unidentified fragments which may belong together. The use of pattern matching techniques to match the edges of the fragments, coupled with use of the information provided in the database as to type of paper, ink, calligraphy, dyes etc., will enable virtual matches between manuscripts physically located in different continents to be tried and tested on the computer screen. It will also open up the manuscripts to scholars interested in paper history, dyes and inks, the development of the book and printing, and other aspects of the manuscripts as objects rather than as texts. The British Library is collaborating with chemists from the Queen's University of Belfast in analysis of the dyes and inks and measurement of the pH of the paper (Gibbs and Seddon 1997). This information will also be added to the database, along with the results of conservation surveys of the manuscripts.

However, the user needs to be able to find the manuscripts of interest in the first place and for this he has to rely largely on categorisation and interpretation, on the mark-up of text and how the information is presented. In a database of this size, free-text searching will be in most cases too slow and imprecise. The choice of the database, its structure and functionality are therefore vital to the success of the Project.

## The database and its functionality

The International Dunhuang Project database must serve three main purposes: it will replace the handlists, conservation records and other tools currently used by the institutions for management of the collections; it will replace the printed catalogues and microfilms used as the primary access sources for scholars; but it will also go beyond this to become a scholarly tool. Charles B. Faulhaber's article 'Philobiblion' is a very interesting account of the sort of problems encountered when designing such a database, and shows the limits to achievable functionality (Faulhaber 1991).

To minimise start-up and maintenance costs, the International Dunhuang Project decided to use an off-the-shelf relational database rather than a specially developed programme. Because the Project did not have the resources to employ specialist computer consultants, the database structure would have to be designed by Project staff, and the system would have to be one which computer-literate staff could use with minimal training. The main considerations in choosing a product were power and flexibility, with the ability to use non-roman scripts and incorporate images. A relational database, 4th Dimension, designed in the late 1980s by ACI Ltd in Paris, was the clear choice, as described by Dr Ulrich Pagel, Curator of Tibetan at The British Library (Pagel 1996). The software company, who have sponsored the Project, provided some assistance with database design. It currently runs on an Apple PowerPC 7600/132 server with both Apples (Quadras and PowerPCs) and PCs as client machines. It could also be run on a Windows PC server, as it is cross-platform.

The functionality of 4th Dimension will be shown here by introducing part of the Project database. The Project plans to use computer capabilities to the full, not only providing a computer equivalent of an illustrated catalogue, but also developing a user-friendly resource containing far more information of use to scholars, conservators, students, and others. Although the screens shown here are prototypes, displaying only some of the information contained in the

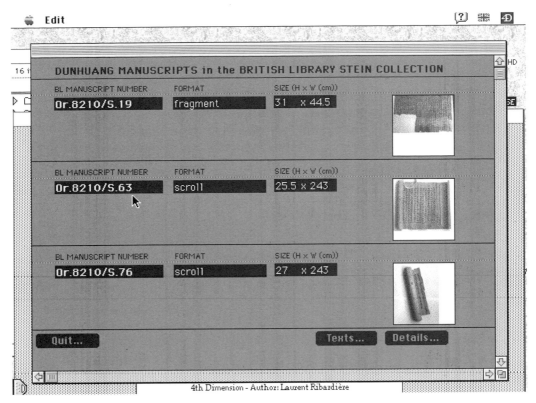

**Above:** Screen 1    **Below:** Screen 2

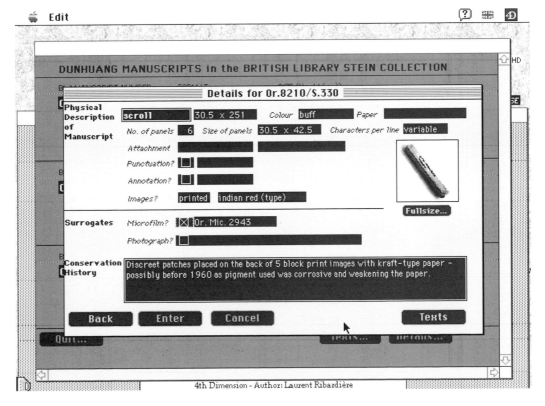

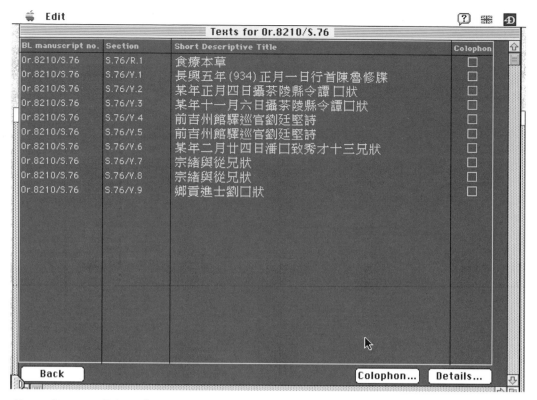

Above: Screen 3    Below: Screen 4

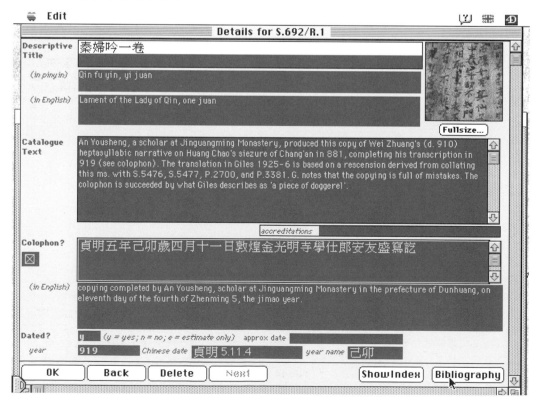

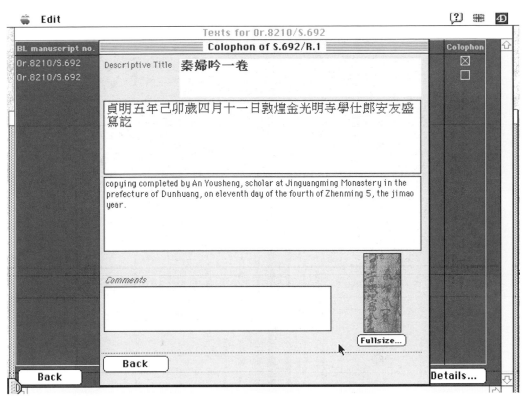

**Above:** Screen 5  **Below:** Screen 6

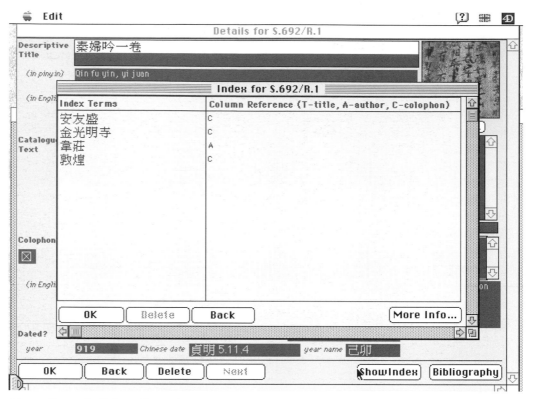

**Above:** Screen 7   **Below:** Screen 8

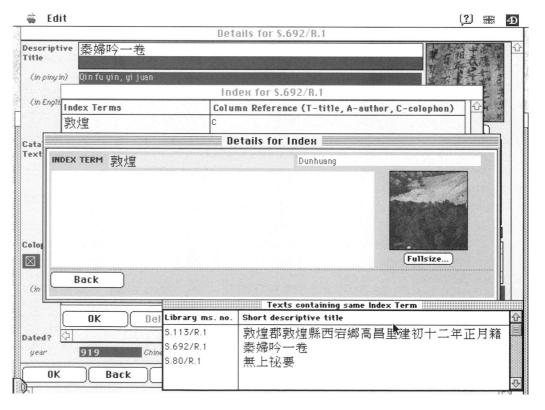

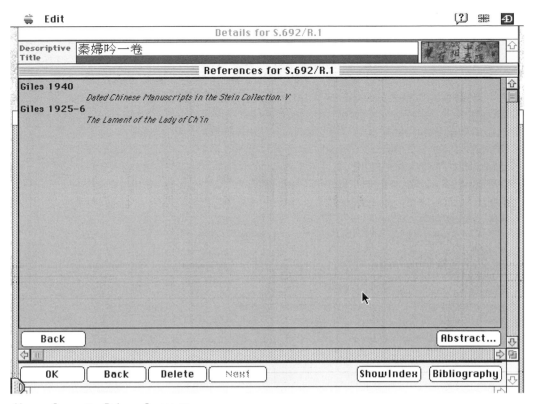

**Above:** Screen 9　**Below:** Screen 10

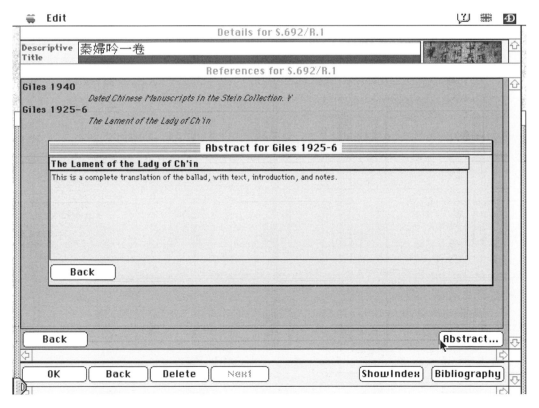

database, and part of the functionality allowed by the structure, they give a flavour of what is possible in this respect.

Screen 1 shows a list of the manuscripts with thumbnails and minimal information. The user can choose to get more information about the object itself (by double-clicking or highlighting the object and then pressing the button marked 'Details') or about the texts on the object (the button marked 'Texts'). These actions take the user to screens 2 and 3 respectively. They can also get to the text information from screen 2. From screen 3 it is possible to call up catalogue information on any of the texts and to look at the text in more detail (screen 4). It is also possible from screens 3 and 4 to call up a transliteration of the colophon with translation and image (screen 5). At any of these stages the user can call up a larger image of the object or the text in question ('Fullsize' button), conduct a search, or print out information.

The database will be accessible to scholars in a manner that will allow them to assist in developing it further. The libraries which hold the manuscripts have few resources or staff and it is not imagined that they will be able to carry out the research necessary to exploit more than a small part of the database's potential. It is therefore essential that outside scholars contribute to the work, helping thereby to create a resource of use to themselves and others. Scholars will be encouraged to correct mistakes or suggest new information on a linked form which will then be sent to the database co-ordinator. Anyone using the database will log-on, giving their full name and other information. This will be linked with the database of Silk Road scholars which is part of the database and when a scholar's suggestions are added they will be marked with initials. The user will then be able to access further information on the contributing scholar. This will enable contradictory information to be put on the database and users will be able to make up their own minds as to its relative value. This is not to say that material will be added without any editing or checking.

One area, for example, in which users will be able significantly to improve the usefulness of the database is in helping to index the texts. At the moment only selected texts are being fully indexed. For the majority of texts only the title and colophon are indexed (for reasons of time). Screen 6 shows the index for the text S.79/R.1. It is possible to search for a specific index term or to sort them alphabetically according to their pinyin transcription. The column numbers shown will be marked on the images of the manuscript so that it will be possible to show the index term in its context.

When the button 'More Info...' is pressed, further information is given on the index term. For example, returning to the information for S.692/R.1, there are four indexed names (screen 7). If one of them, 'Dunhuang', is selected, then screen 8 presents a picture and description of the place. At the same time, a box appears in the lower right-hand corner which lists other texts also containing this index term. Although it may be thought that this would be a slow and cumbersome process because of the relational nature of the data, in fact the structure of the database means that the data relations are not automatic and are only made explicit when necessary so that the processes are performed as efficiently as is possible.

Another resource the database incorporates is a bibliography. A list of books and articles containing information on any text or manuscript is available at the press of a button (screen 9). It is planned, in the case of articles outside copyright restriction, to scan in the entire article. An abstract will be included for other articles and books (screen 10). It will also be possible to link this information to the online catalogues of the institutions so that users will be able to see where they can find the book in question.

There are many other features of the database not shown here and many more potential developments. For example, in order to make the database more accessible to non-specialists, maps of the area in question will be incorporated with images and details of the sites where the manuscripts were discovered, including moving images and sound. Because all the screens are user-designed they can be adapted for any language. The database can be used as the basis for a teaching tool for school children and undergraduates worldwide, so making a new generation aware of this vital historical resource and, it is hoped, encouraging many of them to take up the study of the manuscripts and bring their own ideas to the development of the database.

Further Reading specific to manuscripts:

Gibbs, Perter J. and Seddon, Kenneth R., Berberie and Huangbo, *Ancient Colorants and Dyes* (British Library Studies in Conservation Science: 2), The British Library, London 1997.

Whitfield, Susan and Wood, Frances (eds.), *Dunhuang and Turfan:* (British Library Studies in Conservation Science: 1), The British Library, London 1996.

(For other works cited, see Further Reading: Document Management and Descriptive Data.)

# Excalibur: image-based text storage and searching

Andrew Prescott and Malcolm Pratt

I

The text and image retrieval products manufactured by the American firm Excalibur Technologies Inc. have recently achieved a high public profile (not to say notoriety) as a result of the use of an Excalibur system by the Labour Party's Rapid Rebuttal Unit during the 1997 general election campaign. The Excalibur system used by the Labour Party contains a searchable record of political speeches and other documents which can be kept up to date with a minimum of effort and rapidly searched to provide immediate accurate information on any issue which emerges in the course of a campaign. The British Library had become aware of Excalibur's products sometime before the Labour Party. Excalibur's PixTex/EFS (Electronic Filing System) package had been used in the ELINOR (Electronic Library INformation Online Retrieval) project at De Montfort University (DMU), which was partly funded by The British Library's Research and Innovation Centre. As a new university whose student numbers had grown rapidly and which was based at a number of different sites, the problem of providing DMU students with access to textbooks had become acute. This encouraged DMU to explore how far an electronic library, providing a large collection of information and learning materials in text and image form through desktop workstations, would assist in addressing these issues. Copyright would obviously be a major consideration in developing such a project, but equally important was the very high cost of keyboarding and proofreading a large number of texts. Optical Character Recognition (OCR) technology is not yet sufficiently reliable to produce an accurate copy of the text without careful proof-reading. The cost of providing an adequate user interface to give access to a large number of images of books would have been almost as great as keyboarding. The EFS package allowed DMU to produce searchable versions of over 120 complete published textbooks, as well as course materials, examination papers and journals, simply by scanning in images of the books. Manual intervention was largely restricted to equating page numbers of the electronic files with those of the original books. The chief technical issue was the expense of the software and the difficulty of running it over a network, given that it was proprietary client/server software and that individual user licences were quite expensive.

The success of the ELINOR project encouraged The British Library to investigate potential applications of Excalibur products itself. In 1994, The British

Library installed three experimental workstations running the Excalibur Pix-Tex/EFS system, one in Boston Spa and two in London. In each case the servers were UNIX machines, linked to flatbed scanners. Each server was linked to PCs running the Windows client software. Like all Excalibur projects, EFS uses the adaptive pattern recognition processing (APRP) technology developed by the firm's founder James Dowe III. Dowe was inspired to develop APRP by the way animals use neural networks to recognise different shapes. Excalibur define APRP as a system 'that recognises the presence of patterns in digital data. APRP algorithms, or pattern processors, self-adjust to the data being processed, allowing the data itself to direct the creation of the network, the variables, the "expert rules" and the indexes'. Thus, in searching, EFS does not attempt to match exactly words against words, but looks for patterns in the binary numbers stored in the system. It examines the binary numbers and 'identifies pattern in these numbers. It is these patterns which are the basis of its indexing method not the text strings which are common amongst many other text retrieval systems'.

In carrying out a search for a word like 'Regina', APRP does not look for digits which represent exactly those letters, but for a pattern of digits which looks similar to those generated by that word. Michael Alexander has graphically described this process: 'The engine, based on the neural network concept, actually attempts to mimic how the brain identifies and stores data. This means that the search engine can be taught to recognise the occurrence and inter-linking of patterns in the same way that we human beings might understand a word even though it is misspelt or recognise a bearded man who has shaved off his beard by the shape of his physiognomy'.

The use of this process has some important immediate practical benefits. It makes the searching of large quantities of data considerably quicker. It is not necessary to create the elaborate indexes required by conventional database systems. This makes it possible to search large quantities of unstructured text, and avoids the overhead required in putting that text into a relational database. As Excalibur point out, the 'automated self-organizing pattern indexes' eliminate 'the costly labor of manually defining keywords, building topic trees, establishing expert rules, and sorting and labelling information in database fields'. It also 'avoids the inherent subjective biases of categorical indexes'. Moreover, as Michael Alexander emphasises, one of the chief costs of using large databases such as library catalogues is in the storage of the indexes: 'Depending on the form of indexing used the index may be 150%–250% larger than the original data'. Use of APRP could potentially reduce these costs massively. It would also avoid the need for such major housekeeping tasks as the reindexing of data, which in the case of very large document stores is such a massive task that it is not a practicable proposition.

Because APRP is not looking for exact matches of text strings, it offers the possibility of fuzzy searching in which it looks for a pattern roughly similar to a particular phrase. Excalibur describe this process as follows: 'Fuzzy searching is the ability to retrieve an approximation of a query term or phrase. Excalibur's APRP technology provides searching through a feature referred to as "fault tolerance". Fuzzy searching eliminates the need for people to know the exact spelling of every term they're working with and it eliminates the need to page through hundreds of tables filled with keywords, roots and stems to locate the object of a search'. The user can define the degree of precision of a fuzzy search. A search for 'Regina' with the tolerance set at 100% will retrieve only occurrences of 'Regina'. A tolerance of 80% might retrieve both 'Regina' and 'Refina'. A tolerance of 60% might retrieve both 'Regina', 'Refina' and 'Lafina', and so on. The user can then rank the hits in order of matching, with those closest to 100% at the top.

As is well known, data produced by OCR frequently contains many mis-readings. The use of APRP in theory provides a means whereby such data can be searched to a high degree of accuracy notwithstanding errors in the OCR. Despite the use of APRP, the operations of EFS still depend fundamentally on the quality of the OCR undertaken by the package. The data capture procedure with EFS is as follows. A TIFF image of a page is produced. Images of pages are then converted to text files via the OCR package bundled with the system. Searches are undertaken on binary patterns generated from the OCR text, so that, notwithstanding APRP, very poor-quality OCR will not produce a searchable text. Care has to be taken in the scanning to ensure that the OCR is as good as possible. The tables of hits produced by the system contain the OCR, so that the user has to judge from this whether a reference is worth following up. However, the user has access to both the OCR and the original TIFF image, so that he can obtain access to the original text and is not wholly reliant on the OCR.

A weakness of the EFS package is that the OCR package bundled with it does not perform as well as the best packages currently available on the market. Although reliable searches could be undertaken with ordinary printed or typed text, the OCR package was unable to produce searchable results with very early printing or foreign scripts. An experiment was undertaken with images of 18th-century newspapers produced by the Digitisation of Microfilm project, but the difficulties of applying OCR to an image produced from degraded microfilm and the problems encountered in using the OCR package on 18th-century type forms meant that no worth-while results were obtained. Similarly, the package could not cope with 19th-century German printing. However, results with modern English print and typewriting were good. Attempts have been made to improve the range of material with which EFS can deal by using other OCR packages.

For those involved with information systems in libraries, the chief interest of EFS is probably in the area of what Excalibur describe as 'the conservation of computer resources', in particular the possibility of reducing the storage overhead by eliminating the need for large indexes. However, for curators, these possibilities are less exciting – these issues are very much concerned with what goes on 'behind the scenes'. Retroconversion of data is, however, a much more central concern of curators in collection areas. All curators nowadays recognise the value of having as much information about their collections as possible in machine-readable format. When collection information is in a searchable form, we can start to explore our collections in ways undreamed of by earlier generations. But, for almost every institution, the effort of putting data into such a format almost outweighs the benefits. The costs of defining database structures, supervising the keyboarding of data and then proof-reading it are enormous. OCR is only just starting to achieve the hopes that have been held out for it, as recent projects for the conversion of catalogues for The British Library's Newspaper and Manuscript Collections have shown, but careful proof-reading and checking of data are still required. In theory, EFS, because it will perform accurate searches even if the OCR contains some errors, will allow retroconversion without tears – no need to define record structure, keyboard or proof-read.

The British Library holds the nation's largest collection of seals and seal casts. Seals are among the most intricate and beautiful products of the medieval artist-craftsman but have not received the scholarly attention they deserve. They can provide very important information about medieval society. The increasing use of seals by medieval peasants in the later middle ages was an important indication of their changing social status. The political history of later medieval England has been interpreted in terms of changing patterns expressed by the use of different royal seals. The town seal was an important manifestation of the corporate outlook of medieval towns. Between 1887 and 1900, a massive six-volume catalogue of over 23,000 of the Library's seals was produced by Walter de Gray Birch. This is still the most important single reference work in English on seals. The entries are, however, arranged in a confusing way. They are in what can only be described as a feudal order. The first volume begins with English royal seals in regnal order, followed by the seals of royal officers, ecclesiastical seals, monastic seals, peculiar jurisdictions, religious orders, guilds and military orders. Categories in later volumes include heraldic personal seals, equestrian seals, Princes of Wales, local seals, and noble and other ladies. The lack of detailed name or place indexes makes it difficult to locate seals of a particular person or individual. Moreover, there is no index of seals in accession number order, so that a description of a particular seal cannot be located without re-identifying it and guessing where the description would appear in the catalogue. Birch carefully transcribes the legend around the edge of the seal and gives a full heraldic description of each seal. This information is potentially of great use in identifying seals, but cannot be easily used because it is not indexed.

Birch's catalogue is obviously one that would benefit from being converted to a machine-readable form. However, it is not one of the primary working catalogues to the manuscript collections. Access to the manuscripts in the British Library is primarily through the collection-based catalogues of acquisitions, such as the *Catalogue of Additions to the Manuscripts*, and through the consolidated index to these, the *Index of Manuscripts in the British Library*. Conversion of these primary catalogues must clearly be a higher priority than the conversion of the specialist catalogues of particular categories of material, including not only Birch, but Hughes-Hughes' *Catalogue of Manuscript Music*, Holmes' *Catalogue of the Manuscript Maps, Charts and Plans* and Ward's *Catalogue of Romances*. Priority in the allocation of the limited resources available for retroconversion will naturally be given to the primary catalogues rather than

Birch and the other subject catalogues. In fact, realistically, it is unlikely that sufficient resources will ever be available to contemplate the conversion of Birch and other subject catalogues if conventional keyboarding is used.

An experiment was therefore undertaken to use EFS to produce a searchable version of Birch. The scanning of the catalogue was undertaken by administrative support staff and proved to be a very simple task, completed within a matter of weeks. The only hitch was the difficulty in transferring the images and OCR from the DEC platform at Boston Spa to the Sun workstations in London. The results were excellent. Searches of the catalogue were easily and accurately made. Moreover, it was found that inconsistencies in Birch's original description, which would have required major editorial intervention if a conventional method of converting the catalogue had been used, had no effect on the accuracy of the Excalibur search. For example, at the time that Birch was mounted on EFS, a major project was in hand to rebox the sulphur seal casts, one of the most fragile parts of the collection. It was useful to try and identify all the sulphur seals described in Birch. Unfortunately, Birch sometimes uses 'sulphur' in full, and at other times prefers the abbreviation 'sulph'. This would have had a major impact on search strategy if conventional text string searching had been used, but the fuzzy searching in EFS meant that all these references could be found in a single search. Similarly, inconsistencies by Birch in referring to different collections (he varies between Cotton and Cott, for example) had no impact on the accuracy of the searches.

The use of EFS therefore achieved the conversion of a large catalogue in a matter of weeks with virtually no curatorial intervention. The major problem in using the converted Birch is that the user interface for both the server and client is not simple to use, and would not be suitable for reading room use without providing readers with training. Public access to the converted catalogue has therefore been limited to searches undertaken by staff on request. Having said that, however, it must be stressed that the Windows client would not be particularly complex for an experienced Windows user, and many readers would be able quickly to come to terms with it. A more important long-term obstacle is that the client-server software is relatively expensive and the cost of the large number of user licences which would be required to make the catalogue widely available in the library is prohibitive. However, Excalibur have recently produced a Web client for EFS which may enable the Library to make the converted Birch more widely available.

The results of the trials with Birch were sufficiently encouraging to attempt to convert another catalogue. The *Catalogue of Manuscript Music* by Augustus Hughes-Hughes, published between 1906 and 1909, presents many similar problems to Birch, being arranged according to the type of music with only limited indexes. Some of the lessons learnt in the course of scanning Birch enabled a better result to be produced for Hughes-Hughes. The scanning was undertaken more carefully, with distinctions made through 'zoning' between individual entries, so that a search result takes the user directly to the description of an individual item rather than to the whole page. Again, the results were very encouraging, and a delighted curator of Music Manuscripts was presented in a very short time with a searchable version of one of her most important tools. Similar experiments were also undertaken with the *British Museum Subject Index of Printed Books*, and again EFS appears to have very great potential.

At the moment, it is difficult to convince curators in collection areas that EFS is suitable for the conversion of mainstream catalogues. This is largely because of considerations unrelated to the performance of the software, such as a feeling that the searching procedures are too complex for primary working catalogues in reading rooms, which will be extensively used by readers with limited technical proficiency. However, EFS does seem potentially to have a very important application in the retroconversion of special subject catalogues whose conversion would not otherwise be a practicable proposition. The only limitation on the further development of EFS for this purpose within The British Library is the limited number of user licences which the Library can afford, which makes the converted catalogues at present still difficult of access. Again, however, this may change with the availability of the new Web client.

Catalogues are an elaborate type of text on which to test a system like EFS. It will be recalled that its original use at DMU was for making textbooks more easily available, and there is a similar potential within The British Library for using the system to help to increase access to the millions of texts which it holds. Given the sophisticated search capabilities of the package, another obvious area for experimentation was books which are inadequately indexed. The *Calendar of Letter Books of the City of London* edited by R.R. Sharpe between 1899 and 1912 provides summaries of the registers containing the official correspondence of the city of London, and is one of the chief sources for the history of medieval London, but is poorly indexed. A searchable version of these calendars would potentially be a very useful research tool. Two volumes of this series were scanned and, although their use has so far been limited, it is nevertheless evident that they unlock a great deal of information about medieval London which would otherwise be virtually irretrievable.

A demonstration of EFS to Dr Mark Greengrass of the Department of History of the University of Sheffield, the progenitor of the electronic edition of the papers of the 17th-century philosopher Samuel Hartlib published in 1995, prompted him to consider its potential application to early modern studies. He proposed the establishment of a joint project between the University of Sheffield and The British Library for establishing a searchable corpus of historical sources using EFS, 'A Sword for Excalibur'. An initial requirement was that a detailed analysis of the search capabilities of EFS should be undertaken by an information scientist. It was agreed that Dr Greengrass should jointly supervise with Dr Peter Willetts of the School of Information Studies at Sheffield a M.A. student who would prepare a study of the EFS system. Malcolm Pratt was appointed to this studentship. A copy of the EFS client was installed for him at Sheffield, so that he could access the Boston Spa server. Part of Pratt's M.A. thesis, submitted in September 1995, is reproduced below. His conclusion was that 'The EFS Search Engine appears too good to be true'. At the moment, the EFS system in the Library only holds a few historical works, mounted to assist in testing. It is to be hoped that the Library will be able to add to this in future years, and help achieve Mark Greengrass's vision of a major networked searchable database of historical information. A similar approach is also being used by the Internet Library of Early Journals project, part of the e-Lib programme, which aims to produce a networked searchable corpus of 18th- and 19th-century journals, including the *Gentleman's Magazine*, *The Annual Register* and *Notes and Queries*. This project is also exploring the use of Excalibur to convert these journals to machine-readable form. Excalibur may thus perhaps be able to offer more than rapid rebuttal and prove to be one of the means by which the idea of the 'digital library' can be realised cheaply and practicably.      AP

## II

As part of the assessment of the viability of the British Library's Excalibur Project, it was decided to assess the fuzzy search capabilities of the Excalibur Technologies PixTex/EFS system. This system was linked with the University of Sheffield's Department of Information Studies via SuperJANET WAN and the EFS software was installed on a Pentium computer within the Department to handle and receive the incoming data. After some helpful tuition from British Library staff at Boston Spa, it was possible to use the system and see how the system functioned.

To be able to assess the fuzzy search capabilities a series of controlled tests had to be carried out. An important test for appraising the value of a text-retrieval system are Recall and Precision tests. These would allow us to judge the effectiveness of the EFS search engine. It was decided that a fixed number of search terms would be chosen, which correspond to data stored on The British Library's EFS system. It was further decided that the *Alumni Oxoniensis*, the matriculation lists of Oxford University between 1500 and 1714, would be used for the tests. This data consisted of the biographical details of individuals who had attended Oxford University during the aforementioned period. As the information contained within these lists is made up of alphabetical lists of family names as well as the titles of colleges they attended, professional titles gained, and towns, cities and counties where they lived, 50 terms were chosen for the tests reflecting the spread of the data in the matriculation lists. So college names such as Christ Church, family names such as Smith, major British cites including Nottingham, and professional titles such as Vicar, were all chosen.

Although the PixTex/EFS system offers three search possibilities, content searches were the only appropriate form of searching for the purposes of the assessment of the fuzzy search capabilities of the system. Only content searches allowed for the searching of all of the database or a predefined selection of the database. The British Library's EFS system contained several books at the time of the text. For the purposes of this search only the *Alumni Oxoniensis* was selected. To guarantee a controlled experiment, the search parameters had to be fixed at the same settings for each search. For this assessment of the fuzzy search engine of the PixTex/EFS system, the 'maximum hits' setting was fixed at 200, as was the 'maximum hits to rate'. 'Highlight sensitivity' was set at 5. 'Case sensitive' and 'percentage exact' settings were switched off and the fuzzy search settings were set alternately at 50% and 70% for each set of search terms tested. Although the system allows Boolean and exact searches, these features were not used in these tests.

Recall and Precision tests allow for the evaluation of a text retrieval system's strengths and weaknesses. Recall is defined as the proportion of relevant documents actually retrieved by a search and Precision as the proportion of retrieved documents actually relevant. They are calculated by the following formulae:

$$\text{Recall} = \frac{\text{Retrieved \& Relevant}}{\text{Retrieved \& Relevant} + \text{Not Retrieved \& Relevant}}$$

$$\text{Precision} = \frac{\text{Retrieved \& Relevant}}{\text{Retrieved \& Relevant} + \text{Retrieved \& Not Relevant}}$$

Although there is some debate concerning the value of Recall and Precision testing, such discussion fell outside the framework of this assessment, and it was taken that Recall and Precision are valuable tests. However, as Recall must be assessed with reference to or a knowledge of the size of a database's holdings, and this was not known in the case of The British Library's EFS system, it was decided to calculate only the Precision of the system.

A document was considered to be retrieved by the system when it was shown as highlighted in the search window. The data from the tests was collected on 50 terms. For each term it was found that all the documents retrieved from the searches using all of the pre-selected 50 search terms, at settings of 50% and 70%, to the 200 retrieved document cut off point, all were relevant and none were not relevant. It was therefore found that Precision was 100%. An example of the calculations can be seen below.

### Precision results example

| SEARCH TERM | DOCS | RELEVANT DOCS | PERCENTAGE |
|---|---|---|---|
| Smith 70&50% | 10 | 10 | 100 |
| | 20 | 20 | 100 |
| | 30 | 30 | 100 |
| | 40 | 40 | 100 |
| | 50 | 50 | 100 |
| | 60 | 60 | 100 |

These results were highly unusual. It is more commonplace with text retrieval systems that Precision is never this high. In fact, it is usually the case that with more conventional systems a large number of irrelevant documents are retrieved and that the frequency of the occurrence of non-relevant material would increase the more documents were inspected. As we can see, this did not happen with the EFS system. What is more, with the increase of fuzzy searching level from the 70% setting to the 50% setting it was expected that more non-relevant documents would be retrieved. This also did not occur. Even where the number of documents displayed in the search window were more than those actually highlighted by the system, and so outside the range of our

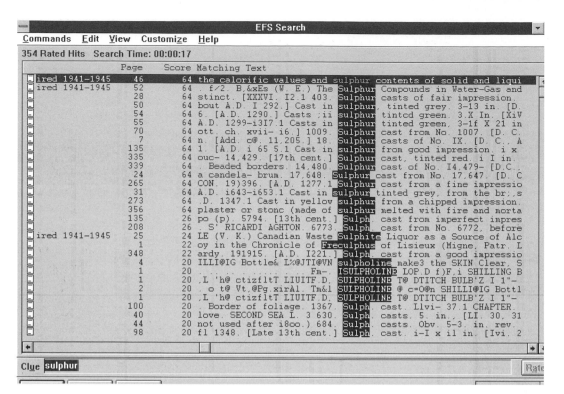

**Above** Screen showing results of search for the word 'sulphur' in Birch's *Catalogue of Seals*, using Excalibur PixTex/EFS.

**Below** Screen illustrating how search parameters may be set in Excalibur PixTex/EFS.

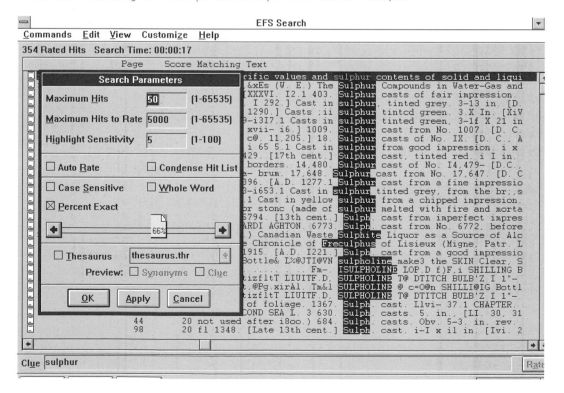

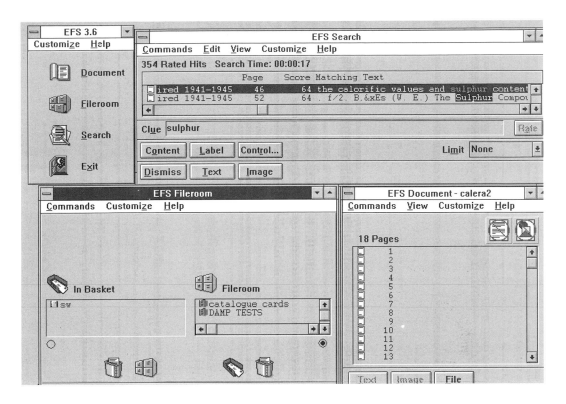

Basic search screen in Excalibur PixTex/EFS.

Precision tests, these terms also clearly seemed to be relevant and within the parameter settings defined at the beginning of the search.

The obvious conclusion to draw from such results is that because the Pix-Tex/EFS system's search engine finds search terms in the database at the binary level, rather than the text-string level, the EFS system is far more accurate. This would be excellent if this was the only possible explanation, but other reasons must be considered. One possible reason is that because of the way the EFS system rates its searches, documents below a certain rating do not appear within the search window. Although this does guarantee that all those documents displayed are relevant it may equally mean that the system does not retrieve documents which are relevant but fall outside the ranking scale owing to OCR error or other reasons of non-recognition. This may be the case, as the system already displays non-highlighted rated documents at the end of the search window. However, as yet no evidence of this can be offered. A further consideration is that perhaps the method of judging Precision in this case was not focused enough and that a more subjective method of judging Precision was needed. Whatever the problems with accepting these results too uncritically, it does appear that the Precision of the system is perfect.

Because of the limited results from the Precision tests, it was decided to examine EFS to discover if there was a relationship between the fuzzy percentage setting and the number of documents retrieved. This would show whether there were any threshold percentage settings at which the fuzzy search engine retrieved more documents. Tests were carried out on 20 of the previously chosen search terms representing the different types of data stored in the system filing cabinets for the *Alumni Oxonienses*. These searches were then carried out following the same method as previously used in the Precision tests, with the exception that there was no cut-off point of 200 set on retrieved records to be examined and that the system was tested at 10%, 20%, 30%, 40%, 50%, 60% and 70% fuzzy settings. The data was then collected for analysis.

In the majority of cases, 85% of search terms input, there was no change in the number of documents retrieved at all the percentage settings. Such figures are consistent with the results from the previous Precision tests where in the majority of cases, 72% of search terms input, there was no difference in documents retrieved between the 50% and 70% fuzzy setting. In a minority of cases the increase in fuzziness did lead to the retrieval of more documents. As can be seen from the following figure, more documents were retrieved for the search term 'Corpus Christi ' as the level of fuzziness increased. This has also been represented as a graph.

### A Fuzzy Percentage and Document Recall Relationship Chart for the Search term 'Corpus Christi'

*Search Term: Corpus Christi*

| PERCENTAGE SETTING | |
|---|---|
| 10% | 620 |
| 20% | 620 |
| 30% | 620 |
| 40% | 619 |
| 50% | 607 |
| 60% | 529 |
| 70% | 529 |

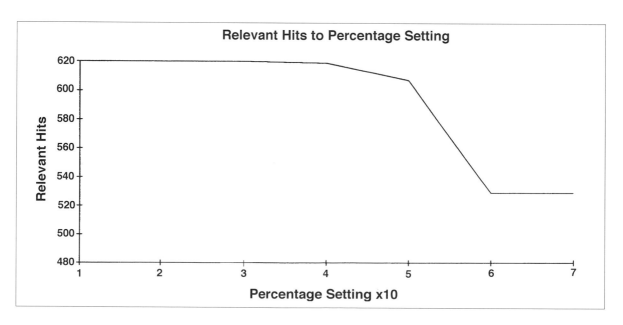

Although this graph and chart in this case represent the exception when retrieving data on the EFS system, it may be worth carrying out further tests on a wider number of search terms to see if this pattern is more common than has been seen here.

The EFS search engine appears too good to be true. Not only does it have 100% Precision within the parameters we have set, its fuzzy search capabilities allow the searcher to increase the percentage of fuzziness so that, in certain circumstances, more documents can be retrieved. This said, other considerations must be taken into account. When searching on the system, a balance must be reached between the number of documents retrieved and the number of documents a searcher may wish to examine at one time. If a searcher wished to see all the documents the system will retrieve, such as the search term 'Nottingham', a fuzzy percentage setting of 50% would display all 234. The increase in fuzziness settings in the EFS system does not guarantee the increase in relevant hits. Where there is an increase in relevant hits, these occur between the setting of 70% and 40%. After 40% no further documents were retrieved. This would suggest that the EFS default setting of 50% is the best for general use. If, however, a searcher wished to see a smaller number then a setting of 70% would retrieve only the top 65 documents. Therefore, the percentage fuzziness setting can be a useful tool to limit document output as well as to find relevant documents. But, despite the availability of the maximum hits setting, EFS will not cut off a search in the middle of a string of hits with the same score. And so, for search terms, like 'Corpus Christi', a far larger number of hits will be retrieved whatever the fuzzy setting. This could be a problem for a searcher, as the sheer weight of material could hinder effective searching or make it at least a laborious process.

These tests would appear to illustrate that many of the claims that Excalibur Technologies have made for their system are true. The benefits of the system's fuzzy search engine above conventional text-string matching systems are clearly demonstrated. Nevertheless, caution should still be exercised when judging the system and undoubtedly more specialised and better defined tests have to go ahead in the future before a full evaluation of the EFS system can take place.

M P

M. Pratt, 'A Sword for Excalibur: Image Based Storage, Historical Database Construction', unpublished M.A. Thesis, University of Sheffield, 1995. Pratt's thesis includes a large number of quotes from text on the Excalibur Web site which was afterwards superseded. Where quotes attributed to Excalibur Technologies cannot be found on Excalibur Web site, they are taken from Pratt's thesis.

(For references to the Excalibur Web site, and to other works cited, see Further Reading.)

# Image – the future of text?

Brent Seales, James Griffioen and Andrew Prescott

Humanities scholars have been used to working independently and making the best of whatever technical resources they have to hand. The first stumbling steps of humanities scholars in using digital imaging to investigate their primary source materials required them to widen their horizons and start working with colleagues from other disciplines. The early experiments of Professor Kevin S. Kiernan of the University of Kentucky in applying digital image processing to sections of the Beowulf manuscript at the British Library during the 1980s depended on the use of a Mipron-D microcodable array-processor at the Coronary Care Unit of the University of Kentucky and subsequently on the use of equipment and staff loaned by Kontron Electronics, the manufacturer of the array-processor at Kentucky. Kiernan's work was inspired by the research of a team led by John Benton at the Jet Propulsion laboratory which had been working on the use of digital imaging to investigate palimpsest manuscripts.

As imaging technology has become more widely available and affordable, it may seem that the need for scientific support of this kind in humanities computing will be reduced, but this is far from the case. Since the questions asked by humanities scholars of their source materials are very varied and complex, they can raise important issues for computer scientists. Humanities scholars will frequently want to use multimedia data – images of different kinds, video and sound as well as alphanumeric data. A data archive for classicists, for example, might include images of papyri, 3-D and video images of artefacts, VRML and CAD reconstructions of buildings, and texts in non-Roman scripts. The development and use of a multimedia archive of this kind presents many challenges for computer scientists.

Humanities researchers will not search an archive of this kind expecting precise 'matches' to already known and recorded information. They are interested in investigating their source materials in innovative and interactive ways. Two reputable scholars may approach a single object in a completely different way. There is no single correct semantic interpretation that can be inferred from the data. Although image data can be laboriously marked up by hand to describe and record different parts of the image, this is not only time-consuming, but limits the user to the interpretation provided by the person who did the marking up. In addition, the type of access required by different users will vary according to their requirements. A researcher making a detailed analysis of a particular piece of sculpture will require high resolution images, perhaps photographed using different types of lighting. The mildly interested art enthusiast will be satisfied with lower resolution, and therefore smaller images.

## Reconnecting science and the humanities

Computer science can aid humanities scholars by providing them with new techniques to investigate their materials. An obvious example is the investigation of palimpsests. A palimpsest is a manuscript in which one text has been erased and a new text written on top. Frequently, the old text is of greater interest than the new one. A method for automatically subtracting the new text from a digital image to reveal the first layer of text would be of great value. There are many areas of manuscript studies where innovative technical approaches of this kind are applicable. During the 18th and 19th centuries, chemical reagents were frequently used to make faded manuscripts more legible. These made the damaged text readable for a few moments, but then left the writing obscured by a dark splodge, impossible to read even under ultra-violet light. An image processing technique which assisted in reading text lost in this way would permit the recovery of important historical and literary texts. The potential benefits of such technologies are not confined to ancient documents. Letter writers in the 18th and 19th centuries sometimes saved paper and postage by writing two texts on each page – the second written at right angles across the first. Again, image processing could be of great value in deciphering these letters.

Humanities scholars have perhaps been overmodest in their expectations of technology. They have been happy to accept that the computer can or cannot help with a particular problem when they have tried a particular (usually proprietary) software package. The idea that computing can be stretched and extended so that it can assist in solving the most intractable problems of humanities research is an unfamiliar one to many scholars in the field. However, this potential is there. The only way in which it can be tapped is by closer cooperation with computer scientists. A closer relationship would be mutually beneficial. Humanities research offers computer scientists a great deal of new test material of an unusual and interesting kind. The need for the availability of 'live' images to assist in work on compression and storage issues is widely acknowledged by computer scientists. As humanities scholars begin to amass large multimedia data archives, of the sort that the *Initiatives for Access* programme generated, they will increasingly be able to offer computer scientists access to precisely this sort of material.

There has been a long-standing assumption that the increasing use of computers by humanities scholars will help reduce the gulf between science and the humanities. In 1984, David Bolter noted that 'Humanists, scholars and creative writers have as yet little use for these machines [computers]. This ... will change, rather rapidly, as they realize that at least text editing by computer is far easier than working with pens, paper, or typewriters'. He went on to express a hope that 'The humanist will not be able to ignore the medium with which he will work daily: it will shape his thought in subtle ways, suggest possibilities, and impose limitations, as does any other medium of communication ... He will choose different problems and be satisfied with different solutions'. One of the ways in which the use of computers could change the outlook of humanities scholars will be that they will find they want to work more closely with computer scientists.

At the University of Kentucky, as Kevin Kiernan amassed the materials for the Electronic Beowulf, he dreamed of being able to explore the digital images in new ways. He teamed up with Professor Brent Seales of the Department of Computer Science at Kentucky, and they began to develop some exciting new tools for exploring the images. They formed a group called GRENDL (Group for Research in Electronically Networked Digital Libraries) to facilitate this collaboration. In order to present some of this joint work and to explore these themes further, Professors Kiernan and Seales organised a major international workshop entitled 'Reconnecting Science and the Humanities through Digital Libraries', which was funded by the National Science Foundation, the University of Kentucky and The British Library. It was held at Kentucky from 19–21 October 1995, and was a successful and memorable occasion which in many ways provided a fitting climax to the *Initiatives for Access* programme. The speakers included leaders in the field of humanities computing, digital library development and computer science from both sides of the Atlantic. The papers will be published shortly. The centrepiece of the workshop was a presentation by Brent Seales of the work he has been doing with Kevin Kiernan, which subsequently formed the basis of a wide-ranging application for research funding to the National Science Foundation in the United States.

The work by the team at Kentucky fell into three broad areas critical to the success of world-wide electronic access to, and the manipulation of, digital multimedia collections: the management of semantic content; dynamic content analysis and reconstruction; and improvements in the efficiency of remote access. This summary of the proposed research will outline its likely importance for humanities scholars, and focus mainly on the investigations into the management of semantic content. A full description of the research will be given in the proceedings of the conference.

### Dynamic content analysis and reconstruction

Given the increasingly large amount of multi-media data in library collections, novel processing techniques must be developed that can examine huge amounts of data quickly and accurately to support dynamic queries for semantic contents that were never envisioned. The University of Kentucky team propose an identification technique that formulates searches using queries that operate in the *compressed domain*. Although compressed, the data is still complete, and so queries that were not anticipated can be formulated and searched on the fly, eliminating the need to compute exhaustively all cues in advance. At the same time, operating in the compressed domain wins an efficiency in space and time that allows more complicated cues to be extracted and searched within a time frame roughly equivalent to searches which had been anticipated. Three-dimensional information is another kind of content that can be extracted in order to recover models of artefacts. Creating digital 3-D models of artefacts is much more difficult, however, than digitising two-dimensional documents. Difficulties stem from the artefact size, sensitivity, and awkwardness in handling. In many contexts, commercially-available approaches (such as laser-based scanners) are unacceptable because of conservation restrictions on handling of the original object. The Kentucky project proposes new methods for reconstructing 3-D shape and texture from video sequences obtained by computer-controllable cameras, under normal, minimally-invasive illumination conditions, which should be acceptable for use on ancient objects.

### Improving the efficiency of remote access

Although world-wide Internet access has become widespread, this access is achieved via a wide range of communication technologies. Most use the infrastructure already available in schools and homes and are, therefore, already being deployed and will have a significant impact on many of those engaged in humanities research and teaching, no matter how computer literate they are. The Kentucky team plan to build on the infrastructure already created by the World Wide Web by mapping their framework for manipulating multimedia data collections onto it. This infrastructure is heterogeneous and suffers from potentially high latencies (which lead not only to slow response times, but also to interruption and breakup of messages), low and/or asymmetric bandwidths, and varying Quality of Service (QoS) guarantees, and this raises several interesting research questions. One area is the incorporation of an intelligent cooperative caching scheme and smart pre-fetching to reduce network load and mask access latency. Another issue of interest to Professor Seales' team is the development of transport-level communication optimisations specifically designed to improve performance over asymmetric bandwidth links and slow-speed links. Finally, the Kentucky project proposes a network layer signalling mechanism that allows dynamic re-negotiation of QoS of an existing connection, coupled with a rate-adaptation algorithm that bases timing of re-negotiation on data flow characteristics.

### Management of semantic content

The information derived from multi-media data is made explicit by a potentially limitless set of processing techniques. Unlike alpha-numeric data, identifying all information contained in multi-media data is not a viable approach, since the semantic information of importance to the user or application is not explicitly available in the data. Instead, the data must be processed to extract the important information. For example, a picture must be processed to determine that it contains a tree, house, or some other semantic object. A second problem associated with identifying semantic content is the fact that the information of importance depends on the application domain or the user's interpretation of what is meaningful. Thus different domains and different users within a domain may view the semantic content differently. Moreover, their interpretation or view may change over time. Embedded semantic information is substantially harder to model and manage than conventional alpha-numeric data because it is rich, complex and subject to variation in interpretation, and so presents future database management system designers with a variety of challenging and important research problems. Perhaps the most challenging problem is that the implicit semantic information must be made explicit, extracted from its embedding.

Professor Seales and his team seek to design and implement a novel framework for defining, manipulating, accessing, searching, and viewing the semantic content found in multi-media data forms. They propose a semantic object approach that tracks the semantic meaning of an object as it is processed and manipulated. The system will also support high-level conceptual information that can only be derived or inferred. Such support will allow humanities scholars to access, modify and derive high-level conceptual ideas, theories and interpretations of the data they study.

For humanities scholars, the most exciting aspects of the research of Professor Kiernan and Professor Seales lie in the development of a method for managing embedded semantics. The other areas of research will considerably improve techniques for handling and accessing large quantities of multi-media data and will make life easier for humanities scholars in using such data, but arguably will not radically change the way in which they approach it.

In 1881, in introducing the facsimile of the important early biblical manuscript, the *Codex Alexandrinus,* one of the first photographic facsimiles of a manuscript, Edward Maunde Thompson, Keeper of Manuscripts at the British Museum and afterwards Principal Librarian, wrote that the publication of the facsimile 'was authorised from a desire to place the text within the reach of scholars in a form free from the errors of the printing press and untouched by the hand'. This remains one of the chief advantages of using images of a manuscript – that there is no editorial intermediary between the user and the text. However, the user cannot use the computer to search and explore images of a text in the same way as with a conventional full-text edition. This is the case even when digital images of a manuscript are available. The user can magnify the text or compare different sections of it, but he cannot find particular words or letters or analyse automatically different features of the manuscript. In order to do this, a copy of the text interpreted into alpha-numeric form is still required, which means the user is still dependent on the viewpoint of the editor who creates that text.

Some manuscript scholars have dreamed of having access to optical character recognition (OCR) technology which will allow a searchable text to be automatically generated from a manuscript. OCR technology is still a long way from achieving this, but such an approach in any case misses the point. Use of OCR would simply mean that the computer does a lot of the donkeywork currently performed by the human editor. One is still dependent on a single view of the text. This editorial text, whether generated by a human or machine, is only concerned with content of the data that is already known and can be defined in advance by some static criteria for recognition. Humanities research is frequently concerned with identifying and investigating information in the material which has not already been defined and is effectively unknown, but which is nevertheless extractable from the image. Moreover, different humanities scholars can have completely different perceptions and approaches to a particular object. The information which requires identification can vary according to the application domain or the user's interpretation of what is meaningful.

This can be seen by considering digital images of the Beowulf manuscript.

An art historian will be concerned with identifying, comparing and analysing the constituent parts of the illustrations and decorated initials in the text. The paleographer will wish to examine the detail of the script in the manuscript, analysing such characteristics as the order in which pen strokes were made, the length of descenders or the curvature of a certain letter-form. On the other hand, an editor will carefully scrutinise text for evidence of erasures, corrections, abrasions and over-writing. All three disciplines will be anxious to establish the codicology of the manuscript, looking at hair-flesh patterns in the vellum, patterns of pricking and ruling and quire signatures to establish how the manuscript was originally constructed. In these examples, it is the application domain, be it art history, palaeography, editing of texts or codicology, which defines its own `view' or interpretation of what is meaningful or important in the data. Moreover, each person within the application domain defines a unique view. Two different art historians may disagree as to the iconographical components and associations of a particular illustration. Two palaeographers may (and almost certainly will) disagree as to the classification and dating of particular letter forms.

A related problem to the domain/user view problem is the fact that views often evolve or change over time. Information important to an earlier generation of scholars is either no longer important or viewed in a different way. Sixteenth-century collectors felt it was acceptable to crop the edges of manuscripts to protect them and improve their aesthetic appearance. Modern scholars however see `the marginal space' of manuscripts as an important area of research in its own right.

## Modelling Object-Oriented Data Semantics (MOODS)

The aim of the research in Kentucky is to develop a highly flexible information management system for multimedia data which recognises and addresses these issues. The system must manage the data, its extracted semantic content, and a set of methods for obtaining new semantic content. This system, known as MOODS (Modelling Object-Orientated Data Semantics), will treat embedded semantic information as objects which can be managed, retrieved and manipulated. MOODS also supports multicomponent data, user/domain specific views (to deal with differences of interest and interpretations), and evolving views (to deal with differences over time). Finally, it takes an innovative approach to the overall system design by integrating a semantic processing engine, database engine, and semantic inference rules to create a system for dynamically identifying and manipulating embedded semantic information and high-level concepts.

In addition to the data and methods (the operations which may be applied to it) found in standard object-orientated systems, each MOODS object contains a semantic specification that defines the meaning of the object. As methods are applied to each object, the object's data, semantic meaning, and available methods all change. Consequently, users view semantic objects as entities that undergo a series of transformations and may have a different meaning and available functionality at each stage. Semantic objects capture and model the

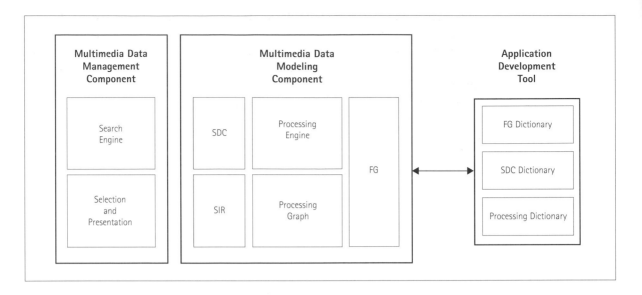

**Figure 1** The components of the proposed MOODS system.

currently known information (meanings) of the data. The way the meaning and functionality change over an object's lifetime is defined by a semantic processing graph defined by an expert of the semantic domain in question (art historian, palaeographer, etc.) A processing graph defines the allowable semantic states an object may traverse. Objects move from state to state via application of logical functions (abstract functions) that are instantiated with a specific function (a specific implementation) when the MOODS system is running. Because semantic objects are defined in terms of logical operations rather than specific functions, the specific functions can be written to be independent of the data they operate on and can be reused by any object.

Figure 1 illustrates the various components of the proposed MOODS information management system. The system consists of two main components: a database and a data modelling component. In addition, an application development tool aids in the construction of modelling systems and facilitates reuse of functions and previously created modelling systems.

The data modelling component distinguishes MOODS from conventional information management systems by providing the capability to extract dynamically semantic information. The processing engine provides each user and application domain with the ability to extract information of importance to that user or domain. It allows user views to change and evolve as new processing techniques become available. Moreover, identifying all semantic information at data entry time requires large amounts of space and limits the scope of future queries to the extracted information. By contrast, dynamic processing reduces the data storage requirements without limiting the amount of semantic information that can be accessed.

The data modelling component consists of five parts, or sub-components. A set of function groups (FG) defines the logical operations that can be applied to the data. The types of semantic information known to the system are represented by a set of semantic data classes (SDC), and a set of semantic inference rules (SIR). The processing graph defines the transformations that a semantic object may legitimately undergo over its lifetime. The semantic inference rules describe high-level concepts as logical relationships between semantic data classes. Finally, a processing engine allows users of the system interactively to apply functions to extract and identify semantic information.

The database component is tightly integrated with the modelling component. Semantic information extracted by the modelling component is automatically entered into the database for searching and browsing via conventional database techniques. Using SIR definitions, the database also supports queries for conceptual ideas and interpretations of data that has not been sufficiently processed or that must be inferred from potentially knowable information. For example, a query for a 'U.S. President' may result in a search for Clinton, Bush, Reagan, etc., generated automatically by reference to an appropriate semantic hierarchy.

The application development tool is an auxiliary tool that aids in the development of new modelling systems. In particular, it maintains a complete database of all known (previously defined) function groups, semantic classes, semantic relationship models, and processing graphs as starting points for the construction of new data models.

A prototype of the MOODS system was developed at Kentucky, and demonstrated with great success at the International Medieval Congress at Western Michigan University, Kalamazoo, in 1995, the Association for Literary and Linguistic Computing/Association for Computing and the Humanities conference at the University of Bergen in 1996, and elsewhere. This showed the potential of the system for dynamically interrogating images of the Beowulf manuscript. Initially, an expert palaeographer can define a data model for extracting particular letters, such as the Anglo-Saxon thorn, from the manuscript. Using the data model, another user can begin processing data to identify this letter form. Users can also define processing paths. One path might be good at identifying letter forms from one type of script, another might be better at a later form of script. Once a good processing path has been defined, future data can be processed automatically using the path. General users of the system may then search the database for specific letter forms. Using the embedded semantic information, the system will return a list of images containing the desired letter forms. Users may then decide to invoke the processing engine on one of the returned images to identify further the specific characteristics of a particular letter. The newly processed information will be entered back into the database and will respond to searches for letter forms with a particular characteristic.

In this way, users are able interactively to search images of text as readily as with tagged alphanumeric data. Moreover, the user is not restricted to the constraints set by the editor of the text – the system can accommodate and record different perceptions of the same text by different scholars. The prototype alone already offers exciting possibilities to medieval scholars. Palaeography is one of the most inexact of humanities disciplines, depending very much on the trained 'eye' of the expert palaeographer to establish the age and affinities of a particular script. Arguments assigning a manuscript to a particular date or place are difficult to document and verify. The way in which the MOODS system allows the reasoning of different palaeographers to be defined more precisely and recorded offers the possibility of a much more rigorous basis to palaeographical interpretations.

This describes the potential of the MOODS system at its simplest level. Establishing lists of forms of letters in a particular manuscript represents perhaps the most basic form of analysis which a manuscripts scholar might wish to undertake. A palaeographer, in dating and localising a manuscript, might wish in addition to distinguish the different scribes responsible for a manuscript or analyse the relationship of their scripts to other manuscripts. Because of the way in which humanities scholars work with their primary sources, content-based access to the data is insufficient, and processing alone cannot establish the desired relationship between semantics and data.

### Supporting semantic inference

To support inferred semantics, the full MOODS system will incorporate a semantic inference rule database as shown in figure 1. Semantic inference rules define the relationship between semantic concepts. Each rule takes the following form: inferred_info<- known_info_expression. In its simplest form, a semantic rule defines an alias for a concept. For example, when speaking of some types of manuscripts, the term 'folio' is used; for other types of medieval manuscripts it is more conventional to use the term 'membrane' instead. Rules can also be used to represent semantic hierarchies. Many semantic concepts are represented in a hierarchical organisation based on 'is a' style relationships where each layer of the hierarchy refines the layer above it. Figure 2 illustrates a very simple semantic hierarchy of famous people. Processing the data to identify its contents typically provides very specific information about the data (e.g. Winston Churchill found in this image), but does not associate higher-level semantics with the image (e.g. a famous English leader). Defining a semantic hierarchy allows the system also to attach high-level semantic concepts to data. To capture more complex semantic relationships, the rules must provide more powerful relations than just aliasing or hierarchising semantics. Expressions must also allow Boolean and comparative operations similar to those used in knowledge representation languages. For example, in analysing the Beowulf manuscript, we might use rules like:

**Figure 2** A very simple example semantic hierarchy of famous people.

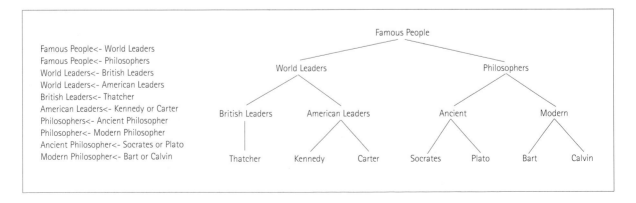

```
multiple_scribes <- (caroline_letter_forms & 1st_recto) &
    (insular_letter_forms & 1st verso)
caroline_letter_forms <- caroline_A  caroline_S caroline_G
insular_letter_forms <- insular_A  insular_S insular_G
```

to capture the concept that the manuscript was written by two or more scribes, as inferred by the occurrence of Caroline letter forms on the first recto and Insular letter forms on the first verso, as exemplified by the identified forms of the letters A, S, and G.

Existing knowledge systems provide rule bases for semantic relationships similar to the semantic rules we wish to provide. Although it is intended to incorporate the expressive language of such systems, MOODS differs from these systems in that our system only knows a small subset of the potentially knowable 'facts' because it does not identify the 'facts' until they are requested.

### Text as image

The concept of MOODS arose directly from The Electronic Beowulf project, and realises many of the views of text implicit in that project. In many ways, The Electronic Beowulf can be seen as an anti-edition. As explained above, rather than seeking to create a definitive editorial text, it dissolves the text into its component parts. Ideally, it would attempt to do this by using images alone, but the need to provide a searchable text means that the CD-ROM will include a transcription of the manuscript. MOODS points towards a way in which The Electronic Beowulf can realise its destiny as an entirely image-based edition.

It may seem that this approach is only viable for medieval texts known only from single manuscripts, where the images can be treated effectively as the main text. However, the MOODS approach will be just as pertinent with entirely different types of material. In the case of a large modern archive containing thousands of documents, for example, it may simply not be practicable to transcribe and index all the material. A means of marking-up and manipulating images of this material will be a far more practicable approach. Thus, the papers of a modern cabinet minister may contain thousands of files and millions of words. A conventional edition would require the transcription and indexing of each word. An electronic edition comprising SGML-tagged text might possibly reduce the effort required in indexing the data (but it should be remembered that the overhead in inserting the SGML tags might be almost as great as with conventional indexing). An image edition in which dynamic searching of images of the text can be undertaken is not only potentially much less labour-intensive but will produce an edition in which the user is not restricted to the view of the documents imposed by the editor or indexer.

Text began as image – in the form of ideograms, hieroglyphs and so on. The modern distinctions between text and image are ones based essentially on the need to migrate information from one medium to another, through such intermediaries as print technology or ASCII text. The need to convert texts into such forms may perhaps in the long term come to be seen as an intermediate technology. When we are able to handle images of the original text as readily as print or ASCII transcriptions, text will again have become image.

# Network services and the way ahead

In any concept of the digital library, the exploitation of the telecommunications network is another vital component. The British Library's development of an online information server accessed over the Internet, **Portico**, was a service innovation which required some technical innovations for the Library context. **Network OPAC and ONE** explores the requirements of remote users for access to catalogues. **Automated Request Processing** describes established services, while **INSIDE** looks into the development of a service only now coming into operation. Perhaps not surprisingly, the challenges which most obviously face these projects were less in solving the technical problems than in the areas of organisation and collaboration with the library and archive community in the development of access structures to digital collections.

By contrast with some of the projects in earlier sections, the networking projects were all attempts to create production standard services which would reach out to the Library's external community. In this way, they were the first steps towards establishing a gateway to the Library's catalogues and information sources. Only through the successful implementation of these services can the Library's longer-term objective of delivering digital documents to its remote users be successful. In **Developing the digital library**, Brian Lang outlines the Library's vision for the future, and the activities which will take us there.

# Portico: The British Library's online information server

**Graham Jefcoate, with additional technical material by Andrew Ford**

Portico is The British Library's online information server providing Internet users with access to information about all aspects of the services and collections of the United Kingdom's national library. By exploiting the latest information technology to this end, Portico formed a natural part of the *Initiatives for Access* programme. Portico is the only corporate online information server that will be operated by the Library for the dissemination of information about its services, collections and events for external Internet users. The information content of Portico falls into the following three categories:

- A 'welcome page' and other top-level or general editorial matter.
- Sectional home pages for the Library's directorates and departments.
- Finding aids for Internet resources with links to external WWW sites.

These are supported by a search engine and an index. Portico's Internet address is at the URL: http://portico.bl.uk.

This brief account of Portico's development concentrates on how the project created a framework for an operational service, emphasising organisational rather than technical issues. Readers with an interest in the current service are referred to the contact points cited on the Portico welcome page at http://www.bl.uk.

In common with many other national libraries and major research institutions, The British Library decided (during late 1993) to establish an online information server on the lines of the Campus Wide Information Servers or Services (CWIS) introduced at many universities. The name given to the server was 'Portico', emphasising its role as the Library's electronic gateway. The service was intended to supply remote users with information about the Library's services and collections in the form of an electronic bulletin board. Portico was originally launched on the Internet in July 1994 as a 'Gopher' delivering plain-text files accessed by selecting topics from menus or through a keyword index. The Gopher format was devised in the late 1980s by computing staff at the University of Minnesota. It offered an ideal system for mounting bulletin-board-type information that could be widely accessed over the Internet using both the Gopher and telnet protocols.

By late 1994 it had become obvious, however, that the future of online information servers lay not with Gophers but with the rapidly developing World Wide Web. Originally developed at CERN, the European high energy physics research centre at Geneva in Switzerland, as a user-friendly means of distributing internal project documentation, the World Wide Web (WWW or W3 for short) is a hypertext-based system supporting interactive links, images, audio and video, as well as the full range of Internet tools (including, for example, file transfer, Gopher, telnet access to remote catalogues and databases, and email). It provides a dynamic format allowing attractive presentation and ease of access to files by means of hyperlinks. The Web makes use of the so-called 'HyperText Transport Protocol' (HTTP) which allows hypertext files to move across the Internet. (More information about the background and development of the World Wide Web can be found at the W3 Consortium's own Web site: http://www.w3.org/pub/WWW/TheProject.html)

As an interconnecting network of networks, the Internet provides clients with access to files on servers world-wide. In common with other Internet applications, the Web is built with the so-called 'client/server architecture'. Files are made available on networked computers acting as 'servers' and can be accessed and downloaded by other computers with the appropriate 'client' software. The client software is called a 'Web browser'. Netscape and its derivatives are currently the most popular browsers and can be downloaded without charge over the Internet. Those with experience of publishing in other media often find the 'client/server' concept difficult to grasp: the presentation of Web pages on the screen (including layout, font, type size, colours in the text fields and even the presence or absence of graphics) is determined by the client software rather than pre-determined by the authors or others making documents available on a server.

As the significance of the World Wide Web became ever more apparent, the Library took the decision to supplement the Portico Gopher with a selection of hypertext pages making use of many of its most attractive features. A small team was assembled in December 1994 with the limited task of creating a prototype Web server as a demonstrator. This team included both staff and consultants with a range of relevant knowledge and skills. A Web adviser, Andrew Ford, provided technical support and built a server environment in which the service could develop. They also created the first pages themselves. Tim Hadlow, the Library's Local Area Network Manager, provided systems support and networking skills. Paula Lonergan, a multi-media designer with experience in CD-ROMs, was responsible for the first page design concept and for the creation of the images. A number of other staff collected or created content.

The prototype Portico WWW service, launched at the Computers in Libraries exhibition at Wembley in March 1995, included text about (and images from) the wider *Initiatives for Access* programme itself, as well as a selection of text, images and audio from current exhibitions. An online tour of the new British Library building at St Pancras proved an especially useful feature. Of the pages on British Library treasures, the 'zoomable' Magna Carta manuscript, devised by Andrew Ford, quickly became one of the most popular. (See Plate 10.) The prototype was extremely well received both by the public and by reviewers. In the first week of the Portico World Wide Web service alone there were some 20,000 transactions on the system.

Following the success of the Portico prototype, a development project was launched with the aim of creating a fully operational service. The project started to build up coverage of British Library services and collections by adding home pages for departments and services, using the experience gained during the original Gopher project. A wider circle of staff and consultants became involved, including (in late 1995) a second technical adviser, Dr Glynn Robinson, and Mark Davies, the Library's first staff 'webmaster'.

The Portico Development Project was managed by British Library Network Services using an adapted version of the PRINCE project management methodology, which is well tested in British public service organisations as a framework for the introduction of new IT-related systems. This methodology calls for a defined set of deliverables and timescales and proved an effective tool for allocating responsibility and resources and monitoring results. With appropriate adaptations, it proved useful in organising the development of a corporate Web site in The British Library context. The project was steered by a board chaired by Neil Smith, Head of British Library Network Services. Graham Jefcoate was project manager and de facto editor, continuing his role on the Gopher project and the Web server prototype project.

The management, development and maintenance of any online information service using the World Wide Web involves a wide range of disparate activities in whatever organisation it might be launched. These activities can be broadly grouped under the headings: 'technical/systems', 'content/editorial', and 'organisation/management'. Each of these activity areas requires special organisational solutions which should ideally be tested during the life of a development project in order to ensure the success of an operational service.

Technical and systems-related activities might include: setting up and running the server itself; establishing appropriate and sustainable server management procedures; maintaining an online service; software maintenance; creating and manipulating graphics, audio and video files; checking the quality of HTML; validating hyperlinks; generating statistics; testing new products and services; ensuring security; and monitoring systems performance.

Editorial or content-related issues cover an equally long list of activities, including: determining design and layout; collecting and collating text, images and audio; co-ordinating content providers; maintaining currency; creating the HTML documents themselves and relevant hyperlinks; implementing style guidelines; and ensuring the quality and consistency of the content.

Finally, a range of wider organisational and management issues also needs to be addressed: representation of the service within the institution; the maintenance and development of links with related projects and activities and with other institutions; keeping abreast of developments and opportunities in the field; creating publicity and ensuring awareness; co-ordinating a training programme and ensuring overall quality.

Each of these activity areas has an important training element: building a major Web site is a learning process for all involved and it is essential to transfer skills and disseminate practical information as widely as possible to those who will need to operate a fully fledged service.

The structure of The British Library made the organisation of these diverse activities especially challenging. The Library is perhaps a uniquely complex institution among national libraries. With services and collections spread across a number of sites in London and at Boston Spa, the physical co-ordination of Library-wide projects presents in itself a major challenge. Moreover, the diversity of functions and activities among those services, and the range of skills and expertise required of its staff, must be greater than in almost any comparable institution. The project needed to establish agreed structures and lines of communication that could be tested and, where appropriate, recommended as a framework for the management of a future operational service.

The Development Project did not attempt to create comprehensive coverage of the Library's diverse activities from the beginning. Rather it concentrated on raising awareness of the potential of the World Wide Web among staff, spreading the skills required to take advantage of it, and creating a framework within which the service could develop. Neither did the Library follow the practice of some other institutions of creating a central editorial team to carry out the task: responsibility for collecting and co-ordinating content was devolved wherever possible on the Library's departments themselves. This was seen by some as a drawback but had the advantage of ensuring staff, as content providers, took 'ownership' of the pages they were creating.

Server management was retained as a central function to ensure overall quality and consistency. The webmaster function was originally carried out by Andrew Ford assisted by Tim Hadlow (later also by Glynn Robinson). In the course of the project, a clear view emerged of the full range of skills and activities needed to develop and maintain the data on the server. This enabled the project to make a case for the creation of the new post of Internet Systems Administrator ('webmaster'). Once appointed, the first incumbent of this post (Mark Davies) was trained by the project's systems advisers over a period of several months. This transfer of skills was an essential prerequisite of establishing an operational service after the close of the project. A number of other staff is currently being trained (late 1996) to support the webmaster.

In September 1993, when a study of the available online information systems was undertaken for The British Library, the World Wide Web was still in its infancy: the National Center for Supercomputer Applications (NCSA) had released the first version of their Web browser, Mosaic, just a few months earlier and world-wide there were only about 50 Web servers operating. Gopher was then the predominant networked information system and seemed groundbreaking in the way that it allowed information throughout the world to be transparently linked together.

Conceptually the mechanisms by which Gopher and the World Wide Web servers operate are very similar. With both systems specialised browser programs are used to retrieve information resources offered by a server program. Each request for a resource is independent of any other request. The major difference between the two systems is in the models of information on which the system designs are based.

The developers of Gopher at the University of Minnesota had a fairly fixed idea of the structure of information: it was to be organised as a hierarchy of menus with the actual information only appearing as text files or images linked to by the menu items. Links to resources can only appear in the menus, not in the documents. However, when Tim Berners-Lee designed the World Wide Web, he envisaged it as an interconnected network of information and recognised that he could not foresee all the possible types of information that might be served. His stroke of genius was to invent a system which, although not in itself revolutionary, was open-ended and all-encompassing. The main features of the Web that set it aside from previous information systems are:

- a universal document naming syntax (URLs) that can address not only documents accessed through Web servers but also those accessed via other systems.
- a simple format for Web documents (HTML), which is based on SGML, an existing, portable markup language. This format includes a hypertext link mechanism, which enables documents to contain active references to other resources.
- the requirement that Web servers should pass explicit information about the type of a document to the browser. With other systems browsers infer the type of a document from its name.

Although today's graphics-rich Web landscape seems much more highly developed than the simple scene that prevailed only two years ago, the changes in technology have been evolutionary. The original framework has proved flexible enough to encompass the details of new technologies such as Java, Shockwave and RealAudio, but the fundamentals remain almost exactly as they were when the Web first appeared.

Given the relative popularity of the Web and Gopher at the time that the Portico service was being developed it was natural that it was first launched as a Gopher service. Gopher was predominantly a text-based service while the Web always had the potential for graphics. It was felt that a text-based service would not discriminate so much against users with less sophisticated computer systems. In the intervening period multimedia PCs have evolved and, as prices for these systems have tumbled, they have come to represent the new, accepted base-line for minimum functionality. Thus the move to a Web-based service in 1995 and the gradual phasing out of the Portico Gopher service have been part of a natural progression. This move was envisaged from the beginning but the speed with which it would occur was certainly not.

The choice of software employed for the Portico service was determined by availability, functionality and quality. In 1994 there was virtually no commercial Web or Gopher software available and the choice was limited to free software. One of the problems with free software is that it sometimes progresses by leaps and bounds with new versions containing many new features appearing almost every week (or even sometimes daily), but at other times may stagnate – even though there might be severe problems with the current version and the developers may not respond to 'bug reports'. On the other hand since the source code to most free software for UNIX is available, anyone with the technical expertise can fix problems or add missing functionality that they require. Such changes are often distributed via Network News and mailed back to the developers who will usually incorporate them into new releases. Where this does not happen and new releases contain desirable new features one has to apply the changes to the new version of the software.

The initial Portico service used the GN Gopher server, written by Professor John Franks of Northwestern University, running on a Sun Microsystems SPARCstation. The GN server is unique in that it will respond both to Gopher requests and to Web requests and can reply with a different version of a document depending on the type of incoming request. It was felt that this feature would be useful in the eventual migration to a Web service. The GN server had a much more active user community than that of the original Gopher server from the University of Minnesota and problems that arose were quickly ironed out.

When the Web service was launched the CERN server was chosen in preference to the NCSA server, primarily on the basis of the quality of the software. The CERN server was written by Tim Berners-Lee in a disciplined, object-oriented style. The NCSA server has been much more popular, especially in the United States, but had performance problems and was the subject of a number of security alerts caused in the main by simple programming errors.

The main problem that recurred during the Portico project was that of document portability. The server was running on a UNIX machine, most documents were written using Microsoft Word on PCs running Windows, and when the Web project started the graphics were created on an Apple Macintosh. Each of these systems differs from each other in the restrictions on the naming of files and the formats for storing information. Some conversion software was available but even that required manual operation and the resultant documents needed to be checked and often edited.

Since the initial deployment of the Portico service, the World Wide Web has become firmly established as a mainstream application and consequently a range of commercial Web products has now become available. It is no longer necessary to hunt the Internet for free software to build a Web site, but given the continuing pace of change of technology, even the new commercial offerings have a short shelf life. One still needs to keep an eye out for new developments that Portico might need to incorporate.

In the jargon of the World Wide Web, Portico is The British Library's 'home page' on the Internet, but the Library's complexity has meant that it functions in effect as a 'host' to a growing number of departmental or sectional home pages for each of its services. This principle was established at the earliest phase of the development project when a small but broadly representative group of departments was invited to be the first to create their own pages. Sectional co-ordinators acted as local project managers liaising with the relevant Portico editors and team. Local efforts were co-ordinated by departmental editors at directorate level. Sections were encouraged to publicise and promote their own pages within their natural user constituencies and beyond.

From this experience, the Library was able to develop detailed guidelines on the design and presentation of pages to be observed by all contributing departments in order to ensure an appropriate and consistent appearance to pages derived from a wide range of sources. These guidelines also set standards for the production of HTML (HyperText Markup Language), the coding language used to create hypertext documents for use on the World Wide Web.

In general, the Library has aimed at a rather 'conservative' style on Portico's pages, reflecting its role as a leading resource for scholarship, research and innovation. Portico seeks to avoid complex sequences of pages, meretricious design features, special formatting, jargon or obscure terminology. It has not been anxious to be in the forefront of Web design, rather incorporating useful innovations once they have been tested elsewhere. In general, Portico has been 'content-driven' rather than 'technology-' or 'design-driven'. Quite deliberately, the Portico 'welcome page' has been kept relatively simple in design and content to ensure ease of downloading. Simplicity of design has mean that Portico pages can be read using as wide a number of available browsers as possible.

To help co-ordinators organising the work within their sections, a checklist of possible actions was drawn up. They were encouraged to consider setting up a sectional working party as a means of involving managers and colleagues and of making sure everyone who needed to be consulted felt involved in the project. It was equally important to establish the authorship and 'ownership' of particular pages: who would be responsible for their content and for keeping them up-to-date? At the same time, they were advised to request the installation of HTML editing tools for local use. These are installed and supported centrally by the Library's Information Systems staff.

Once these necessary organisational steps had been taken, departments could turn to the task of assembling material and ideas. They were advised to check for existing sources of documentation in digital formats: for example, Gopher documents and word-processing files used for text on leaflets or in articles. Other documents, including older material, could be retyped or scanned using Optical Character Recognition (OCR) equipment. Illustrative material would also be required: each section was asked to find an identifying image for use on its welcome page and (reduced) as a 'clickable' thumbnail on all the dependent pages. Sections were also encouraged to locate and consider analogous pages either in Portico itself or at other WWW sites so they could benefit from existing examples. They might also wish to build appropriate links to such sites into their hypertext pages.

A sectional home page comprises a sectional 'welcome page' and a suite of subsidiary pages linked from it. Apart from text and menus, Portico pages carry a number of images and links to other appropriate pages at external sites. The sectional 'welcome page' determines the structure of the home page as a whole. Apart from the identifying image, this page should carry a brief sectional 'mission statement' followed by a short menu of dependent pages. Departments were encouraged to establish a sectional email account to enable users to interact. They were also asked to consider an online feed-back form.

During any one quarter, the Portico team aims to process about four or five sectional home pages, building gradually to the widest possible coverage of the Library's services and collections over a period of about two years. If this appears a relatively long gestation period, it should be reflected that the Library's directorates and departments are often as large and diverse as many other independent organisations. A single service might well develop a suite of 50 or 60 pages.

Once drafted, pages are placed in a test area on the server for review by local managers and staff and by central editors. After going 'live' on the server, more work had to be undertaken to ensure staff in the section felt they had a stake in its own home page, and in particular that they knew its URL. This needed to be added to departmental stationery and business cards, and publicised elsewhere as appropriate. The sections were also urged to promote their home page to the wider world through the 'usual channels' it used to inform its user constituency about its activities (bulletin boards; email discussion lists; professional or specialist journals; newsletters and so on). Other Web sites might be invited to make appropriate links. Finally, staff should ensure the home page featured in courses, exhibitions, visits and all publicity material.

Portico was developed as a partnership between the content providers (editors, co-ordinators and contributors) and the systems administrators (the network managers, webmaster and technical consultants). The project attempted to involve as wide a circle of staff as possible in the developing service, establishing its role and securing its place in the Library's corporate culture.

Not unexpectedly, knowledge of the uses and potential of networked information was very unevenly spread among managers and staff. The prototype proved a useful tool in raising awareness and capturing the imagination of staff, users and the wider public.

The project was closely co-ordinated with a parallel project to raise awareness of the Internet in general, to promote its use in supporting and enhancing Library services, and to widen staff access to it. By late 1996, over 500 staff were regular users of the Internet, with Web browsing software loaded onto their office PCs. The Portico welcome page always appears first when activating the Web browser and Portico was always used as a 'starting point' in any Internet-related training. The addition of a World Wide Web resource guide, with hyperlinks to around 100 significant sites, ensured staff recognised Portico as their personal gateway to the Internet.

Once staff had seen the potential of the Web, and had been able to evaluate it themselves, more and more areas of the Library expressed interest in establishing their own sectional 'home pages'. During the development phase, about five to six sections were 'processed' at any one time during any one quarter.

One of the project's most important early 'deliverables' was a set of guidelines on house style, page design and layout. Training in the use of HTML was arranged centrally, and HTML editing tools were installed for local editors and contributors where required. Among the further deliverables were a search engine and a statistics-gathering facility.

In addition to style and content, the project addressed a wide range of issues relating to the management and functionality of the operational service itself. A management structure was proposed with a Management Board representing the editorial, systems and service interests. The content providers are responsible for creating the content of Portico and for ensuring its currency and quality. Each directorate has its own editor who co-ordinates the work of local sectional co-ordinators. Editorial efforts are co-ordinated by a central editor (currently Dr Bart Smith) based in the Library's Press and Public Relations department. The central editor liaises closely with the webmaster, who is based in the Library's Information Systems directorate. The webmaster maintains the data on the server and develops its functionality. This structure reflects the corporate nature of the Portico service.

The Portico Development project aimed to create a framework for a British Library corporate online information server that provided Internet users with information about British Library services, collections and events that is accurate, timely and appropriate. Interest in Portico both within the Library and, more importantly, among its 'target audience' of Internet users, has been growing steadily. The service is already accepted as a normal part of the Library's work and a primary means of communicating with its users and the wider public. User feedback has been largely favourable. At present (late 1996) well over a third of a million transactions are logged on the growing number of Web pages each month. It is often cited as a model of a national library online information service.

Portico's success and the increasing acceptance of the World Wide Web as an Internet tool have encouraged the Library to examine the Web as an interface to other online services, such as its prototype network OPAC, the BLAISE service, and document ordering and delivery services. The Library is also examining the Web as a medium for internal communication (the so-called Intranet function).

The experience of the Portico project was also of direct relevance to Gabriel, the developing online service of the Conference of European National Librarians on the World Wide Web providing a gateway to the online resources of Europe's national libraries. The project management of Gabriel was also based at The British Library and the two projects developed on parallel lines. With its wide range of functions and activities distributed across over 20 sites at two locations, The British Library provided a model for the development of a WWW service based on even more disparate and geographically dispersed institutions. (The Gabriel URL is: http://portico.bl.uk/gabriel/en/welcome.html.)

The Portico Development Project was formally wound up on 31 March 1996 when the new operational service came into being. That the framework to launch the service had been created in the short space of a year was entirely due to the enthusiasm and expertise of the Portico team and staff throughout the Library. Expectations about the new service are high. The challenge now is to ensure Portico is adequately supported, receiving the resources it needs to sustain the current service and to take full advantage of future developments in the digital library field.

# Network OPAC and ONE

**Christopher Easingwood, Neil Smith and Jan Ashton**

The British Library's Strategic Objectives, *For Scholarship, Research and Innovation*, lay great emphasis on the improvement of access to our collections and the provision of British Library services to remote users. The British Library will work towards:

> *'a set of library services which offer maximum access through full use of new technology, both on our own sites and, over electronic networks, to other major libraries and users'*

The catalogue is fundamental to gaining access to the collection of any library. The two *Initiatives for Access* projects which seek to increase our understanding of the requirements for remote user access to our catalogues are the Network OPAC and the European Library Plan project OPAC Network in Europe – ONE.

## The Network OPAC

The British Library has developed its own OPAC (Online Public Access Catalogue) which has been in operation in its reading rooms since 1993. The Library's requirements for its OPAC included both sophisticated searching facilities across several catalogues and the capability to interface with a Reader Admission system and an Automated Book Request System. This resulted in an advanced modular system based on a client/server architecture distributed over two separate levels of servers. The user terminals are personal computers running a sophisticated Windows OPAC client connected by Ethernet LANs to multiple user servers. These user servers are in turn connected over the Library's Wide-Area Network to a single data server that holds the catalogues running under the BRS/Search retrieval software. This 'client/server-client/server' model utilises the TCP/IP communications protocol across the Library's network.

As part of the *Initiatives for Access* programme, the Library wanted to examine the possibilities of providing remote access to the Library's catalogues. The project became known as the Network OPAC and contributes to the Library's objective to 'provide a simple means of access to the Library's collections and its services via electronic networks'. Because of the architecture of the Library's OPAC, in terms of being a distributed client-server system, it was relatively straightforward to substitute the Library's own internal network with JANET – the UK academic network running the TCP/IP protocol which forms part of the global Internet. This meant that we could provide access from PCs in universities, running the Windows client software, to the Library's catalogues. For a full technical description of the Library's OPAC, see *The British Library's Catalog Is On-Line* published in Byte magazine and available on the Web (URL: http://www.byte. com/art/9505/sec8/art1.htm).

The Network OPAC was launched as a trial service to the UK academic community in April 1994 and has been in use in over 200 academic and research institutions in the UK until its closure in June 1997. The Network OPAC service was the responsibility of the Library's National Bibliographic Service (NBS). The catalogues that could be accessed up until the end of May 1997 were:

- General Retrospective Catalogue of Printed Books
- Current Catalogue of Printed Books
- Science Technology and Business Current Catalogue
- Printed Music Current Catalogue
- Document Supply Centre Books Catalogue 1980-

These catalogues provide access to over seven and a half million records of the Library's holdings.

When a site registered for the Network OPAC service it received client software to run on IBM compatible PCs under Windows. This gave the user the Graphical User Interface that is available to users in the reading rooms in the Library. The interface recognises the importance of browsing as an essential tool to allow the user to gain access to the wealth of material in the catalogues. This is especially relevant to the Library's catalogues as they contain a very wide range of material types and therefore different cataloguing treatment. Standard OPAC direct searching facilities were also provided, together with the ability to enter searches for material in African, Cyrillic, Greek and Hebrew scripts and to display the full native character set of the records retrieved.

As part of the trial we researched the use of the service and looked at developments for a successor system (possibly based on Z39.50/SR protocols – see more below) and at extending the user base, possibly to include overseas users. Initially we decided to broaden the user base to include not only academic or research institutions but a number of public library, commercial and individual users. We also invited a small number of overseas institutions who expressed an interest in the service to take part in this extended trial.

Since registration was on a site basis rather than by individual user, it was up to each site to decide how access was offered to the Network OPAC within the institution. This ranged from sites where there was a dedicated Network OPAC terminal in a Public Access area, to sites which networked the software so that academics could have access from their own PCs.

NBS produced a variety of materials intended to support the service. These ranged from an online user guide giving information about the catalogues, how to search for material and how to go about locating and borrowing items once you have identified them, to leaflets and posters to help publicise the service within the institutions, to the setting up of an electronic mail discussion list to provide a forum for users to discuss issues between themselves and with NBS staff. The electronic mail list was hosted on the JANET Mailbase system and was called *lis-bl-nopac*.

**OPAC 97**

As a result of the trials the Library developed a simple Web interface to its catalogues called OPAC 97, which was made available in May 1997. OPAC 97 is provided free of charge to users world-wide who have access to the Internet and a copy of any of the standard Web browsers (e.g. Netscape, Internet Explorer) and no additional client software is required. (See Plate 11.) The service offers access to two additional Document Supply Centre catalogues, serials and conferences, with an overall total of over eight and a half million records. A direct link to the Document Supply Centre allows registered customers to order loans and photocopies online, and users not registered with the Centre can request photocopies of journal articles or conference papers through the LEXICON service directly via OPAC 97. OPAC 97's functionality is currently limited in certain ways, such as in its treatment of character sets and the lack of direct access to the index. These and other issues will be addressed in a later OPAC service which begins development in autumn 1997. OPAC 97 can be directly accessed at: http://opac97.bl.uk.

### ONE – OPAC Network in Europe

Having made the Network OPAC available, the Library was keen to examine the possibilities for remote access to catalogues offered by a new standard – Z39.50. Through the *Initiatives for Access* programme, the Library pursued this objective through a collaborative project which is part of the European Commission's Library Plan. This project is OPAC Network in Europe (ONE).

ONE is funded under the Library Plan, to a level of 2.4million ECU (about £1.7million; $2.6million). It started in February 1995 and is scheduled for completion in October 1997. Within the context of the Library Plan it is a large-scale project: 15 partners in 8 countries will provide between them over 7000 person days. The original project plan had no fewer than 240 tasks, though this has been reduced slightly recently following recommendations from the first project review. The organisation with the perhaps unenviable role of controlling all this work is Oslo College-BRODD, Norway.

The 15 partners are (C = Coordinator, P = Partner, A = Associated partner):

- AUSTRIA: Joannneum Research (P) , Steierermärkische Landesbibliothek (A), Steiermärkische Landesmuseum Joanneum (A)
- DENMARK: Dansk BiblioteksCenter (P) , Nationalmuseet (A)
- FINLAND: Helsinki University Library – TKAY (P)
- GERMANY: Die Deutsche Bibliothek (P)
- THE NETHERLANDS: Pica (A)
- NORWAY: BIBSYS (A) , BRODD (C) , Nasjonalbiblioteket (P), Universitets-biblioteket Oslo (A)
- SWEDEN: LIBRIS (P)
- UK: The British Library (P), Crossnet Ltd (P)

More information about the project is provided at a Web site maintained by BIBSYS at the following URL: http://www.bibsys.no/one.htm

The project's aim is to provide users with better ways to access library OPACs and national catalogues and which will stimulate and facilitate interworking between libraries in Europe. The project is based on the use of the Z39.50 standards which enable users to search widely different computer systems across networks and offer end-users the promise of greater ease of use through a solution to the proliferation of different user interfaces to library catalogues.

The project will produce high-quality software which will be put into the public domain. The software produced will address issues of diverse record formats and character sets which are currently barriers to seamless access across distributed databases. ONE will contribute to the development and enhancement of the SR/Z39.50 standards. The project will also produce new systems for user assistance which will make it easier for users in one country to access catalogues in another. Entry point software will also be produced which will allow users to dial-in to a single point to access any of the participants' OPACs.

## What is Z39.50?

Z39.50, to quote the title page of the protocol itself, 'specifies a client/server based protocol for Information Retrieval'. It is worth bearing in mind that *information retrieval* is fundamentally what Z39.50 is all about. In Z39.50 parlance, the server is known as *the target*; the client becomes *the origin*.

What problem is Z39.50 trying to solve? Libraries have for many years been using automated information retrieval systems. All major library system suppliers provide modules for accessing the library's own OPAC. Many information providers have provided access to their catalogues through some form of automation. The problem for the end-user is that interfaces to these catalogues may be entirely different: the information is stored in a different way, with different sets of rules for searching. Z39.50 overcomes these problems and makes it possible for a user of one system to search and retrieve information from other systems without knowing the search syntaxes that are used by those other systems. In other words, it offers a means of translating the different search languages developed by the different library system suppliers and online database hosts. The library can provide one piece of software which will enable the user to access any Z39.50 compliant database anywhere in the world.

The Z39.50 protocol achieves interoperability by converting between any native client syntax and the native syntax of any server. Thus a request to undertake an author search is translated into the standard protocol structure by the Z39.50 client and transmitted to the server over the network. The server receives this protocol structure and translates it into its own native search language and carries out the search. The search results are similarly translated into the protocol structure and sent to the client, which then translates from the protocol to its native system and displays the results to the user. In this way, implementors have only to construct a conversion from their native system to the protocol.

Z39.50 has been accepted as a NISO standard and has gone through several versions. The latest version, which we are implementing in Project ONE, is Version 3, which was ratified in July of last year. The protocol is maintained on behalf of the international information community by the Library of Congress. The Maintenance Agency monitors input from the Z39.50 Implementors Group, the ZIG, whose membership is open to anyone with an interest in Z39.50. It operates a busy discussion list, and organises meetings at least twice a year.

Though there was, perhaps, a suspicion that the ZIG was dominated by Americans, more Europeans have become involved and the group recently committed itself to meeting in Europe at least once a year.

For further information about the ZIG, the Maintenance Agency and a list of all sorts of useful Z39.50 resources, including information about Project ONE and other European projects, try the Web site maintained by the UK Office of Library Networking at:

http://ukoln.bath.ac.uk/z3950.

### Z39.50 features

Let us look briefly at the information retrieval features specified in Z39.50 – all of which will be implemented in at least some of the systems being developed within the ONE project.

- SEARCH – sent by the end-user at the origin. Z39.50 allows the user to search by around 100 access points, called use attributes in Z39.50 terminology (author, title, publisher etc.) and caters for varying degrees of sophisticated searching techniques.
- PRESENT – the target sends back retrieved records in response to the search request.
- SCAN – allowing the user to browse through the indexes held on the target. There are not all that many implementations of SCAN in the Z39.50 world but a number of ONE partners, including the Library, are implementing it.
- SORT – enabling the user to specify the order of records.

Other features provide for the development of systems which provide the end-user with information about the duration of a search session, and how many records have been displayed – this may be very important if the user is being charged for access. The access control facility allows for more sophisticated user identification and password options – it can be used to permit access only to a certain range of services. Finally there is a range of Extended Services – these are defined in the protocol as '*task type,* related to information retrieval, but not defined as a Z39.50 service'. Execution of the task by the target is outside the scope of Z39.50 and is carried out by other application software. The most significant of the extended services is *Item Order* which allows the client to submit an order request to the server – a number of partners within ONE view Item Order as one of the main components of the Z39.50 based service they hope to provide.

Finally, a mention for EXPLAIN. One of the key new features of Version 3, EXPLAIN allows an origin to obtain detailed information about the implementation of target. Some of this will be in the form of straightforward human-readable information provided for the end-user showing, for example, information about the size of the database being searched; when it was last updated; contact information; opening hours, etc. Some of the EXPLAIN data can be taken by the origin and used to dynamically configure the user-interface – depending on the data sent the number of access points presented to the end-user can be altered: there is no point in prompting the user to enter a Library of Congress Subject Heading if the server doesn't allow it.

## ONE: Service Objectives

The two main service objectives can be expressed as follows:

- link library users in partner institutions to the information resources available in each other's catalogues
- develop pan-European services which can be extended to include resources world-wide through the Internet

## ONE: Technical Objectives

The technical objectives are as follows:

- link together existing Z39.50 implementations in the participating institutions
- enhance existing Z39.50 implementations – implementors' agreement
- develop Z39.50 kernel software (based on DBV-OSI project)
- develop a 'neutral' client package – the Neutral Entry Point
- develop a toolkit – MARC conversion, character conversion
- develop a stand-alone PC client

All of the above deliverables will be put into the public domain at the end of the project.

A key point for the deliverables is the use of the DBV-OSI development software. This is a project funded not by the EU, but by the German government under the auspices of Die Deutsche Bibliothek. We are extremely fortunate that we have been able to re-use the software within the ONE project – it has provided us with high-quality software and came ready-made with most of the features we required. The software was developed in conjunction with Crossnet Ltd in the UK, a company which is also part of the ONE project.

A major deliverable from the ONE project is the Neutral Entry Point (NEP), which is being developed by DBC. The concept of the NEP is to provide Z39.50 services to users who do not have access either to a library system which supports Z39.50, or to a stand-alone client. Acting as a gateway, the NEP will be installed on a UNIX machine and will enable users to access the ONE servers by using Telnet or a WWW browser.

At the same time ONE is working on the development of tools which, it is hoped, will overcome some of the fundamental problems encountered when exchanging bibliographic records between different countries in Europe – namely the proliferation of different MARC formats, and the different character sets in use. A MARC conversion utility is being developed by BRODD which will support the translation of all the different MARC formats in use within the project (FINMARC, DANMARC, UKMARC etc.) into both USMARC and UNIMARC.

Similarly we are looking for a long-term solution to the thorny issue of character set support. The project is required by the EU to come up with a solution based on the use of UNICODE (ISO-10646). A decision was taken to use the deliverables from another EU-funded project, CHASE. CHASE will translate from the local character set used in the client software into ISO-10646, and send the information to the remote server in that character set. The server will perform the search and use CHASE to convert the results from *its* local character set into ISO-10646; this is received by the client which then uses CHASE again to convert from ISO-10646 to its local character set. This means that a client and a server both implementing CHASE need to know nothing about the local character sets in use.

Last, but by no means least, a Windows stand-alone client will be built.

## Current status of the project

So at what stage is the project now? In March and April of 1996 thorough testing took place between all the partners; and The British Library, for its part, also involved the wider Z39.50 community in the form of library system suppliers in the UK, and ZIG members in North America.

At the same time we began specifying the second version of the servers, which basically meant choosing which remaining Z39.50 features we wanted to incorporate – each partner chose on the basis of their own specific service requirements. A key aim of the project is the successful implementation of EXPLAIN, which is being implemented by all partners. Implementors Agreements were drawn up – one specifically for EXPLAIN, and another covering the remaining features. Implementors Agreements define a common way of dealing with the options to be implemented and ensure a high degree of interoperability between the partners' systems. In addition, an agreement was drawn up covering the handling of BIB-1 use attributes.

Since then partners have been working on implementing the new features in the servers, as well as fixing problems reported from the first phase of testing. At the same time the final stages of work on the toolbox modules are taking place, as well as work on the NEP and the stand-alone client. Some partners are also developing their own clients.

Testing of the second versions of the servers is due to take place during March and April 1997. The project culminates in a major trial service during which each partner will involve real users in testing each of the servers on offer. We believe that only by involving users can we get a proper idea of the value of Z39.50 in providing real services. It is important to stress that the main aim of the project is to facilitate an operating service between the partners – so as well as the complex technical issues we have had to address service, marketing and licensing issues.

## The British Library and Z39.50

As part of the exploitation plan of the project all partners indicated from the start how they planned to use the deliverables from the ONE project. As far as the Library is concerned, we believe that Z39.50 offers the potential to provide a range of services both for our own readers and remote users, and for the users of other organisations who wish to access The British Library's collections.

As far as access to the Library's catalogues is concerned, the Library's Strategic Objectives – which describe the type of services the Library intends to provide by the year 2000 – stress the importance of increasing remote access to our catalogues for the benefit of the majority of the population who are unable to visit our reading rooms and, indeed, for users outside of the UK.

To this end the Library is working closely in the UK with CURL – the Consortium of University and Research Libraries – to investigate the best way of providing wider access to our OPAC catalogues. This is in the context of wider discussions on the establishment of a National Bibliographic Resource (NBR). The use of Z39.50 could provide the key building block in the development of a NBR based on the catalogues of CURL members, of The British Library, and other national collections such as the National Library of Wales and the National Library of Scotland. For more information about CURL's COPAC, and to look at the work they have already done in providing Web access to their members' databases, check out http://copac.ac.uk/copac/

The Library has also indicated the importance of using the Internet to provide visitors to the reading room with access to non-British Library catalogues. Our Information Systems Strategy says:

*'By the year 2000 the British Library ... will provide access to the world's catalogues through a single gateway leading from the online catalogue...'*

# Automated Request Processing

**Andy Ekers**

The British Library Document Supply Centre at Boston Spa (BLDSC) currently receives over four million requests every year. Over 70% of these are now received by one of a number of electronic methods. The computer systems that support the processing of these requests are collectively known as the Automated Request Processing or ARP systems.

There are three main groups of systems within ARP.

1. Automated Request Transmission. The receipt of automated requests is supported by a group of systems known collectively as Automated Request Transmission or ART. The most popular ART system is ARTTel (Automated Request Transmission by Telecommunications).

2. Core Automated Request Processing. Once the requests are received another group of systems processes the electronic messages to produce the printed and bar-coded forms used by BLDSC. These are collectively known as the Core Automated Request Processing systems (CARP). A key part of the CARP system is AUTOMATCH.

3. Automated Request Monitoring. Finally there are a number of systems that allow BLDSC to monitor the progress of requests and notify customers of dispatch or non-supply. These are collectively known as the Automated Request Monitoring Systems.

### Automated Request Transmission – ART

Automated requesting at Boston Spa goes back to 1975 when the ARTTelex System was introduced to process requests received from all over the world via the telex network. Since then we have introduced a number of automated methods for customers to transmit their requests to the Document Supply Centre. Chief among these is the ARTTel system first introduced in the late 1970s. Initially access was via a single 300 baud direct dial telephone line. This was improved in 1983 by providing a link to British Telecom's PSS network, now known as GNS or Global Network Services. In 1987 an ARTTel link to the Joint Academic Network (JANET) was added. ARTHost, also introduced in the late 1970s, allows customers using database hosts such as Blaise, Dialog, ESA, DIMDI and Datastar to send requests direct to BLDSC.

A number of hardware improvements were introduced in the late 1980s and early 1990s, including moving the entire ART system to a VAX/VMS environment. This required a complete re-write of the software. At the same time the British Telecom link was upgraded to a 9600 baud dataline and an additional back-up link to JANET was installed.

In 1990 the Replies Intray service was introduced allowing customers to view their coded reply messages online. In 1993 Version 2 of the ARTTel System was introduced. This provided a much more user-friendly system and included a number of new features such as confirmation of receipt and customer access to files transmitted during the previous two months. At the same time further ART services were introduced: namely ADD Addresses which allows delivery to a third party, and Shipped Messages which confirms that material has been dispatched. The direct dial connections were also upgraded to cope with communications up to 9600 baud with full error correction on two lines.

In 1994 the software for the ARTHost systems was completely revised to improve its speed and efficiency. The processing of OCLC requests was integrated with the main ARP systems.

In 1995 we launched two new services. ARTEmail enables customers to obtain the full ART service via electronic mail, and includes the ability to send requests and receive the Replies Intray messages. Direct Internet access to ARTTel enables Internet users to connect direct to our ARTTel service via a telnet link. By the end of 1995, all customers using direct dial (PSTN) access to ARTTel Version 1 had upgraded to Version 2. We therefore closed Version 1 and, in early 1996, upgraded access to ARTTel Version 2. This now has six direct dial lines capable of communicating at up to 28.8 Kbps.

During 1995 and 1996 much of the work on ARP has been directed towards linking it to the developing INSIDE system in all its flavours: CD-ROM, Windows and Web. The CD-ROM version uses ARTTel to transmit orders to BLDSC and to receive replies. Integration of ARP with the online Windows and Web versions of INSIDE is designed to be much closer. Once the customer has placed an INSIDE order the system will pass it direct to ARP. ARP will then process the order as an automated request so that it can be satisfied by BLDSC staff. ARP is also used to pass reply messages back to the INSIDE system and to control the billing and registration operations.

### Core Automated Request Processing – CARP

Once they are received via the ART systems electronic requests undergo a number of processes culminating in the production of printed request forms. These processes are supported by the CARP systems. Between 1975 and 1989 the main function of the CARP system was to check the format of the electronic message, add the customer's address using their transmitted customer code, and print the result onto request forms for processing by staff in BLDSC. The system did nothing with the request information. However, as the proportion of electronic requests increased, the benefits of using the request data to make request handling and monitoring more effective became clear.

During the early 1980s planning for a much enhanced ARP system began. This culminated in the introduction of a new CARP system in August 1989. A number of developments and enhancements to this system have been carried out during the following years especially in relation to automatically matching and sorting the electronic requests. This development is expected to continue for some time.

The heart of the system introduced in August 1989 is the printing of a bar-code on the request form and the creation of a database file of automated requests. This master file is central to the whole ARP system and enables the Automated Request Monitoring systems *(see below)* to function. It holds more than a year's worth of data consisting of more than five million requests.

The other major innovation during the early 1990s was the introduction of AUTOMATCH. This system takes each electronic request in turn and identifies and matches its bibliographic content so that the ARP system is able to detect whether the request is for a monograph (book), a serial or a conference. If the item is a serial AUTOMATCH goes on to identify exactly what the full serial title is and the appropriate BLDSC shelfmark. AUTOMATCH is also able to identify other fields within the bibliographic content of the request such as the Year of Publication, Volume, Part and Pages required. Recently AUTOMATCH has been extended to identify requests at the article level for items held on the ADONIS CD-ROM system. Work is now under way to extend success in matching serial titles to matching individual monograph titles.

Following identification by AUTOMATCH another part of the CARP system sorts each request to one of a number of printing streams. These streams are allocated on the basis of the geographic location of the item within BLDSC. Within each stream the requests are sorted according to the storage areas' requirements. For example, requests for one of the serial stores are sorted by shelfmark and date of publication. These streams of requests are then printed by the remote printing system. Laser printers, connected to the remote printing system, are situated at various points throughout the Library. On demand the operator at any remote station can print out the stream of requests for that storage area. The remote printing sites stretch further than the Boston Spa site; some are based in the Library's London operations and are connected to the ARP system via our internal network.

AUTOMATCH has replaced a tedious manual sorting operation with a fast and efficient system for delivering requests to the right part of BLDSC in the order required. Many enhancements to improve further the accuracy of matching and electronically link the output to CD article stores are planned.

## Automated Request Monitoring – ARM

The Automated Request Monitoring system comes into play once the requested item has been located at the shelf. Serial parts from 1988 onwards have a bar-code attached when they are added to stock. This barcode contains information to identify that part, such as its shelfmark and year of publication. As soon as the required item is fetched from the shelf the barcode on the serial part and on the request form are wanded into the Fetch Wanding system. If the item does not have a barcode (for example older serials or books) then various methods are used to allocate default data. The data collected by this system serves four purposes:

- For copyright fee paid requests it enables the Library to charge the customer a royalty fee for each request. The fee charged depends on the item supplied.

- It enables the Library to report to the Copyright Licensing Agency and to publishers what fees have been collected so that the relevant payments can be passed on.
- For all serial parts it provides management information on the usage.
- It traps request forms that have been used incorrectly (for example when an item has already been supplied on the same form) or fraudulently (for example when a form has previously been reported as lost).

If the request has been fulfilled successfully the item is sent out from our dispatch department. At this point the barcode on the attached request form is wanded again. The Despatch System uses this information to update the relevant record on the Master file and update the billing systems. If for some reason the request has not been satisfied the form is wanded into the Replies System. The operator allocates one of a number of standard coded replies (e.g. NOT means 'We do not hold this title') and the system updates the record. The Replies System then sends this information to the customer in a variety of ways. For customers who prefer their replies by post the system prints Request Status Report statements daily. Others prefer to access the information online or by e-mail through the Replies Intray. As well as receiving coded replies in their Intray, customers can opt to receive Shipped Messages (*see above*).

The fourth main part of the ARM system is called View Request. This is used internally in BLDSC to view information relating to each request that has been processed during the previous year. It is particularly useful to customer services staff when answering queries from customers relating to specific requests. Future plans for the ARM system involve extending it to a fully fledged circulation control system.

# INSIDE – an integrated searching, ordering and delivery service

**Richard Roman, with a technical note by Lynne Chivers**

The British Library Document Supply Centre (BLDSC) is located at Boston Spa near Wetherby in Yorkshire and has been operational for over 30 years. Recognising the need for a centre of excellence for collecting and making available the world's research material, the government of the day decided that such a centre should be established with plenty of physical space to grow and develop as the collections themselves developed.

Today, the BLDSC makes a major contribution to research throughout the world. It supplies material to more than 19,000 customers who in turn serve millions of individual researchers with information to meet their specific research requirements. Nearly four million requests are sent to the BLDSC every year from customers around the world: some three million from the UK and one million from abroad. Customers range from major academic institutions and international corporations to small commercial firms.

The breadth and depth of the collection have been central to the success of the BLDSC. The main criterion for acquisition is that items are likely to be requested by customers in higher education, research, business and industry. Serials are collected irrespective of subject and language. English-language books are acquired, wherever published, while foreign-language books are bought on a selective basis. Other categories taken are British official publications, European Community material, unrestricted report literature, theses, conference proceedings, oriental material, translations into English and music scores. Table 1 shows the BLDSC's annual intake and total holdings.

TABLE 1. HOLDINGS AT THE BLDSC

|  | HOLDINGS | ANNUAL INTAKE |
|---|---|---|
| JOURNALS (SERIALS) | 247,000 | 47,000 |
| BOOKS (MONOGRAPHS) | 2,998,000 | 41,852 |
| REPORTS IN MICROFORM | 3,850,000 | 110,000 |
| OTHER REPORTS | 500,000 | 25,000 |
| US DOCTORAL THESES | 451,000 | 6000 |
| UK DOCTORAL THESES | 112,000 | 6000 |
| CONFERENCE PROCEEDINGS | 335,000 | 16,000 |
| TRANSLATIONS | 557,000 | 9000 |
| LOCAL AUTHORITY MATERIAL | 28,000 | OVER 1000 |
| MUSIC | 129,000 | 3500 |
| CYRILLIC SCIENCE AND TECHNOLOGY BOOKS | 220,000 | OVER 1000 |
| ROLL MICROFORM | OVER 1700 MILES | |
| MICROFICHE | 300,000 | |

In an increasingly technological age one of the major questions asked within The British Library is 'How can this unparalleled collection be made more easily available and readily accessible?'

Nobody knows precisely where information technology will lead us over the next few years. The development and astonishing growth of the Internet and of companies involved in multimedia products suggest that the traditional publishing and information dissemination models are no longer appropriate. It is for this reason that The British Library has decided to take a step-by-step approach. As new forms of disseminating knowledge become available, The British Library will harness evolving technologies and develop appropriate systems and means of communication.

A number of separate initiatives have been undertaken of which the *Inside* service is one important thread. *Inside* is both a concept and the name of a product. The concept is remote digital access to the collections of The British Library. The product is a specific service which links electronic searching of The British Library's holdings with a direct order facility and a choice of delivery options. Searching The British Library's holdings can be conducted from one's own desktop computer from anywhere in the world at the touch of a button.

## The database

The 20,000 most requested journals from the BLDSC are catalogued down to article title level and put onto a database. A variety of other information is also captured including the journal title, the ISSN, the authors (up to 10 authors for any one article), the publisher and the date of publication. Individual papers in the 16,000 conferences that are collected by the BLDSC each year have also been added to the database which is updated daily. It takes no more than 72 hours for a journal to be fully indexed and available on the database from the time that it is first received in the Library.

The database is notable both for the range of topics included and for its international coverage. One unique feature is that coverage is based on customer demand. Thus, it is highly responsive to developments and changes amongst the world's researchers.

The strength of the database is one of the key aspects of the *Inside* service. Each month the database increases by some 200,000 new articles and 13,000 conference papers. However, this is seen only as a first stage. Consideration is being given to how it can best be further enhanced and enlarged. This will develop in two ways; first by discussion and consultation with researchers with special interest groups such as the pharmaceutical and medical industries and second, because The British Library has a responsibility to the wider community, by considering developments for the common good.

## The searching facilities

Three different methods of accessing the database are being developed. A number of CD-ROM products are already available, and an online Windows and a Web version are currently being tested for launching in 1997.

April 1996 saw the successful launch of two new CD-ROM products; *Inside*

*Science Plus* and *Inside Social Sciences and Humanities Plus*. These two CD-ROMs are published monthly and include data from the previous six months. The ordering and delivery options (see below) are fully developed .

The CD-ROMs have been developed in co-operation with the commercial company RTIS over a number of years and include a number of valuable features which enable the librarian or information manager to regulate use. Not the least of these is the ability to flag up an institution's own library holdings so that a particular article can be ordered from one's own library rather than from the BLDSC. Another valuable development is the ability to make notes against any particular article. These can be shown whenever the reference is called up. For example, it may be noted that a colleague already has the article and there is no need to re-order it.

The development of both online access via a Windows interface and via the World Wide Web access is progressing well. Beta trials were conducted with several major national and international companies and academic institutions throughout autumn 1996. These technical trials tested installation, functionality and the general robustness of the systems in preparation for the UK launch.

*Inside on-line* will build on the successes of the existing services by adding to the 20,000 current journals access to the 16,000 conferences. The British Library is working closely with software specialists Dataware Technologies to design the user-friendly Windows system.

The *Inside on-line* interface uses drag and drop functions to move the user through the various stages of searching, ordering and delivery. These options are represented on-screen by in-tray, pending and out-tray features. The office metaphor is maintained throughout with the use of on-screen notepads, folders and lists. Traditional Boolean searching has been hidden by the use of icons, which give a simple visual representation of the relevance of citations. This allows the information specialist to construct complex searches and the non-specialist to develop search techniques quickly.

### Ordering facilities

Essential prerequisites for the success of *Inside* are guaranteed availability of requested documents and their rapid delivery. All documents included in the database that have been received by the BLDSC during the previous six months are available only as photocopies. No loans are allowed so that it can be guaranteed that the item requested will be in stock and can be delivered promptly.

A dedicated team is being established to process all requests within guaranteed time-scales. These include two hour fax back; 12 hour fax back; overnight post and courier. Discussions are also well advanced with major publishers to allow electronic delivery.

Document delivery charges include payment of a service charge and of a copyright fee. All costs will be shown before the customer purchases the document so that a close watch on expenditure can be maintained. As noted above, *Inside* offers a local management facility. An appointed local manager can authorise all use of the system through the allocation of passwords and can maintain control over budgets. For example, a large commercial concern may wish to give each researcher his or her own budget whilst an academic institution may wish to limit the ordering facilities to the librarian and only allow students to search the database. All this is possible at the local level.

### The future

Future plans for *Inside* are to continue to develop the holdings database to make as much of The British Library's collections available as possible, and to provide specialist information services to particular professions, areas of study and research interests.

The move to electronic delivery of documents wherever possible is also progressing rapidly. Tests have been run in developing a virtual library and discussions are being held with a number of potential partners to add further value to ensure that The British Library continues to be at the forefront of world-wide dissemination of knowledge.

RR

### Trial Electronic Data Store of journals – TEDS

The article above mentioned the possibility of electronic delivery of journal articles to BLDSC's customers around the world. Building on the idea of scanning and faxing documents, BLDSC are considering introducing a process whereby images of regularly requested journal articles would be held within an electronic document database. The electronic versions, together with bibliographic data, would be supplied by the publishers and the database would be an optional source of articles for copyright fee paid requests received by ARP (the Automated Request Processing system). Where allowed by publishers, library privilege requests could also be filled using TEDS as a source.

A feasibility study involving a trial system is being conducted (see outline diagram below), for which a number of publishers have agreed to supply journals in electronic format.

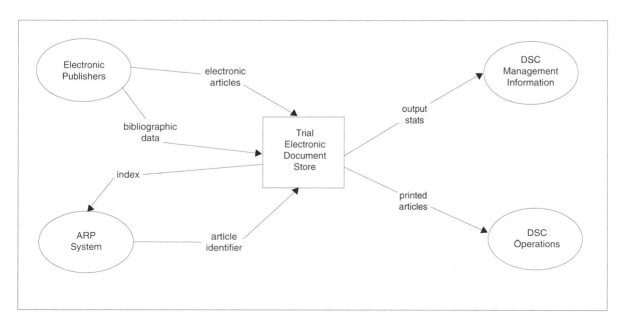

The trial electronic document store, known as TEDS, builds up an index to documents based on the bibliographic data supplied by publishers. Copies of the articles held either in TIFF image or Acrobat PDF format are either stored directly in the database, or a reference to the article in a remote document store is recorded. A copy of the TEDS index is passed to the ARP system to be added to the Automatch index.

When a request for an article is received by ARP, the Automatch software identifies the article as being held in TEDS and passes the identifier of the article to TEDS. The TEDS software then retrieves the article's image files either from its own database or, if appropriate, from a remote database via the Internet, and prints out the article.

A monthly report is produced for BLDSC's Management Information Team listing which requests have been satisfied via TEDS to enable auditing of electronic document supply.

It is expected that the service provided to customers via TEDS will be more efficient and provide a higher-quality product than the traditional photocopy service. Depending on the outcome of the feasibility study, a full-scale system will be built and may be linked to automated electronic document delivery.

LC

# Developing the digital library

**Brian Lang**

The British Library's international reputation is based on its unparalleled collection of books, manuscripts and other printed publications. The Library is committed to providing direct access to those primary sources in its reading rooms, and to continuing to improve the standard of its reading room services. It is also committed to the steady enhancement of its collection of printed books and manuscripts by purchase and acquisition by other means. The Library must also, however, in order to fulfil its role as the national library of the United Kingdom, develop adequate collections of publications in digital and other non-print media. It must also be capable of providing services based on such new publication technology.

As digital publications are appearing in increasing volume, a major aim of The British Library's *Initiatives for Access* programme has been to gain greater experience of the new technologies involved in providing digital services.

The learning process took us beyond strictly IT matters. The likely impact on the organisation as well as the implications for the human and financial resources which will be needed to translate pilot projects and demonstrators into sustainable services have also been studied, as have the rewards and challenges of working in partnership with external organisations and suppliers. This book has given an account of the projects, setting out our experiences in a way which we trust will be useful to others involved in library technology, digital publishing, and the provision and management of digital services and resources. In this concluding chapter, I will describe how The British Library is moving ahead in its digital library development activities, drawing on the lessons learnt from the *Initiatives for Access* programme.

### What is the digital library?

The digital library is the widely accepted term describing the use of digital technologies to acquire, store, preserve and provide access to information and material originally published in digital form or digitised from existing print, audio-visual and other forms. The goal of the digital library is to improve, for all our users, access to The British Library's collection however it might develop in the future. The digital library will involve a number of partner organisations who will contribute expertise and resources to the project.

The digital library will be more than a programme for delivering services to our remote users. While it is true that we will be able to provide such users with a new range of services, we also wish to enable our reading room users, in the new St Pancras building and in our other reading rooms, to have full access to the complete range of materials in the Library's collection, digital or otherwise.

The digital library will also provide us with benefits in terms of the conservation and preservation of our collection – particularly items which are fragile, of high value, or are heavily used – through the use of digital surrogates. It is significant, however, that this approach will help us move towards one of our major strategic objectives – the realisation of a single collection, whether acquired through legal deposit or purchase and whether stored at Boston Spa or in London. Finally, it will provide us with the technical means to accommodate material added to our collection through the extension of the statutory deposit legislation to non-print materials.

The digital library is therefore an integral part of the Library's overall vision of the way it will in future fulfil its responsibilities as the national library of the United Kingdom. As I wrote in the Foreword to The British Library's Information Systems Strategy:

'We do not envisage an exclusively digital library. We are aware that some people feel that digital materials will predominate in libraries of the future. Others anticipate that the impact will be slight. In the context of The British Library, printed books, manuscripts, music, sound recordings and all the other existing materials in the collection will always retain their central importance, and we are committed to continuing to provide, and to improve, access to these in our reading rooms. The importance of digital materials will, however, increase.'

By the year 2000, we expect that The British Library will be an international centre of expertise in the use of digital materials as well as a major component within a global digital library. We will simultaneously provide access to a wide range of electronic materials produced outside the Library and make the Library's collections and catalogues available in electronic form.

Key elements of a digital library, which we hope will be in place by the year 2000, are:

– the collection of a wide variety of materials in digital form, either through purchase, licence agreements or by legal deposit;
– the provision of information about the Library's services and collections to remote users over electronic networks;
– access to British Library electronic services by remote users and access to remote sources by British Library readers and staff through integrated gateway services;
– commercial services which are able to provide electronic surrogates, whether text, images or sound, of items in the Library's collection;
– a variety of electronic publications in a number of media, published particularly over networks and on CD-ROM, which will exploit the potential of imaging and other technologies to provide new means of exploring and accessing items in the Library's collection;
– integrated access in the Reading Rooms to a wide range of electronic products in a variety of media (via networks, on CD-ROM, etc.) of research value;
– networking and imaging technologies to support and enhance all aspects of the Library's basic operational services;
– networking and imaging technologies to facilitate closer co-operation with other bodies;

– expertise within the Library for the application of new technologies to library activities and bibliographical research of all kinds.

### Three critical principles and the Library's digital collection

The Library considers there to be three principles guiding its digital library developments:

#### *The digital collection may be created and produced in a variety of different places, but will be accessible as if it were a single entity.*

In the new digital library world, two new tenets will be central – that a library's digital 'collection' will comprise material from a variety of sources, and that the user must be presented with an homogeneous view of those disparate sources. The sources of the digital collection will comprise material digitised from the library's analogue originals; digital materials added to the collection through purchase – primarily in CD-ROM form; and material to which access rights have been acquired, but which reside on systems outside the direct control of the library and which are accessed via global networks. A major service aim for the library must be that the user is presented with a view of this varied collection as if it were a single entity.

#### *The digital collection will be organised/categorised/indexed for easier access than is possible from its original point of production.*

Fundamental to the use of any collection is the catalogue. New digital materials will pose new questions to the cataloguing community. The cataloguing of a 'physical' digital item – e.g. a CD-ROM – presents relatively few difficulties when compared to the challenges presented by the identification and recording of the new kinds of digital publications possible today and which will become commonplace tomorrow. The successful resolution of these problems will be essential if we are to be able to guide the user through the distributed digital library collection.

#### *The digital collection will be stored and maintained in such a way as to ensure that it will continue to be available long after the period of its immediate currency.*

A research library needs to retain material so as to provide future researchers with a rich corpus of source material. The British Library has the added responsibility of preserving the national published archive. The archival retention of digital materials presents complex problems, mainly because of the often symbiotic relationship between the data and the hardware/software system that provides access to it.

Our digital collection will be built from a number of sources: the digitisation of some of our existing collection materials; the acquisition of published digital materials through purchase and other means; and, the legal deposit of digital materials published in the UK.

Partly through the *Initiatives for Access* programme, we have accumulated a digital store of many gigabytes, including the Electronic Beowulf; some of the

Library's Treasures (including the Magna Carta, the Sforza Hours, and the Leonardo Notebook); part of the Burney collection of newspapers; part of our photographic collections (including Indian Miniatures and Canadiana); the Gandhari fragments and Dunhuang manuscripts. While a consistent selection policy will need to be developed, a significant digital store has nevertheless been brought together.

The Library already has a large collection of CD-ROMs, purchased by various Library departments. The Library also has one of the world's largest collections of patents in digital form. Held on CD-ROMs, it is anticipated that by the year 2000 all patents published throughout the world will be in digital form only. Finally, the National Sound Archive (NSA) has an enormous collection of audio CDs and digitised surrogates of older material. In addition, new methods of access based on licence agreements with rights holders will be pursued whereby access is to a remote electronic store maintained by the rights holder. This will provide economic and IT benefits to the Library in terms of access to online electronic journals which may be continually updated.

The Library has made a case to government for the extension of statutory deposit to digital UK publications. The proposal applies initially to CD-ROMs, and a demonstrator project was established in order to model and test the entire procedure from receipt to user access. The cataloguing aspect of the CD Demonstrator Project is reported here in the case study by Sandie Beaney and her colleagues.

### Digital library developments and the UK government's Private Finance Initiative

The British Library is a non-departmental government body, funded mainly through grant-in-aid from the Department of National Heritage. At present, the level of grant-in-aid is around £85 million per year, but the Library generates an additional £35 million per year comprising revenue from its priced services, sponsorship, and from other funding bodies such as the European Commission's Library Plan. For the future of digital library development, two factors are significant: first, demand for our current services based on print materials is increasing; secondly, it is very unlikely that grant-in-aid will be increased to pay for the digital library developments. How then will we fund the considerable investments in IT infrastructure and systems, marketing and customer support, and acquisition of rights to digital materials?

The major expenditure will be in the development of the digital library systems – the IT infrastructure which will be required – and the provision of marketing and user support. The Library will be seeking the necessary investment through the UK government's Private Finance Initiative.

The Private Finance Initiative (PFI) was launched by the UK government in 1992 as a new method of public sector procurement. PFI is based on the principles of allowing both private and public sectors to concentrate on doing what they are likely to do best. Thus, the public sector acts as an enabler and guardian of public services which are provided by private sector management, creativity and capital investment.

In essence, PFI allows public sector organisations to make use of private sector expertise and resources in providing public services. It provides for a new business relationship between public and private sectors, based on common goals of improvement of the quality of public services, and best value for taxpayers' money. The private sector is enabled to invest in products and/or services that will earn it an attractive return and which will also benefit the public interest. Value for money is achieved primarily through the optimum transfer of risk to the private sector.

There are several different kinds of PFI partnership. These include:

- Financially free-standing projects, where a private sector organisation undertakes the project on the basis that costs will be recovered entirely through charges to the final user.
- Services sold to the public sector, where the cost of the project is met wholly or mainly by charges from the private sector service provider to the public sector body which let the contract.
- 'Joint Venture' projects, where the cost of the project is met partly from public funds and partly from other sources of income, with overall control of the project resting with the private sector.

In October 1995, the Library selected Andersen Consulting, through competitive tender, to undertake a study on partnership options for the digital library. Andersen Consulting were asked to produce recommendations on how the Library should maximise revenue-earning and investment opportunities through PFI to achieve its strategic and business objectives for the digital library.

To be successful, any PFI arrangement made by the Library will have to:

- create an environment in which the private sector can find profitable opportunities which do not compromise the Library's objectives;
- provide value for money for the UK Treasury, especially through the transfer of risk to the private sector partner.

The first essential steps in a PFI procurement are to advertise the public sector requirement and invite bids. Bids are evaluated and shortlisted according to how they match the requirements. Negotiations are then entered into with the shortlisted bidders until a best and final offer is received. Contract negotiations then take place. The Digital Library PFI project is taking an additional initial step through a 'market sounding' exercise. The market-sounding process will invite discussion with interested private sector organisations prior to the issuing of the full Invitation to Tender. This is because the digital library requirements are sufficiently complex that the Library needs to test the market in order to obtain a more informed view of what the private sector will be interested in and who the major players are likely to be.

This process results in the following indicative timetable:

- Informal Discussions with interested parties, and definition of the Invitation to Tender document – up to six months;
- Issue of formal Invitation to Tender and negotiations with prospective partners – nine to twelve months;
- Development of new services – six to nine months;

- Launch of new services – two months.

The overall timescale is between two years and 30 months.

We do not know as yet what the Digital Library PFI partnership will look like. This depends partly on the responses received during the market-sounding phase but also because, in PFI procurement terms, we cannot specify a solution – we can only give our requirements.

However, the Library has looked at possible partnership attributes. It is likely that we shall be dealing with a consortium of companies which together can provide the various kinds of resource – IT, marketing, financial, etc. – we need. This consortium would require a revenue stream to offset its investment, and so they might be interested in document supply and patent delivery services. The Library might in turn expect them to market those services to new sectoral or geographic markets, such as North America and the Pacific Rim.

We would also expect that the consortium might bring in other partners to develop other aspects of the digital library, for example a multimedia publisher wishing to license items in the Library's collection for a series of CD-ROMs.

## The British Library's Digital Library Programme

The Digital Library Programme consists of three main strands: the Digital Library PFI Development Project, the Demonstrator Project for processes resulting from the extension to legal deposit to non-print publications, and the Digital Datastore Development Project.

Considerable resources will be needed for the Library to achieve its digital library goals. The resources required are unlikely to be forthcoming from government in the form of additional grant-in-aid, and cannot be reallocated from other Library activities. The strategy has therefore been to fund development through partnership and collaboration. In particular, we need to involve the private sector to provide IT solutions and other technical expertise. In order to obtain this partnership, the Library is considering the PFI and the Digital Library PFI Development Project is managing the appropriate procedures.

The legal deposit Demonstrator Project will shadow the entire process to which a digital item would be subject if it were to be deposited with the Library. One aim is to demonstrate to the Department of National Heritage that the Library will be capable of handling and exploiting non-print publications. Its supplementary aims and objectives include:

- development of in-house expertise in processing non-print materials received through legal deposit;
- encouragement to operational directorates to streamline the processing of non-print materials;
- feedback from staff and users;
- specification of the technical requirements, staffing and costs of a full-scale system.

The Digital Datastore Development (3D) Project is an attempt to define the Library's business and technical requirements for the use of digital data. A substantial amount of work on the former was carried out by Library staff in the second half of 1995. The 3D Project has the following aims:

- To supply the Digital Library PFI Development Project with sufficient information about the Library's business and technical requirements to enable it to produce a comprehensive specification.
- To ensure that the existing digital material within the Library's collections continues to be maintained, preserved and made available for use.
- To provide a suitable corporate framework for the continuing development of digital library activity at a directorate level which will accord with the Library's strategic developments.
- To consolidate and develop the technical expertise already present in the Library to ensure that it maintains its position as a major player in the national and international library and information world, a number of initiatives for the use of digital material are under way or planned. Some, such as those for document supply or services for visitors and readers, have emerged in business plans. Others are coming forward as opportunities reveal themselves, either through the exploitation of data created under the *Initiatives for Access* programme, or as a greater understanding of the potential of the technology permeates the organisation and potential partner institutions.

The *Initiatives for Access* programme was established to help The British Library gain greater experience in the new technologies which libraries will use to offer their users services based on digital information. The driving forces of the increase of digital information and the ubiquity of the Internet are leading libraries, particularly research libraries, to develop and make greater use of the digital library concept. The challenges are substantial, not least the search for funds to develop and implement the new activities and services. If libraries succeed, then their contributions to the national research effort, scholarly endeavour and economic competitiveness will be greatly enhanced. The goal of the Digital Library Programme is much too important for failure even to be considered. The question is not whether the digital library should be developed, but how.

# Afterword: Places and spaces

**Lorcan Dempsey**

*Yet there is nothing more provincial or more transient than the up-to-the-minute vision. Never did a people more need the book.*

DANIEL BOORSTIN

*What characterises the new system of communications, based in the digitised, networked integration of multiple communications modes is its inclusiveness and comprehensiveness of all cultural expressions. Because of its existence, all kinds of messages in the new type of society work in a binary mode: presence/absence in the multimedia communication system. Only presence in this integrated system permits communicability and socialisation of the message. All other messages are reduced to individual imagination or to increasingly marginalised face-to-face subcultures. From society's perspective, electronically-based communication (typographic, audiovisual, or computer-mediated) is communication. ... But the price to pay for inclusion in the system is to adapt to its logic, to its language, to its points of entry, to its encoding and decoding.*

MANUEL CASTELLS

*People should think not so much of the books that have gone into the National Library but rather of the books that have come out of it. A library, after all, feeds the people that go in there.*

SEÁN O'FAOLÁIN

*Technology ... expels from movements all hesitation, deliberation, civility ... Not least to blame for the withering of experience is the fact that things, under the law of pure functionality, assume a form that limits contact with them to mere operation, and tolerates no surplus either in freedom of conduct, or in autonomy of things, which would survive as the core of experience, because it is not consumed by the moment of action.*

THEODORE WIESENGRUND ADORNO

Early in this collection, Mike Alexander and Andrew Prescott mention the consternation at the introduction of electric lighting into the Reading Room of the British Museum. If electric light was a Trojan Horse, then enemy troops have been pouring from it ever since, and at no time in more numbers than at the present. Today, electric light has been joined by optic fibre and innovation touches not only the environment of the library, but what is at the core of its identity and purpose: the accumulation, preservation and communication of knowledge, imagination and learning.

It may seem glib to suggest that the library should be medium-neutral. It is glib because the book (and other documents) is so much a part of life and thought, because its form and shape make it so well adapted to the reading and living habits of its users, because the curatorial traditions of libraries are so bound up with the book as object. It is glib also because of the truth of what Boorstin asserts in his first sentence above and the shallowness of our alternative visions. We are in the middle of poorly understood change for which we have few real guides. Much discussion about the future is conducted in terms of high-level summary labels which have little explanatory power. We have little in the way of usable electronic libraries or, indeed, much sense of what shape they will take or how they will mesh with the interests of their users.

Yet, for all our difficulty in taking a long perspective, we know a glass network spans the globe which is putting in place the material base for new ways of working, communicating and learning. This glass network is creating the first global information economy, 'an economy with a capacity to work as a unit in real time on a planetary scale'. Commercial and research activity is increasingly carried out in global digital spaces, and any organisation that wishes to operate as a significant provider of business intelligence or research resources must be visible in those digital spaces. Not to be there will be to be marginalised. To be marginalised means that potential users are deprived of valuable resources, and that books, journals and other resources are kept from their readers. It means, to pursue O'Faoláin's analogy, that the library fails to nourish and is less than it should be.

As the library continues to organise the assembly places where readers are brought into fruitful contact with resources that inspire and inform, it must become a service organised around physical places and digital information spaces. It must be alert to the various needs of the materials it handles, to the various interests of its current and future users, and to the various wider contexts of change. The British Library provides access to the national intellectual record; it is uniquely placed to show how the intellectual record, deeply and richly organised, can enrich emerging digital spaces and the lives of the people who assemble there.

## Place – the library as building and collection

For most readers the library is a place, a building, and the collection it houses. The quotation from Boorstin comes from an essay accompanying a book of photographs, of libraries of all types and sizes, which I acquired at the same time as I began writing this piece. The photographs are by Diane Asseo Griliches and the book seems to come most alive in the pictures of the great reading rooms: the Library of Congress, the Bibliothèque Sainte-Geneviève, and the Bibliothèque Nationale. (Surprisingly, the electrically lighted Reading Room of the British Museum is not pictured here.)

These put the reader at the centre of a great vault, beyond which it is easy to believe that the world's knowledge is arrayed ready to be called up as if waiting for that one moment of use. They are personal because each reader has a private space, manifest in the pool of light thrown by the desk lamp, and intimate because each reader is in a private relationship with the collection and builds their own world upon it. However, they are also social: they are visibly great knowledge exchanges, each an inclusive 'hive-like dome', which support social flow and assembly. And they are monumental in that they seemed to collect for all time and for all places, making them timeless and apart. Libraries are unlike museums or theatres; their role is not spectacular. The private, intimate relationship of the reader with the library collection and the experiences it engenders makes it easier for the library to enter the fabric of people's lives. This is not only true of large national or research libraries – but of all types of libraries. And much of the power of great libraries arises where this relationship is enhanced by places which arbitrate in right measure the personal and the social, the intimate and the monumental.

The catalogue has a special place. Much of the collection is hidden: it exists as potential. Discovery in the catalogue makes it actual. The catalogue acts as a surrogate for the collection, and, for the dedicated library user, searching the catalogue is continuous with the wider accumulation of knowledge. It suggests the size of the collection, the mass that still needs to be prospected. The traces of its creators can be seen in the styles, over time, of the individual entries. Griliches includes a photograph of a card catalogue from Boston Public Library and describes it in personal terms 'This solid, well-used wooden veteran has a personal attraction and a kind of lasting beauty that a computer can never have. I wanted to make its portrait before it disappears.' A portrait comes from a dialogue with a life: the catalogue has a life that is bound up with the lives of previous users and those that have created it. She includes a caption from Barbara Tuchman: 'For me the card catalogue has been a companion all my working life. To leave it is like leaving the house one was brought up in.' And so, it is not difficult to understand how for many people, automation of the catalogue represents, in a real way, a 'withering of experience' as described by Adorno.

This is especially so as it is seen as a prelude to further change, which not only signals a changing relationship to particular physical places, but the disappearance of the craft, the tacit knowledge, which is a part of their use, and a part of the use of the collections they house. Put this way, developments are part of a larger reordering of experience.

It is interesting to counterpose the quotes from Adorno and Castells. Castells talks proleptically of the digital media's 'inclusiveness and comprehensiveness of all cultural expressions'. Castells is discussing an environment one of whose characteristics is to be at the end of the trajectory Adorno describes: an 'informationalised' society, in which business, cultural and personal activities are mediated by the network, in which technology acts on information to achieve ends. Doors open automatically; chips control household appliances; money is disappearing; shops dispose product lines around their floors based on sales information. We resist the full reach of what Castells proposes even as we recognise the trend.

However, it leads to disjointedness at several levels: the transitions between the library as place and the library as digital information space, between the collection of codices and the hypertext scroll, are jerky. The short timescale of

*Initiatives for Access* has coincided with significant change: it was a period which saw the rapid penetration of the Internet and the emergence of the Web. It is difficult to take a long perspective; such a reordering of experience will take time to work through and we cannot now discern the outcomes. We may not yet have a sense of digital reading rooms shaped to the measure of working and learning – their domes, alleys and cells of knowledge – but it is important that this work has begun.

## Change

Castells distinguishes between the *space of places* and the *space of flows* made possible, but not caused, by the network. In the space of flows, flows of information transform relationships, and allow a general reshaping of organisations, work and behaviour according to a networking logic, a logic based on addition at the edges, decentralisation, horizontal integration around process. He suggests that there is at once a global integration facilitated by the network, but, at the same time, a fragmentation between those connected and those not connected.

One can base a reductive description of the changes facing libraries on this distinction. Think of repositories of knowledge and the flows between them and their users. Libraries currently organise repositories in the space of places, large stores of physical items, around which patterns and practices of management and use have developed. They still largely manage 'atoms', individual physical items which need to be created, packaged, transported, distributed, fetched; items which have mass and have to be massively duplicated. Flows are limited, and constrained by place and time and mass. There is shallow resource sharing: the flow of materials between libraries is marginal to overall activity. There is limited entry into the space of flows, which is about 'bits', about the 'global movement of weightless bits at the speed of light', about, in fact, *being digital*.

Take a simple example: a project group wishes to discover journal articles and books about Roman Bath. In a well-stocked library, they can scan the shelves. Say they want to do a more thorough 'discovery' of material. They can look in the catalogue. They can look in databases on CD-ROM. They might have access to some remote databases over the Internet. But each of these is delivered through a separate interface, they may have to move between machines, they may have to print out or write down results. Once they have discovered a selection of materials, they have to find out where they are. Typically, they will have to return to the catalogue and redo searches for the desired items. Say they are in a library which has an arrangement for reciprocal borrowing with several neighbouring libraries. They will have to redo searches for unfound items in those libraries. They might bring other items to the Inter-library Loan (ILL) department, where they may have to write down the details again. Then the ILL staff may repeat some of the operations already carried out by the users, to verify and to locate items. Requests may then be sent to The British Library for materials. Bibliographic details may be re-keyed for transmission.

What happens is that there are a variety of boundaries – between functions, between users and library – which are not interconnected by systems, and across which there are intermittent and inefficient flows. In fact, the flows are achieved by human effort: multiple human visits to different systems and multiple transcriptions which waste time and impose barriers to full use.

Although extensively automated, the library focus, as in other sectors, has tended to be of particular place-based tasks, catalogue and circulation, or of flows within hierarchical non-interconnected circuits, ILL and cataloguing for example. There is limited flow of data between processes and consequently limited reorganisation of activities. Existing library places are vertically integrated; although they now use networks extensively, the logic of their organisation is place-based: the management of multiple individual physical repositories.

In digital information spaces, there will continue to be repositories of information but the emphasis shifts to the flows between them and between them and their users. These repositories may contain metadata – catalogues and other data which assists in the discovery, use and exploitation of resources – or resources themselves. In this environment, the activities of discovery, locate, request, deliver, currently carried out in multiple incompatible circuits need to be brought into a common framework of communicating applications.

The British Library offers record, document and reference services into the space of flows. Indeed, the Document Supply Centre has been organised around the space of flows of an earlier network system, the mail. *Initiatives for Access* has begun the process of further integrating scholarly British Library resources, so that the user of the future will be able to reach deep into collections of books, maps, sound, and other resources.

### Space – the library as a manager of digital information spaces

What has to be done to make access to the intellectual record within an achieved digital information space if not a complete reality, then something more than the very preliminary and partial experience it now is? We need to manage repositories, flows and control, and we need to bring these together in viable digital environments, supporting hospitable 'information landscapes'. Information landscape is a useful term in that it highlights the need to consider a wide range of resources and services within a common frame of reference. A piecemeal approach will fail to deliver the benefits.

*The management of repositories.*  We have little experience of managing large-scale mixed media digital repositories in open networked environments. Repositories will be based on digital surrogates of existing resources and on material published in digital form. They will contain a variety of resource types with different characteristics and requirements – engineering models, geospatial data, sound, image collections, manuscripts. Resources will have to be identified within one of the emerging naming schemes; support for version control, copyright management, and transparent content negotiation will have to be in place. Materials will be differently encoded. The paper journal article is atomic – its content is only available to the human reader. It can be converted to bits by being scanned – this will allow it to be exchanged more easily, but its content is still only available to the human reader, it is 'atomic' to the program which transfers or displays it. Structure could be added, and applications built which understood more of its content, and exploit the semantic information the tagging conveys. Structure allows applications to do smart things with it. It can be indexed and searched on particular tags, selectively output to various media, and is amenable to a wider range of processing, coming more alive within the space of flows. Metadata to support discovery, but also preservation, copyright management, client access, and commercial activities will have to be created and managed. Appropriate metadata will have to be exported into resource discovery systems, initially local catalogue repositories, but beyond that into emerging distributed discovery services. Effective disclosure of resources will be key, and integral with effective disclosure will be data to support use, re-use and exploitation. The British Library and other large research institutions contain materials managed within practices from various curatorial traditions: archives, maps, books, patents, and so on, which will have to be managed and accessed within a common framework. Most metadata currently exists at the item level: metadata at collection level and other levels of aggregation and granularity will also have to be provided to facilitate effective high-level navigation of collections, and for those collections where item-level description is uneconomic or impracticable. The content of repositories will have to continue to be available to human users long after the technical apparatus of its creation and publication have been superseded.

*The management of flows.* Flows consist of resources themselves, but also the service requests and messages that support distributed services. Searches against databases, result sets, item requests and orders; billing, charging or authorisation data; and others: these will flow between applications and repositories. A protocol framework for managing these flows is being put in place. This includes protocols for search and retrieve, for service and document request, for ordering and payment, for authentication and authorisation, for delivery and subsequent collation and re-use.

*The management of control.* Technologies for supporting market mechanisms are immature. Open distributed control in the digital information space is still a research and development challenge, which will require generic business and technical solutions. Clients need to be able to prove who they are when challenged. The usefulness of an information landscape will be severely reduced without distributed authentication services which mean that the client need only 'prove' themselves once. Multiple challenges (passwords) erect fences in the landscape which inhibit use. Authorisation information – what services does the client have access rights to – needs to be exchanged. The integrity and privacy of exchanged data, involving the use of encryption and other services, may be an issue. Together with services for billing, paying and copyright management these will be required to support a market for information products and services; they will provide the controls that allow charged-for resources to release their value into information landscapes effectively.

*Bringing it all together – the information landscape.*   The challenge is significant and intriguing: to present the user with services organised around their information uses and natural ways of working and not around the constraints of location, mechanics of interaction, or medium. In time, it must be possible to search, locate, deliver, collate, and create in productive ways, unconstrained by the clumsy, mechanical apparatuses that currently hinder operations. We are only beginning to imagine what such landscapes might be like in practice and putting in place the infrastructure necessary to support them. The landscape will support navigation of collections and services, it will hide the user from the variety of underlying protocols or mechanisms, it will consolidate and negotiate. It is here that access to place and digital space will be brought together. A reader may request an item to be delivered: the system will decide whether this needs an HTTP get, an ILL request, or a note saying to go to the reference collection. A user wishes to discover whether items are available: the system will present some options for searching, will open up a Z39.50 connection, or a Web browser, or whatever is required. And so on …The World Wide Web provides a premonition of what such a landscape might be, but it is shallow. A layer of software, or middleware, which hides underlying difference and which allows the transparent addition of services and resources will provide the basis for the landscape. It will be based on metadata and protocol support, incorporating an increasingly deeper semantic understanding of resources themselves. In future, the structure put in place to support the landscape will support the operation of agents, which relieve the user of routine and repetitive tasks, and visualisation techniques, and other access technologies. It will be defined in terms of logical user services (e.g. reference services, current awareness, document requesting, and so on), and, ideally, will be independent of the underlying physical implementation of those services (e.g. CDs, Web indexes, catalogues, text repositories, etc.). The importance of a standards-based approach is clear. The British Library may create a landscape for its users. But other libraries, large firms, universities and other organisations will similarly be creating landscapes for other, overlapping, constituencies: they will want to easily incorporate British Library services alongside others.

*Initiatives for Access* has been exploring the creation and management of repositories and the management of flows. The Digital Library Programme is well-placed to make a significant contribution to our understanding of these issues in real world services.

## Conclusion

The focus of this book has been on the necessary first steps in the construction of a viable digital environment. At the same time, The British Library has been involved in the construction of one of the most significant library 'places' the world will have seen, a building in which the main objective is to 'create an easy commerce between the lone scholar and the huge building mass required to house the collections, all the fellow (rival?) researchers and the general public …'. It is an enterprise emphatically set against the 'withering of experience': the architect, Colin St John Wilson, discusses scale, how to accommodate the demands for personal space with flow, of daylight as a source of ambient light, and closes by describing the 'difficult to define "body language" that responds to the invitation to touch (the travertine barrier, the leather handrail, the oak-ribbed carapace of the column) …'. He hopes that the arrival in nearby St Pancras of the Channel Tunnel Rail Link will make the courtyard a social assembly place, the clock tower a rendezvous point. St John Wilson acknowledges the influence of Alvar Aalto – himself a creator of libraries – and endorses Aalto's view that a building should be judged not on the day of its opening but after 30 years of use.

The next 30 years, a generation, will say much about the ability of The British Library to act as a central social and learning place in the heart of a great world city. It will also say much about its ability to organise a social and learning space within the emerging global space of flows.

Brian Lang describes the ambitious aims of the Digital Library Programme, which will build on the results discussed here. Boorstin says that 'And yet, all this may make us the first generation qualified to grasp so poignantly the wonderful, the uncanny, the mystic simplicity of the book'. One senses from the essays collected here that Michael Alexander, Andrew Prescott and their colleagues understand the pressure of these words, that their enterprise is motivated by a wish that the Library remains true to its mission and that readers and collections will benefit by being brought together. We can be confident that they will work towards the construction of an assembly place which will be rich in experience, and which will, quietly, be a monument to their endeavour.

## Acknowledgements

Lorcan Dempsey directs the UK Office for Library and Information Networking (UKOLN) at the University of Bath. UKOLN is funded by The British Library and the Joint Information Systems Committee of the Higher Education Funding Councils. He is responsible for the views expressed here.

# Glossary of terms

**Ablative:** A process of write-once optical recording in which a laser creates microscopic holes or pits in a thermally sensitive recording material consisting of a tellurium-based thin film coated on a glass or plastic surface. When read by a laser, areas of an **optical disk's** surface that contain holes/pits will reflect light differently, thereby permitting identification of recorded **bits**. See **recording process**.

**Access:** In data processing, the process of retrieving data from memory.

**Access time:** A term that describes: 1) the time it takes to get an instruction or a unit of data from computer memory to the processing unit of a computer; or 2) the time it takes to get a unit of data from a direct access storage device to computer memory.

**Algorithm:** A formula for solving a problem; a set of steps in a specific order, such as a mathematical formula or the instructions in a computer program.

**ANSI:** American National Standards Institute. A highly active group affiliated with the International Standards Organisation (ISO); ANSI prepares and establishes standards in a number of technical disciplines, including transmission codes (e.g., **ASCII**), protocols, storage media (tape and diskette), and high-level languages (e.g. FORTRAN, COBOL)

**APRP:** Adaptive Pattern Recognition Processing

**ARTTEL:** Automated Request of Transmission by Telecommunications

**ASCII:** American Standard Code for Information Interchange. American National Standard binary-coding scheme consisting of 128 eight-bit patterns (seven bits plus a parity check bit) for printable characters and control of equipment functions.

**Backfile conversion:** Scanning older existing document holdings for image processing and retrieval.

**Back-up copy:** The process of making a copy of index or image data files for use in the event that the original is lost, damaged, or destroyed.

**Bandwidth:** The throughput or ability to move information to or from a device. Bandwidth is measured in quantities of data – usually bits per second.

**Bi-metallic alloy media:** A write-once **recording process** which features a disk consisting of two metal-alloy layers sealed in plastic to protect against oxidation and contaminants. A laser beam records information by fusing the two layers together, thereby creating a four-element layer that represents the 'one' **bits** in digitally coded data. The two layers are left unfused to represent 'zero' bits. When such disks are read by a laser, the fused layers will reflect light differently than the unfused layers.

**Binary:** A computer code using two distinct characters, normally 0 and 1.

**Binary scanner:** An optical reader that scans and converts images into **digital** form. A binary scanner records each **pixel** as only black or white. See **grey-scale scanner**.

**Bit:** Contraction of Binary digIT. The smallest unit of data a computer can process. Represents one of two conditions: On or Off, 1 or 0, Mark or Space, Something or Nothing. Bits are arranged into groups of eight called **bytes**.

**Bit map:** A method of representing images by assigning an individual memory location for each picture element (**pixel**).

**Bitonal:** Having picture elements (**pixels**) that are only one bit deep. A bitonal image has two intensity values (1 and 0), corresponding to black and white. See **binary scanner**.

**BLAISE:** British Library Automated Information Service

**Bookmark:** In Web browsers, setting a bookmark allows the users to easily return to that specific page

**bpi:** **Bits** per inch. Measure of the density of information storage on media.

**bps:** **Bits** Per Second. In serial data transmission, the instantaneous bit speed with which a device or channel transmits a signal. Sometimes confused with baud.

**Byte:** A group of **bits**, processed or operating together. An electronic data-processing term that is used to describe one position or one character of information. The most common byte is eight bits long. A byte has 256 different possible combinations of eight binary digits.

**CALS:** Computer Aided Acquisition and Logistics Support. A Department of Defence initiative supporting the electronic interchange of data and documents (including engineering drawings) between contractor, government agencies and end users.

**CARP:** Core Automated Request Processing

**CCITT:** International Telegraph and Telephone Consultative Committee. Abbreviation of the French name for the committee which, among other things, issues standards for facsimile, including **Group 3** and **Group 4** digital standards which include data **compression** and **decompression**.

**CCD:** Charge Coupling Device

**CDI:** Compact Disk Interactive

**CD-ROM:** Compact Disk- Read Only Memory. A high-capacity optical storage device that can read but not write data.

**CD-R:** Recordable Compact Disk which, when recording has completed, is 'fixed up' to provide a disk playable in any audio compact disk player and never recorded again

**COLD:** Computer Output to Laser Disk. Technique for the transfer of computer-generated output to **optical disk**, such that it can be viewed or printed without use of the original program.

**COM:** Computer Output to Microfilm. Microforms containing data produced by a recorder from computer-generated electrical signals.

**Compatibility:** The characteristic of data-processing equipment by which one machine may accept and process data prepared by another machine without **conversion** or code modification.

**Compressed file:** Refers to final digital file image storage required after **compression**. Smaller file sizes are generally preferred to maximise storage media use and facilitate data access.

**Compression:** A software or hardware process that 'shrinks' images so they occupy less storage space, and can be transmitted faster and easier. Generally accomplished by removing the bits that define blank spaces and other redundant data, and replacing them with a smaller algorithm that represents the removed bits..

**Computer system:** A configuration, or working combination, of computer hardware, software, and data communications devices.

**Continuous tone:** An image that has all the values (0 to 100%) of grey (black and white) or colour in it. A photograph is a continuous tone image.

**Conversion:** Procedure in which one format is transferred to another format, e.g., paper to microfilm, microfilm to electronic information.

**CQL:** Corpus Query Languages

**Curie Point:** A transition temperature marking a change in the magnetic properties of a substance, esp. the change from ferromagnetism to paramagnetism.

**DAT:** Digital Audio Tape

**Data backup:** To create a duplicate copy for security or disaster recovery purposes.

**Data communication:** The movement of encoded information using electrical transmission systems; the transmission of data from one point to another.

**Database Management System (DBMS):** A software program that acts as a computerised filing cabinet full of information which comes with a superior indexing system.

**Decompression:** The process of decoding a compressed image and expanding the data to its original format.

**Desktop Imaging System:** A single-user set-up for image processing.

**Digital:** Use of binary code to record information. 'Information' can be text in a binary code, e.g., **ASCII**, or images in a bit-mapped form, or sound in a sampled digital form or video.

**Digital data:** Data represented by **binary** codes.

**Digital image:** Image composed of discrete **pixels** of digitally quantised brightness or colour.

**DIS:** Draft International Standard

**Domain name:** A name that identifies an Internet Server.

**Download:** To receive data (usually a document or software) from another computer over a network.

**dpANS:** Draft proposed American National Standard

**DPI:** Dots per inch. Measure of output device **resolution** and quality, e.g., number of pixels per inch on a display device. Measures the number of dots horizontally and vertically.

**DSC:** Document Supply Centre (based in Boston Spa, Yorkshire)

**DTD:** Document Type Definition

**Dye polymer:** A **recording process** of write-once optical recording in which a laser's energy is converted into heat to form pits in a polymer which contains an infrared-absorbing dye. Information is recorded by the laser which operates at the dye's absorption wavelength.

**EBCDIC:** Extended Binary Coded Decimal Interchange Code. An eight-bit computer code used to represent 256 numbers, letters, and characters. Developed by IBM and used primarily in IBM equipment. See also **ASCII**.

**EDAC:** Error Detection And Correction. Operation that includes all phases of identifying and dealing with data errors, including direct-read-after-write and error correction codes.

**EIM:** Electronic Information Management.

**eLib:** Electronic Libraries Programme. In 1993 the Higher Education Funding Bodies in the UK invited proposals for projects which would 'transform the use and storage of knowledge in higher education institutions'. Fifteen million pounds was initially allocated to the 'Electronic Libraries Programme', managed by the Joint Information Systems Committee on behalf of the funding bodies. A series of waves of funding, proposals and projects has resulted in the eLib programme consisting of around 60 projects.

**Enhancement:** Technique for processing an image so that the result is visually clearer than the original image.

**Enterprisewide Imaging System:** Large system

with hundreds of users in different buildings; it can consist of several integrated department imaging systems.

**FDDI:** Fibre Distributed Data Interface. An ANSI standard for a 100 megabit-per-second **LAN** using fibre-optic cabling.

**FIF:** Fractal Image Format

**FIPS:** Federal Information Processing Standard

**Firmware:** A set of software instructions set permanently or semi-permanently into the read only memory (ROM) of a computer chip.

**FTP:** An abbreviation for file transfer protocol, which determines how files are exchanged via computer.

**GIF:** Graphics Interchange Format

**Gigabyte:** GB. A unit of measure that is the equivalent of $2^{30}$, or one billion bytes.

**Grey-scale scanner: Scanners** with grey-scale capability detect how dark or light a **pixel** is and pass this information on to the computer. The more bits of data the scanner records for each pixel it scans, the more levels of grey. For example, a one-bit-per-pixel scanner records only black or whites, a two-bit-per-pixel scanner records four levels of grey, and a four-bit-per-pixel scanner records 16 levels of grey. See **binary scanner**.

**Group 3:** CCITT compression technique which applies run-length encoding to a single horizontal line at a time.

**Group 4:** CCITT compression technique that efficiently compresses digitised images both horizontally and vertically (two dimensions).

**Halftone:** Technique of reproducing continuous-tone illustrations by photographing the image through an etched screen.

**HTML:** Hypertext Markup Language provides the codes used to format hypertext documents on the web.

**Hypertext:** A type of document that contains links to other documents, or other places in the same document. In hypertext, you click on a linked word or phrase to jump to the segment it refers to.

**ICR:** Intelligent Character Recognition. Advanced form of **OCR** technology that may include capabilities such as learning fonts during processing, or using context to strengthen probabilities of correct recognition.

**IfA:** Initiatives for Access programme. The British Library's programme of digitisation and networking projects.

**Index:** At its simplest, it is a descriptive set of data associated with a document for locating the document's storage location. In a more complex and demanding role, indexing can be used to consolidate documents that may not be, at first glance, related, or that may be stored in different locations, or on different media. Indexing stored documents is the great intellectual challenge in document retrieval. Anyone can scan a piece of paper, the hard part is devising an indexing scheme that describes every possible parameter of each document for later searches, comparisons and processing.

**Information system:** The organised collection, processing, transmission, and dissemination of information in accordance with defined procedures, whether automated or manual. Sometimes called a record system. Electronic records are generally scheduled by information system, whereas non-electronic records are generally scheduled by series.

**Integration:** Combining various pieces of hardware and software, often acquired from different vendors, into a unified system.

**ISDN:** Integrated Services Digital Network is a service offered by some telephone carriers that handles both data and voice communication over the same line. The bandwidth of ISDN is greater than the fastest modem speeds.

**ISO:** International Standards Organisation

**ISSN:** International Standards Serial Number

**JBIG:** Joint Bi-level Image Group. Algorithm standard under development by a CCITT/ISO Committee, or a bi-tonal compression algorithm which has potential applications in database management systems that are composed of black and white halftoned photos and text.

**JPEG:** Joint Photographic Experts Group. Algorithm standard under development by a **CCITT/ISO** committee for a general-purpose compression technique for colour and grey-scale image applications.

**Jukebox:** Automated device for housing multiple **optical disks** and one or more read/write drives.

**Laser printer:** A printer device that uses a laser beam to generate an image that is developed with toner and fused to paper using heat and pressure.

**LCSH:** Library of Congress Subject Headings

**Local Area Network (LAN):** A system for linking together computers, terminals, printers, and other equipment, usually within the same office or building.

**Longevity:** The useful shelf life expectancy of optical data disks before writing (pre-write), plus the estimated post-write data life span.

**Lossless:** Image and data compression applications and algorithms, such as Huffman Encoding, that reduce the number of bits a picture would normally take up without losing any data.

**Lossy:** Method of image **compression**, such as **JPEG**, that reduces the size of an image by disregarding some pictorial information.

**Magnetic disk cache:** Temporary storage on magnetic disk for quick retrieval of frequently used documents.

**Magneto-optical:** An optical **recording process** that is rewritable. The recording or 'write' process uses a laser beam to heat a pre-magnetised site on the media's recording surface. This causes a reversal of the magnetic polarity, resulting in subtle reflective differences sensed as digital data by the 'read' laser beam. The process is reversed to erase the data.

**MARC:** Machine Readable Cataloguing

**Megabyte:** MB. A unit of measurement equivalent to $2^{20}$ or about one million bytes.

**Metadata:** Words that describe the properties of an object (e.g., publishing date, author's name, number of pages in a book).

**Modem:** MOdulator-DEModulator; a device that encodes and decodes **digital** data for transmission as analogue signals over a particular medium, such as telephone lines, coaxial cables, fibre optics, or microwaves.

**MPEG:** Motion Pictures Experts Group. An image compression scheme for full motion video proposed by the Motion Picture Experts Group, an ISO-sanctioned group. MPEG takes advantage of the fact that full motion video is made up of many successive frames, often consisting of large areas that do not change – like blue sky background. MPEG performs 'differencing' noting differences between consecutive frames. If two consecutive frames are identical, the second does not need to be stored.

**Multifunction:** An optical data disk storage system that accepts removable, double-sided 5.25-inch optical media in both write-once and rewritable formats.

**OCR:** Optical Character Recognition or Reader. The ability of a scanner with the proper software to capture, recognise, and translate printed alphanumeric characters into machine-readable text. Most OCRs work by using either Pattern Matching or Feature Extraction.

**ONE:** OPAC Network Europe

**OPAC:** Online Public Access Catalogue

**Open System Architecture:** Proponents of open systems are seeking to standardise computer equipment and processes so that data contained in one machine or system can be transferred or communicated easily to another. Such standards may address purely physical concerns (whether a plug fits into a particular socket or how fast electrical impulses are sent through a cable) or higher order logical concerns (so that, for instance, one word-processing program can recognise footnotes or chapter headings created by another word-processor as discrete elements with specific characteristics).

**Optical digital data disk:** A form of **optical disk** used to store and retrieve digital data or digital image information.

**Optical disk:** A direct access storage device that is written and read by laser light. Certain optical disks are considered Write Once, Read Many (**WORM**), because data is permanently engraved in the disk's surface either by gouging pits (ablation) or by causing the non-image area to bubble, reflecting light away from the reading head. Erasable optical drives use technologies such as the **magneto-optical** technique, which electrically alters the bias of grains of material after they have been heated by a laser. Compact disks and laser (or video) disks are optical disks.

**PFI:** Private Finance Initiative. The Private Finance Initiative was launched by the British government in 1992 as a new method of public sector procurement. PFI is based on the principles of allowing both private and public sectors to concentrate on doing what they are likely to do best. Thus, the public sector acts as an enabler and guardian of public services which are provided by private sector management, creativity and capital investment.

**Phase change:** A **recording process** in which a laser beam records information by heating selected areas of the recording layer until its glass-transition temperature is reached. A crystalline-to-amorphous or amorphous-to-crystalline transition occurs in heated areas, accompanied by a change in their reflection characteristics.

**PhotoCD:** Standard for compression of images, developed by Kodak

**Pixel:** A sort of acronym for picture element. Also called a Pel. When an image is defined by many tiny dots, those dots are pixels. On the printed page, each pixel is one dot. On colour monitors, though, a pixel can be made up of several dots, with the colour of the pixel depending on which dots are illuminated, and how brightly.

**PRINCE:** Project in a Controlled Environment. A widely used methodology for managing IT projects.

**RAID:** Redundant Arrays of Inexpensive Disks. A storage technology in which information is split up between multiple hard disks. This hardware configuration holds gigabytes of data, and is capable of storing and retrieving information faster than ordinary hard disks.

**Raster image data:** A line or array of **pixels**, as depicted on a CRT monitor, that corresponds to the original scanned image. The number of lines per inch is a function of the scan resolution (e.g., 200 dots per inch equals 200 lines per inch). The resulting scanned image contains a large number of pixels that collectively form a **digital image** or **bit-map** image.

**Read/write head:** Component that records and senses data on a magnetic or optical disk.

**Recording process:** The means of inscribing and storing digitally coded information generated by computer systems. There are two approaches to recording: rewritable and write-once, read-many (**WORM**). Within these two categories are several recording processes. **Phase change** and **magneto-optical** are rewritable. **Ablative**, **bi-metallic, dye-polymer**, and **thermal bubble** are WORM recording processes.

**Resolution:** 1. Measure of imager output capability, usually expressed in dots per inch. 2. Measure of halftone quality, usually expressed in lines per inch. The higher the resolution, a greater amount of detail may be shown.

**Rewritable optical disk:** A recording medium that, unlike **WORM disks**, can be erased, written over, and otherwise re-used. Both **magneto-optical** and **phase change** technology are currently used.

**Run-length code:** A method of redundancy reduction (data **compression**) used by **digital** facsimile transmitters to enhance speed. When image patterns of an original are converted into digital signals, all black and white areas on a page are reported as a series of ones (black) and zeros (white). The number of white spaces between black elements (number of zeros between ones) is assigned a number, or run-length code. The unit assigns a short code to represent each space encountered, rather than reporting all of the individual white spaces (zeros), and the most frequently used run-length codes are given the shortest binary numbers. Run-length coding may be performed horizontally across the width of the page (one-dimensional) or vertically (two-dimensional).

**Scanner:** Device that converts a document into binary (digital) code by detecting and measuring the intensity of light reflected from paper or transmitted through microfilm.

**SCSI:** Small Computer System Interface. Industry standard for connecting peripheral devices and their controllers to a microprocessor. The SCSI defines both hardware and software standards for communication between a host computer and a peripheral.

**Server:** Computer dedicated to operating some portion of a total system, such as a database server, image server, or fax server.

**SGML:** Standard Generalized Mark-up Language. A language for describing documents that facilitates the exchange of text among systems. The Department of Defence mandated that its publishing systems support this standard.

**SQL:** Structured query language. A relational database language developed by IBM and standardised by **ANSI**.

**TEI:** Text Encoding Initiative

**Terabyte:** A unit of measurement equivalent to $2^{40}$ or about one trillion bytes.

**Thermal bubble:** A **recording process** of write-once optical recording in which highly focused laser beam evaporates a polymer layer to form bubbles or bumps on a thin film composed of precious metals, such as gold or platinum. The bubbles open to form pits which reveal a reflective under layer.

**TIFF:** Tagged Image File Format. A standardised header or tag that defines the exact data structure of images to be processed. TIFF is supported by many desktop publishing and graphics programs.

**Transfer:** The act or process of moving records from one location to another, especially from office space to agency storage facilities or Federal records centres, from one Federal agency to another, or from office or storage space to the National Archives for permanent preservation.

**TSS:** Telecommunications Standardisation Sector

**Turnkey System:** An integrated configuration of preselected hardware and pre-written software designed to accomplish a particular information-processing task. The term is most often applied to dedicated computer systems that use minicomputers or microcomputers.

**URL:** Uniform Resource Locator. An address for a Web site that is unique to that site.

**WAIS:** Wide Area Information Service. A type of server that provides search access to text-based databases and ranks results based on relevance to the search. Based on **Z39.50**.

**Watermarks:** Marks on an object to identify the source institution in order to discourage unauthorised use. The mark may be either visible or invisible in normal printing or display

**Work flow:** In imaging software, a program that tracks the progress of a document from its entry into the system through the various departments in the organisation to its final destination.

**WORM:** Write-Once, Read-Many. **Optical disks** which store user data (write) and are accessible (read) when needed. Information recorded on WORM disks is considered permanent, in that the disks are not rewritable like magnetic media. See **recording process**.

**Z39.50:** A retrieval protocol which allows client applications to query databases on remote servers, retrieve results, and perform other retrieval-related functions

**Zoom:** To enlarge a selected portion of an image displayed on a screen.

# Further reading

## Digital Libraries and the Electronic Book

Association for Computing Machinery (ACM), *First ACM Conference on Digital Libraries 1996*. Programme available at http://fox.cs.vt.edu/DL96/

R. Atkinson, 'Library Functions, Scholarly Communication, and the Foundation of the Digital Library: laying claim to the control zone', *The Library Quarterly* 66:3 (July 1996), 239-65

C. Bailey, *Scholarly Electronic Publishing Bibliography*. Available at: http://info.lib.uh.edu/sepb/sepb.html

P. Barker, 'Electronic Books and Libraries of the Future', *Electronic Library* 10.3 (1992), 139-49

D. Bearman and J. Perkins, *Standards Framework for the Computer Interchange of Museum Information* (Silver Spring: Museum Computer Network, 1993)

S. Birkets, *The Gutenberg Elegies: the fate of reading in an electronic age* (New York: Fawcett Columbine, 1994)

W. P. Birmingham, E. H. Durfee, T. A. Mullen and M. P. Wellmann, 'The distributed agent architecture of the University of Michigan Digital Library', AAAI Spring Symposium on Information Gathering in Heterogeneous, Distributed Environments 1995. Also available from: ftp://ftp.eecs.umich.edu/people/wellman/aaai-infogath-ss95.ps

J. Bolter, *Turing's Man* (London: Duckworth, 1984)

J. Bolter, *Writing Space: the computer, hypertext and the history of writing* (Hove and London: Laurence Erlbaum Associates, 1991)

British Library, *Initiatives for Access News* (1994-6)

British Library Research and Development Department: *Information Technology in Humanities Scholarship: British achievements, prospects and barriers*, BL R&D Report 6097 (London: The British Library and British Academy, 1993)

A. E. Cawkell, *This is IT* (London: ASLIB, 1992)

C. Butler, *Computers and Written Texts* (Oxford: Blackwell, 1992)

W. Chernaik, C. Davis and M. Deegan, *The Politics of the Electronic Text* (Oxford: Office for Humanities Communication Publications, 1993)

W. Chernaik, M. Deegan and A. Gibson, *Beyond the Book: Theory, Culture and the Politics of Cyberspace* (Oxford: Office for Humanities Communication, 1996)

*Communications of the Association for Computing Machinery (ACM)* 38.4 (April 1995). Issue devoted to digital libraries

*Computer* (May 1996). Issue devoted to the US Digital Libraries initiative. Available at: http://www.computer.org/pubs/computer/dli

*Digital Libraries 94: Proceedings of the First Annual Conference on the Theory and Practice of Digital Libraries*. Available at: http://www.csdl.tamu.edu/DL94/

*Digital Libraries 95: The Second Annual Conference on the Theory and Practice of Digital Libraries*. Available at: http://www.csdl.tamu.edu/DL95/

*Evaluation of the Electronic Libraries Programme: Synthesis of Annual Reports* (London: Tavistock Institute 1997). Available at: http://www.ukoln.ac.uk/elib/wk_papers/

E. Fox, *Sourcebook on Digital Libraries: Report for the National Science Foundation*, Tech Rep. TR-03-35, Computer Science Department, Virginia Tech (Blacksburg: Virginia Tech, 1993). Also available at http://fox.cs.vt.edu/DLSB.html

E. Fox., ed., *Rethinking Libraries in the Information Age: Lessons Learned with Five Digital Library Projects*. Available at: http://fox.cs.vt.edu:80/talks/UNC96/

J.-P. Genet and A. Zambolli, eds., *Computers and the Humanities*, European Science Foundation (Aldershot: Dartmouth, 1992)

P. Graham, *Bibliography on Electronic Library Issues*. Available at: http://aultnis.rutgers.edu/texts/ElectLibBib.html

P. Graham, 'Requirements for the Digital Research Library', *College and Research Libraries* 56:4 (July 1995), 331-9. Also available at: http://aultnis.rutgers.edu/texts/drc.html

S. Harnard, 'Post-Gutenberg Galaxy: The Fourth Revolution in the Means of Production of Knowledge', *Public-Access Computer Systems Review* 2.1 (1991), 39-53. Also available at:

http://infotrain.magill.unisa.au/epub/Resources/Bibliography/Harnad9.txt

H. Harris, 'Retraining Librarians to Meet the Needs of the Virtual Library Patron', *Information Technology and Libraries* 15:1 (March 1996), 48-52

*Information Services & Use* 16:3/4 (1996) (Special issue: British Library treasures)

*Journal of American Society of Information Scientists*, 44.8 (September 1993). Special issue on digital libraries.

M. Katzen, ed., *Scholarship and Technology in the Humanities: proceedings of a conference held at Elvetham Hall, Hampshire, 9-12 May 1990* (London: Bowker Saur, 1991)

S. Kenna and S. Ross, eds., *Networking in the Humanities: proceedings of a second conference on scholarship and technology in the humanities held at Elvetham Hall, Hampshire, 13-15 April 1994* (London: Bowker Saur, 1995)

K. S. Kiernan, ed., *Reconnecting Science and the Humanities in Digital Libraries. A Symposium Sponsored by the University of Kentucky and the British Library*. Available at: http://www.uky.edu/~kiernan/DL/symp.html

M. Lesk, Home Page: http://www.lesk.com/

Librarians' Association of the University of California, *New Horizons in Scholarly Communication*. Available at: http://www.ucsc.edu/scomm/index.html

R. Martin, ed., *Scholarly Communication in an Electronic Environment: Issues for Research Libraries* (Chicago: ALA, 1993)

C. Mullings, M. Deegan, S. Ross and S. Kenna, *New Technologies for the Humanities* (London: Bowker Saur, 1996)

P. Paviscak, S. Ross and C. Henry, *Information Technology in Humanities Scholarship: Achievements, prospects, and challenges – the United Sates focus*. American Council of Learned Societies Occasional Paper no. 37 (New York: American Council of Learned Societies, 1997). Also available at: http://www.acls.org/op37.htm

H. Rheingold, *Virtual Reality* (New York, London: Summit Books, 1991)

H. Rheingold, *The Virtual Community: Homesteading on the Electronic Frontier* (Reading: Addison-Wesley, 1993)

S. Ross, 'Intelligent Graphical User Interfaces: Opportunities for the Interface between the Historian and the Machine', in I. Kropa, P. Teichenbacher and G. Jaritz, eds., *The Art of Communication: Proceedings of the 8th International Conference of the Association for History and Computing* (Graz: Akademische Druck and Verlagsanstalt, 1995)

J. Weiss, 'Digital Copyright: Who Owns What?', *New Media* 5:9 (September 1995), 38-43

*Other useful URLs include:*

Ariadne: http://www.ariadne.ac.uk/

Arts and Humanities Data Service: http://ahds.ac.uk

The eLib Electronic Libraries Programme: http://www.ukoln.ac.uk/services/elib/

Copyright and Fair Use: http://fairuse.stanford.edu

D-Lib magazine: http://www.dlib.org/dlib.html *OR* http://hosted.ukoln.ac.uk/mirrored/lis-journals/dlib/

EC Telematics for Libraries programme: http://www2.echo.lu/libraries/libraries.html

Humanities Research Institute, University of Sheffield: http://www.shef.ac.uk/uni/academic/D-H/hri/

IBM Digital Library: http://www.software.ibm.com/is/dig-lib/

IFLA, *Digital Libraries: Resources and Projects*: http://ifla.inst.fr/II/diglib.hum

International Institute for Electronic Library Research, De Montfort University: http://ford.mk.dmu.ac.uk

The Library of Congress: http://www.loc.gov/

Museum Computer Network: http://world.std.com/~mcn/

National Digital Library Federation: http://lcweb.loc.gov/loc/ndlf/

National Technology Alliance: http://www.nta.org/

NSSN Standards: http://www.nssn.org/

The Online Computer Library Center (OCLC): http://www.oclc.org/

Rank Xerox: http://www.parc.xerox.com/parc-go.html

The Research Libraries Group (RLG): http://www.rlg.org/

The UK Office for Library and Information Networking: http://www.ukoln.ac.uk/

University of Michigan, Humanities Text Initiative: http://www.hti.umich.edu/

University of Virginia Library, Electronic Centers: http://www.lib.virginia.edu/ecenters.html

University of Virginia Institute for Advanced Technology in the Humanities: http://jefferson.village.virginia.edu/

### Digital Imaging and Multimedia

R. Bagnall, *Digital Imaging of Papyri: A Report to the Commission on Preservation and Access* (Washington D.C.: Commission on Preservation and Access, 1995)

D. Bearman, ed., *Hypermedia and Interactivity in museums: proceedings of an international conference* (Pittsburgh: Archives and Museum Informatics, 1991)

W. E. Benemann, 'Reference Implications of Digital

Technology in a Library Photograph Collection', *Reference Services Review* 22:4 (1994), 45-50

'Beowulf Bests Dragons In Cyberspace', *National Geographic* 186:6 (December 1994)

H. Besser and J. Trant, *Introduction to Imaging: Issues in Constructing an Image Database*. Available at: http://www.gii.getty.edu/intro_imaging/

A. Cawkell, *Indexing Collections of Electronic Images: a review,* British Library, Research and Development Department Research Reviews 15 (London: The British Library, 1993)

A. Cawkell, *A Guide to Image Processing and Picture Management* (Aldershot: Gower Press, 1994)

A. Cawkell, *The Multimedia Handbook* (London: Routledge, 1996)

M. Deegan, S. Lee and N. Timbrell, *An Introduction to Multimedia for Academic Use* (Oxford: University of Oxford, 1996)

K. Donovan, 'The Anatomy of an Imaging Project: A Primer for Museums, Libraries, Archives and other Visual Collections', *Spectra* (newsletter of the Museum Computer Network) 23:2 (Winter 1995/1996), 19-22

N. Elkington, ed., *Digital Imaging Technology for Preservation: Proceedings from an RLG Symposium, March 17 and 18 1994* (Mountain View: RLG, 1994)

M. Ester, *Digital Image Collections: Issues and Practice* (Washington D.C.: Commission on Preservation and Access, 1996)

T. Feldman, *Multimedia in the 1990s* (London: The British Library, 1990)

A. Hamber, 'The Vasari Project', *Computers and the History of Art* 1:2 (1991), 17-33

A. R. Kenney, *A Testbed for Advancing the Role of Digital Technologies for Library Preservation and Access* (Washington, D. C.: Commission on Preservation and Access, 1993)

A. R. Kenney with M. Friedman and S. Poucher, *Preserving Archival Material through Digital Technology: final report* (Ithaca, N. Y.; Cornell University Library, 1993)

A. R. Kenney and S. Chapman, *Tutorial: Digital Resolution Requirements for Replacing Text-Based Material: Methods for Benchmarking Image Quality* (Washington D.C.: Commission on Preservation and Access, 1995)

A. R. Kenney and S. Chapman, *Digital Imaging for Libraries and Archives* (Ithaca, N. Y.: Cornell University Library, 1996)

A. R. Kenney and S. Chapman, 'Digital Conversion of Research Library Materials: A Case for Full Informational Capture', *D-Lib Magazine* (October 1996): http://www.dlib.org/dlib/october96/cornell/10chapman.html

S. Ketchpel, *Annotated Bibliography of Digital Library Related Sources*. Available at: http://robotics.stanford.edu/users/ketchpel/annbib.html

K. S. Kiernan, 'Digital Image Processing and the *Beowulf* manuscript', *Literary and Linguistic Computing* 6:1 (1991), 20-27

K. S. Kiernan, 'Digital preservation, restoration, and the dissemination of medieval manuscripts', in A. Okerson and D. Mogge, eds., *Scholarly publishing and the electronic networks: gateways, keepers, and roles in the information omniverse* (Washington D.C.: Association of Research Libraries, 1994), 37-43. Also available at: http://www.uky.edu/~kiernan/BL/kportico.html

K. S. Kiernan, 'Old Manuscripts, New Techologies', in M. Richards, ed., *Anglo-Saxon Manuscripts: Basic Readings* (New York: Garland, 1994), 37-54

K. S. Kiernan, 'The Electronic Beowulf', *Computers in Libraries* (February 1995), 14-15

K. Kleve, E. Ore and R. Jensen, 'Literalogy: On the Use of Computer Graphics and Photography in Papyrology', *Symbolae Osloenses* 62 (1987), 109-29

T. Kuny and G. Cleveland, *Digital Libraries: Myths and Challenges*. Available at: http://www.nlc-bnc.ca/ifla/IV/ifla62/62-kuny.pdf

C. Lynch and L. Lunin, eds., *Perspectives: Advanced Applications of Imaging*. Special issue of *Journal of American Society for Information Science* (September 1991)

A. Prescott, '*The Electronic Beowulf* and digital restoration', *Literary and Linguistic Computing* (forthcoming)

J. Reilly and F. Frey, *Recommendations for the Evaluation of Digital Images Produced from Photographic, Micrographic and Various Paper Formats*. Available at: http://lcweb2.loc.gov/ammem/ipirpt.html

P. Robinson, *The Digitization of Primary Textual Sources* (Oxford: Office for Humanities Communication, 1993)

M. Thaller, ed., *Images and Manuscripts In Historical Computing* (St Katherinen: Halbgraue Reihe zur Historischen Fachinformatik, A 14, 1992)

C. L. Sundt, ed., *Issues in Electronic Imaging*. Special issue of *Visual Resources* 10:1 (1994)

*Other useful URLs include:*

Adobe: http://www.adobe.com/

ELISE project: http://severn.dmu.ac.uk/elise/

Getty Information Institute: http://www.ahip.getty.edu/

Harvard University film scanning project: http://preserve.harvard.edu/resources/digitization/colormicrofilm.html

Kodak: http://www.kodak.com/digitalImaging/digitalImaging.shtml

Kontron Elektronik: http://www.kontron.com

Project Open Book (Yale University): http://www.library.yale.edu/preservation/pob-web.htm

Vasari Enterprises: http://www.brameur.co.uk/vasari/

### Document Management and Descriptive Data

M. Alexander, 'Retrieving Digital Data with Fuzzy Matching', *Library Association Record, Technology Supplement* 96:9 (1994), 21-2.

L. Alschuler, *ABCD...SGML: A User's Guide to Structured Information* (London: International Thomson Computer Press, 1995)

P. Ames, *Beyond Paper: The Official Guide to Adobe Acrobat* (Mountain View: Adobe Press, 1994)

S. Beaney and L. Carpenter, 'The indexing and retrieval of digital items' *Information Services & Use* [Special issue: British Library treasures] 16:3/4 (1996), 209-21

N. Blake and P. Robinson, eds., *The Canterbury Tales Project: Occasional Papers*, nos. 1-2 (Oxford: Office for Humanities Communication, 1993, 1997)

L. Burnard, 'What Is SGML and How Does It Help?', *Computers and the Humanities* 29:1 (1995), 41-50

P. Conner, 'Hypertext in the Last Days of the Book', *Bulletin of the John Rylands University Library of Manchester* 74 (1992), 7-24

P. Delany and G. P. Landow, eds., *Hypermedia and Literary Studies* (Cambridge, Ma.: MIT Press, 1991)

L. Dempsey, 'ROADS to Desire: some UK and other European Metadata and Resource Discovery projects', *D-Lib Magazine* (July-August 1996). Available at: http://hosted.ukoln.ac.uk/mirrored/lis-journals/dlib/dlib/dlib/july96/07dempsey.html

L. Dempsey and S. Weibel, 'The Warwick Metadata Workshop: a Framework for the Deployment of Resource Description', *D-Lib Magazine* (July-August 1996). Available at: http://hosted.ukoln.ac.uk/mirrored/lis-journals/dlib/dlib/dlib/july96/07weibel.html

W. V. Egmond, 'Principles for Computer Catalog Descriptions of Medieval Scientific Manuscripts', in Folkerts and Kühne (1990), 109-122

W. V.Egmond, 'The Future of Manuscript Cataloguing', in Stevens (1991), 153-158

*Electronic Bodhidharma*: http://www.iijnet.or.jp/iriz/irizhtml/irizhome.htm

Charles B. Faulhaber, '*Philobiblion*: Problems and Solutions in a Relational Database of Medieval Texts', *Literary and Linguistic Computing* 6:2 (1991), 89-96

M. Folkerts and A. Kühne, eds., *The Use of Computers in Cataloguing Medieval and Renaissance Manuscripts* (Algroismus: Studien zur Geschichte der Mathematik und der Naturwissenschaften: 4), (Munich: Institut für Geschichte der Naturwissenschaften, 1990)

E. Gaynor, 'From MARC to Markup: SGML and Online Library Systems' in *From Catalog to Gateway, Briefings from the CFFC* 7 (1996), a supplement to *ALCTS Newsletter* 7:2 A-D (1996). Also available at: http://www.lib.virginia.edu/spec-col/scdc/articles/alcts_brief.html

C. F. Goldfarb, *The SGML Handbook* (Oxford: Oxford University Press)

P. Graham, *The Dublin Core and the Warwick Framework*. Available at: http://aultnis.rutgers.edu/pgperstuff/PGTalkDubCore.pdf

N. L. Hahn, 'The Future of Computerised Manuscript Catalogues. A Proposal', in Folkerts and Kühne (1990), 41-56

E. van Herwijnen, *Practical SGML* (Dordrecht: Kluwer Academic Publishers, 1990)

N. Ide and J. Veronis, eds., *Text Encoding Initiative: background and context*. Special numbers of *Computing and the Humanities* 29:1-3 (1995)

Graham Jefcoate, 'Getting the Message from Gabriel', *Library Technology* 1:2 (April 1996), 33-4

A. Kenny, *The Computation of Style: an introduction to statistics for students of literature and humanities* (Oxford: Pergamon, 1982)

C. Lagoze, C. Lynch and R. Daniel, *The Warwick Framework: a Container Architecture for Aggregating Sets of Metadata*. Available at: http://cs-tr.cs.cornell.edu/Dienst/Repository/2.0/Body/ncstrl.cornell%2fTR96-1593/html

G. P. Landow, *Hypertext: the Convergence of Contemporary Critical Theory and Technology* (Baltimore: Johns Hopkins University Press, 1992)

G. P. Landow, ed., *Hyper/Text/Theory* (Baltimore: The Johns Hopkins University Press, 1994)

Hope Mayo, 'Standards for Description, Indexing, and Retrieval in Computerized Catalogs of Medieval Manuscripts', in Folkerts and Kühne (1990), 19-40

Hope Mayo, 'MARC Cataloguing for Medieval Manuscripts: An Evaluation', in Stevens (1991), 93-152

T. Meadows, 'OCR Falls Into Place', *Imaging Business* 2:9 (September 1996)

P. Oddy, *Future Libraries, Future Catalogues* (London: ASLIB, 1996)

*Optical Character Recognition in the historical discipline: proceedings of an international workshop organised by the Netherlands Data Archive, Nijmegen Institute for Cognition and Information*

(St Katherinen: Halbgraue Reihe zur Historischen Fachinformatik, A 18, 1992)

Ulrich Pagel, 'Automated Cataloguing of Tibetan Manuscripts and Blockprints', *IIAS Newsletter*, 9 (Summer 1996), 15

C. Sperberg-McQueen and L. Burnard, eds., *Guidelines for Electronic Text Encoding and Interchange* (TEI P3) (Chicago: ACH-ACL-ALLC, 1994)

W. M. Stevens, *Bibliographic Access to Medieval and Renaissance Manuscripts: A Survey of Computerized Data Bases and Information Services* (Primary Sources and Original Works: 1 (3/4)), (New York: Haworth Press, 1991)

W. M. Stevens, 'Sources and Resources for History of Science to 1600: A Survey of Computer-assisted Catalogues for Original Sources in Manuscripts', *Nuncius: Annali Di Storia Della Scienza* 9.1, 239-264

*Other useful URLs include:*

ASIANDOC mailing list: http://zorba.uafadm.alaska.edu/philo/ebti/EBTI-home.html

Berkeley project on Finding Aids for Archival Collections: http://sunsite.berkeley.edu/FindingAids

British National Corpus: http://info.ox.ac.uk/bnc/

Center for Electronic Texts in the Humanities (CETH): http://www.ceth.rutgers.edu/newhome.html

Consortium for the Computer Interchange of Museum Information (CIMI): http://www.cimi.org/

Dublin Core Metadata Element Set Home Page: http://purl.org/metadata/dublin_core

ELINOR project at De Montfort University: http://ford.mk.dmu.ac.uk/Projects/ELINOR/ (includes a full bibliography of publications relating to ELINOR)

Excalibur Technologies: http://www.excalib.com/rev2/contents.html

Internet Early Journals Project: http://www.bodley.ox.ac.uk/ilej/

The SGML Web Page: http://www.sil.org/sgml/sgml.html

Softquad: http://www.sq.com/

Text Encoding Initiative: http://www-tei.uic.edu/orgs/tei/

## Networks

L. Dempsey, *Libraries, Networks and OSI: a review with a report on North American Developments* (Bath: UKOLN, 1991)

L. Dempsey, R. Russell, J. Kirriemuir, 'Towards Distributed Library Systems: Z39.50 in a European Context', *Program* 30:1 (January 1996), 1-22

P. Flynn, *The World Wide Web Handbook* (London: International Thomson Computer Press, 1995)

A. Ford, *Spinning the Web* (London: International Thomson Publishing, 1994; 2nd edition, Andrew Ford and Tim Dixon, 1996)

P. Graham, *What is a URx? What Do I Need to Know About It?* Available at: http://aultnis.rutgers.edu/pgperstuff/PGtalkURx.pdf

G. Jefcoate, 'Gabriel: Gateway to Europe's National Libraries', *Program* 30:3 (July 1996), 229-38

B. Kelly, *Running a WWW Service.* Available at: http://www.leeds.ac.uk/ucs/WWW/handbook/handbook.html

D. Kovacs, *Directory of Scholarly and Professional Electronic Conferences.* Available at http://www.n2h2.com/KOVACS/

C. Lynch, *The Z39.50 Protocol in Plain English.* Available at: http://ruff.cs.umbc.edu:1080/courses/491/wais/plain.english.txt

C. Lynch, 'Information Retrieval as a Network Application', *Library Hi-Tech* 8:4 (1993), 57-72

C. Lynch and C. Preston, 'Internet Access to Information Resources', *Annual Review of Information Science and Technology* (*ARIST*) 25 (1990), 263-312

R. Russell, 'Z39.50 and SR: an overview', *VINE* 97 (December 1994), 3-8

N. Smith, ed., *Libraries, Networks and Europe: a European Networking Study* (London: The British Library, 1994)

G. Tseng, *Library and Information Professional's Guide to the Internet* (London: Library Association, 1997)

S. Weibl, 'The World Wide Web and Emerging Internet Standards for Scholarly Literature', *Library Trends* 43:4 (Spring 1995), 627-34

I. Winship and A. McNab, *The Students' Guide to the Internet* (London: Library Association Publishing, 1996)

*Z39.50 FAQ.* Available at: http://www.iti.gov.sg/iti_service/irg/irg.faq.html

*Other useful URLS include:*

Coalition for Networked Information: http://www.cni.org/

European projects involving Z39.50: http://ukoln.bath.ac.uk/z3950/europroj.html

National Initiative for a Networked Cultural Heritage (NINCH): http://www-ninch.cni.org

PURL home page: http://purl.oclc.org/

## Digital Preservation

D. Bearman, ed., *Archival Management of Electronic Records* (Pittsburgh: Archives and Museum Informatics, 1991)

D. Bearman, *Electronic Evidence: Strategies for Managing Records in Contemporary Organisations* (Pittsburgh: Archives and Museum Informatics, 1994)

L. Burnard and H. Short, *An Arts and Humanities Information Service: report of a feasibility study commissioned by the Information Services Sub-Committee of the Higher Education Funding Councils* (Oxford: Office for Humanities Communication, 1994)

J. Coleman and D. Willis, *SGML as a Framework for Digital Preservation and Access* (Washington D. C.: Commission on Preservation and Access, 1997)

Commission on Preservation and Access and Research Libraries Group, *Preserving Digital Information: report of the Task Force on Archiving of Digital Information* (Washington D.C.: Commission on Preservation and Access, 1996). Also available at: http://lyra.rlg.org/ArchTF/

P. Conway, *Preservation in the Digital World* (Washington, D.C.: Commission on Preservation and Access, 1996)

C. Dollar, *Archival Theory and Information Technologies: the impact of information technologies on archival principles* (Ancona: University of Macerata, 1992)

P. S. Graham, *Intellectual Preservation of the Third Kind* (Washington, D.C.: Commission on Preservation and Access, 1994). Also available at: http://aultnis.rutgers.edu/texts/cpaintpres.html

M. Hedstrom, 'Understanding Electronic Incunabula: A Framework for Research on Electronic Records', *American Archivist* 54:3 (1991), 334-54

Michael Lesk, *Preservation of the New Technology. A Report of the Technology Assessment Advisory Committee to the Commission on Preservation and Access* (Washington, D. C.: Commission on Preservation and Access, 1992)

P. Lyman, 'Invention, the Mother of Necessity: Archival Research in 2020', *American Archivist* 57:1 (1994), 114-25

J. Mohlenrich, ed., *Preservation of Electronic Formats: Electronic Formats for Preservation* (Fort Atkinson, Wi: Highsmith Press, 1993)

National Preservation Office, Conference Proceedings 1995-7 (forthcoming)

S. Ross, 'Opportunities in Electronic Information', in B. Brivati, A. Seldon and J. Buxton, eds., *Contemporary History: A Handbook* (Manchester: Manchester University Press, 1995)

S. Ross and E. Higgs, *Electronic Information Resources and Historians: European Perspectives* (St Katherinen: Halbgraue Reihe zur Historische Fachinformatik, 1993; and as British Library R&D Report 6122)

J. Rothenberg, 'Ensuring the Longevity of Digital Documents', *Scientific American* (January 1995), 42-7

D. Stinson, F. Amell and N. Zaino, 'Lifetime of KODAK Writable CD and Photo CD Media', *SIG-CAT Discourse* 9 (January 1995), 1

J. W. C. Van Bogart, *Magnetic Tape Storage and Handling: A Guide for Libraries and Archives* (Washington D.C.: Commission on Preservation and Access and the National Media Laboratory, 1995)

V. I. Welch, 'The Role of Standards in the Archival Management of Electronic Records', *American Archivist* 53:1 (1990), 30-43

*Other useful URLs include:*

Commission on Preservation and Access: http://clir.stanford.edu/cpa/

National Preservation Office: http://portico.bl.uk/services/preservation

PADI (Preserving Access to Digital Information): http://www.nla.gov.au/dnc/tf2001/padi/padi.html

### Standards and Standards Bodies
### American National Standards Institute (ANSI ONLINE)

http://www.ansi.org/

The American National Standards Institute is a private-sector, non-profit, membership organisation located at 11 West 42nd Street, New York, New York 10036 (Telephone: 212 642 4900; Telefax: 212 398 0023).

### International Standards For Information Services, Libraries, And Publishing

http://www.niso.org/internat.htm

Resources/Publications: *The Information Standards Quarterly, NISO Press Catalog,* and the *TC 46 Experts Sign-Up Sheet* contain summaries of the activities of TC 46 and descriptions of the subcommittees and International Standards that have been adopted as American National Standards.

### International Standards Organisation (ISO)

http://www.iso.ch/welcome.html

ISO maintains a home page that provides a catalogue of international standards and drafts which can be searched by keywords or reference numbers; plus ordering information. Additional information includes a list of ISO members, TCs, general information about ISO and the work of its committees, and the ISO 9000 Forum.

***ISO 12083 Electronic Manuscript Preparation and Markup (SC4).*** An SGML implementation for books, serials, and journal articles. It has been adopted in the United States as

NISO/ANSI/ISO 12083. This standard is available in print and electronic form from NISO Press.

***ISO 9706 Paper for Documents – Requirements for Permanence (SC 10).*** The standard describes a chemical wood paper with alkaline sizing and calcium carbonate filler and is similar to ANSI/NISO Z39.48 – 1992.

***ISO 3166 Codes for the Representation of Names of Countries (WG 2).*** This standard establishes the two and three character and numeric codes assigned to countries and other geopolitical entities of the world; it has been adopted in the United States as NISO/ANSI/ISO 3166.

***DIS 690 – 2 Bibliographic References – Electronic Documents or Parts Thereof (SC 9).*** The standard describes a prescribed order and the conventions for referencing electronic documents (monographs, databases, software, serials, bulletin boards, and e-mail).

*CD 11620 Library Performance Indicators (SC 8).* The proposed standard contains a basic set of performance measures based on existing library practices.

*Z39.50 Information Retrieval Application Service Definition and Protocol Specification (SC 4).* The proposed new standard will be an international adoption of ANSI/NISO Z39.50 – 1995.

### Library and Publishing Standards

http://www.faxon.com/Standards/StandardsMenu.html
This menu points to information on the Faxon World Wide Web server related to standards in the serials and publishing industry. It also provides selected links to other servers with valuable standards-related information.
The Faxon Company, 15 Southwest Park, Westwood MA 02090; phone: 617 329 3350

### National Information Standards Organisation

http://www.niso.org/
The National Information Standards Organisation is a non-profit association accredited as a standards developer by the American National Standards Institute, the national clearinghouse for voluntary standards development in the US. NISO's Voting Members and other supporters include a broad base of information producers and users including libraries, publishers, government agencies, and companies that provide information services. NISO is a leader in shaping international standards
NISO has developed standards such as Z39.50 (Information Retrieval), 12083 (an SGML Tool), Z39,2 (Information Interchange Format), Z39.53 (Codes for the Representation of Language), and Z39.18 (Scientific and Technical Reports).

### AIIM International. Document Imaging Standards

http://www.aiim.org/industry/standards/
AIIM plays an essential role in creating national and international standards, promoting their use, and disseminating them to users worldwide. Participation in the Standards Program is open to anyone. Members and other industry professionals play a key role in developing standards.

### Data Interchange Standards Organisation

http://www.disa.org/
ASC X12 – Accredited Standards Committee X12
In 1979, ANSI chartered the Accredited Standards Committee (ASC) X12 to develop uniform standards for interindustry electronic interchange of business transactions— electronic data interchange (EDI).

### Quality, Guidelines & Standards for Internet Resources

http://coombs.anu.edu.au/SpecialProj/QLTY/Qlty-Home.html
The purpose of this and related documents is to keep track of the leading sources of information dealing with the standards, measures and management procedures aimed at the improving quality of the networked information facilities.

### TEI Guidelines for Electronic Text Encoding and Interchange

http://etext.virginia.edu/TEI.html
These Guidelines are the result of over five years' effort by members of the research and academic community within the framework of an international cooperative project called the Text Encoding Initiative (TEI), established in 1987 under the joint sponsorship of the Association for Computers and the Humanities, the Association for Computational Linguistics, and the Association for Literary and Linguistic Computing.

### The Library of Congress Web page for the Z39.50 Maintenance Agency

http://lcweb.loc.gov/z3950/agency/
This page includes documentation and information related to the development and ongoing maintenance of the Z39.50 standard (ANSI/NISO Z39.50-1992, ANSI/NISO Z39.50-1995, and development of future versions of Z39.50), as well as information related to the implementation and use of the Z39.50 protocol.

### eLib standards guidelines

http://ukoln.bath.ac.uk/elib/wk_papers/stand2.html
This document provides recommendations for the selection and use of standards in eLib projects.

# Contributors to The British Library Initiatives for Access programme

## British Library staff and consultants

Sebastian Airey, Education Service
Michael Alexander, Information Systems
Nigel Allum, Science Reference and Information Service
Robin Alston, Humanities and Social Sciences
Helen Andrews, Document Supply Centre
Stephen Andrews, Document Supply Centre
Jan Ashton, National Bibliographic Service
Bob Aspey, Document Supply Centre
Andy Atkinson, Information Systems
Heather Aylesbury, National Bibliographic Service
Janet Backhouse, Department of Manuscripts
Stephen Bagley, Cataloguing
Chris Baile, Information Systems
Chris Banks, Music Library
Peter Barber, Map Library
Phil Barden, Document Supply Centre
Kate Barnes, Education Service
Paul Baxter, Science Reference and Information Service
Sandie Beaney, Cataloguing
John Bennett, Information Systems
Janet Benoy, Exhibitions Service
John Billingsby, Document Supply Centre
Jane Bishop, Science Reference and Information Service
Alan Boarder, Information Systems
David Bradbury, Document Supply Centre
Andrew Braid, Document Supply Centre
Mike Bremford, Information Systems
Barbara Brend, Education Service
Anthony Brickell, Information Systems
Richard Briggs
Karen Brookfield, Education Service
Michelle Brown, Department of Manuscripts
Chris Browne, Information Systems
Roger Butcher, Information Systems

Pat Byrne, Science Reference and Information Service
Derrick Byrne, Collections and Preservation
Tom Cain
Peter Carey, Photographic Service
Richard Carpenter, Humanities and Social Sciences
Leona Carpenter, Information Systems
Cindy Carr, Document Supply Centre
Jane Carr, Public Affairs
Matt Cherrill, Reproductions
Lynne Chivers, Information Services
Richard Christophers, Humanities and Social Sciences
Daniel Clarkson, Information Systems
Martin Clayton, Humanities and Social Sciences
Hugh Cobbe, Music Library
John Conway, Audio-Visual Services
Julian Conway, Department of Manuscripts
Sharon Cooke, Science Reference and Information Service
Annette Cooper, Information Systems
Doug Cooper, Science Reference and Information Service
Peter Copeland, National Sound Archive
Graham Cranfield, Humanities and Social Sciences
Mike Curston, Document Supply Centre
Jeremy Cutler, Department of Manuscripts
Chris Dance, Information Systems
Mark Davies, Information Systems
Martin Davies, Humanities and Social Sciences
Pete Davis, Document Supply Centre
Chris Devlin, Information Systems
Brett Dolman, Department of Manuscripts
John Draper, Research and Innovation Centre
Pat Earey
Christopher Easingwood, Information Systems
Stuart Ede, National Bibliographic Service

Andy Ekers, Information Systems
Jon Ellis, Science Reference and Information Service
Martin Ellis, Information Systems
Phil Farlow
Charles Farrell
John Fines
Nick Flinders, Science Reference and Information Service
Andrew Ford, Information Systems
Dave French, Collections and Preservation
Mandhir Ghidda
Annie Gilbert, Reproductions
Kevin Gladwell, Information Systems
John Goldfinch, Humanities and Social Sciences
Christopher Gravett
Richard Gray
John Griffin, Humanities and Social Sciences
David Grinyer, Information Systems
Tim Hadlow, Information Systems
Christine Hall, Department of Manuscripts
Lotte Hellinga, Humanities and Social Sciences
Robin Herford
Barbara Hobey, Collections and Preservation
Helen Hodgart, Information Systems
Michael Hoey, Collections and Preservation
Brian Holt, National Bibliographic Service
Barry Horne
Kathy Houghton, Publications
Caroline Howes, Document Supply Centre
Clive Izard, Audio-Visual Resources
Marie Jackson, Press and Public Relations
Peter James, Information Systems
Steve Jarvis, Information Systems
Graham Jefcoate, Humanities and Social Sciences
Crispin Jewitt, National Sound Archive
Tony Johnson, Information Systems
Vanita Kalia, Science Reference and Information Service

Brian Kefford, National Bibliographic
Service
Chris Kelsey, Collections and Preser-
vation
Ed King, Collections and Preservation
Katy King, Document Supply Centre
Brian Lang, Chief Executive
Marcella Leembruggen, Humanities
and Social Sciences
Stephen Lilgert, Document Supply
Centre
Joanne Lomax, Special Collections
Paula Lonergan, Public Affairs
John Long, Information Systems
Serena Lovelace, National Sound
Archive
Martin Lunn, Document Supply
Centre
Scot McKendrick, Department of Man-
uscripts
John Mahoney, Information Systems
Robert Marcus, National Sound
Archive
Graham Marsh, Photographic Service
Ian Mason
Richard Masters, Information Systems
Rebecca May
Margaret Meserve, Humanities and
Social Sciences
Richard Moore, Cataloguing
Gavin Mortlock
Kevin Mouncey, Information Systems
Caroline Mulcahy, Science Reference
and Information Service
Martin Nail, Research and Innovation
Centre
David Newton, Science Reference and
Information Service
Nick Newton, Information Systems
William Noel
Andrew Ogilvie, Photographic Service
Michael O'Keefe, Oriental and India
Office Collections
Sheila Ormerod
Mark Page
Ulrich Pagel, Oriental and India Office
Collections
John Palmer
Greg Payne, Information Systems
Maria Petrou, Science Reference and
Information Service
Sharon Phelan, Science Reference and
Information Service
Andrew Phillips, Humanities and
Social Sciences
Hazel Podmore, Collections and
Preservation
Laurence Pordes, Photographic
Service
Pamela Porter, Department of

Manuscripts
Andrew Prescott, Department of
Manuscripts
Alice Prochaska, Special Collections
Jonathan Purday, National Biblio-
graphic Service
Janet Rarugel, Reproductions
Nick Redfern
Marjorie Reeves
Andrew Rennard, Information Systems
Gillian Riley, Document Supply
Centre
Glyn Robinson, Consultant
Richard Roman, Document Supply
Centre
Susan Rose
Alan Routley, Information Systems
Vicky Roy, Document Supply Centre
Jagvinder Sanger, Information Systems
Des Seal
Charlotte Sexton
Graham Shaw, Oriental and India
Office Collections
Simon Shaw, Information Systems
Graham Sherfield
Sue Simpson
Sue Skelton, Cataloguing
Bart Smith, Press and Public Relations
Neil Smith, Information Systems
Brian Snookes
Somalatha Somadasa
Nigel Spencer, Document Supply
Centre
Andrea Stubbs, National Bibliographic
Service
Jonathan Summers
Andrew Swires, Document Supply
Centre
Anne Sykes, Cataloguing
David Tranter, Information Systems
Vic Verrall, Document Supply Centre
Stephen Vickers, Document Supply
Centre
Penelope Wallis, Education Service
Ben Walsh
Alan Ward, National Sound Archive
Richard Watson
Roger Watson
David Way, Publications
Lali Weerasinghe, National Sound
Archive
Mike Wheatley, Information Systems
Peter Whitfield
Susan Whitfield, Oriental and India
Office Collections
Chris Wild, Information Systems
Joyce Williams, Information Systems
Carl Wilson, Information Systems
Jane Wilson, Science Reference and
Information Service

Slawek Wojcik, Information Systems
Anne Young, Publications
British Library Corporate Design
Office

**External contributors**
(Principal contacts only are listed)

*2AR*
Chris Haden
Simon Jones
Kevin Roxburgh
Jane Whitman

*ADC*
Alan Shepherd

*Bath University*
Chris Knight

*Biblioteca Nazionale Centrale
Rome*
Guiliana Sciascia
Pasqualino Avigliano
Maurizio Mavilia
Angelo Busato

*Birkbeck College*
Barry Coward

*British Academy*
Seamus Ross

*British Museum*
Rowena Loverance

*Capital Planning Information Ltd*

*Center for Advanced Research
and Teaching in the Humanities*
Charles Hiestand

*Consiglio Nazionale delle
Richerche, Rome*
Annamaria Campanile
Antonio De Leonardis
Annunziata Fazio
Marco Campanile
Enzo Iegri

*Dataware UK Ltd*
Tony Dodd

*De Montfort University*
Marilyn Deegan
Peter Robinson

*Excalibur Technologies*

*Exponent Electronic Publishing
Services*

**Footmark Media Ltd**

**Hoskyns**
Chris Parker
John Sefrin
Nick Binns

**Houghton Library, Harvard University**
Leslie Morris

**IBM, UK Ltd**
Rod Coppock
Martec Imaging Ltd
Chris Haden
Simon Jones

**iBase Image Systems**
Peter MacGregor
Bob Hamilton

**Image Associates**
Paul Southey
Leslie Stump

**Instituto da Biblioteca Nacional e do Livro, Lisbon**
Maria Valentina Sul Mendes
Maria Matilde Paula
Rui Louriero
Luis Carlos Peixoto

**London Guildhall University**
Deian Hopkin

**Kansas University**

**Koninklijke Bibliotheek, Bibliotheque Royale Brussels**
Elly Cockx-Indestege
Annie de Coster
Bart Op de Beeck
Sophie Basch
Jean-Luc Tilliere
Nadine Bonnet

**Koninklijke Bibliotheek, The Hague**

Gerard van Thienen
Jos Uljee
Erik de Groot

**Middletreat Ltd**
Ian Witham

**Miranda Gray Illustration**

**Morse Computers**

**Newcastle University Open Connections**
Di Bindman
Helen Johnston
Ellen Peacock
Joanne Stemp

**Open University**
Sadler Johnson
Mike Peterson
Steve Bannister

**Oxford University Computing Services**
Lou Burnard
Dominic Dunlop
Gavin Burnage
Scotty Logan

**Oxford University Library Automation Service**
David Cooper

**Prestige Network**
Shawn Khorrassani

**Primary Source Media**
Cristina Ashby
Geoff Couldrey
Paul Lewis
Nick Allen
Mike Moore

**Quorum Information Service**

**Republic Ltd**
Gordon Plant

**Royal Library, Copenhagen**

**University of Bologna**
Guy Aston

**University of Glasgow**
Seamus Ross

**University of Kentucky**
Kevin S. Kiernan
Michael Ellis
David Hart
Danette Shupe
C.J. Yuan

**University of Lancaster**
Meg Twycross
Paul Williams

**University College of St Martin, Lancaster**
Pamela King
**University of London Computing Centre**
Kevin Ashley

**University of Northumbria at Newcastle**
Margaret Graham

**University of Sheffield**
Norman Blake
Mark Greengrass
Michael Hannon
Michael Pidd
Malcolm Pratt
Estelle Stubbs
Peter Willett
Nigel Williamson

**University of Washington**
Professor Richard Solomon
Steve Graham

**University of Westminster**

**Western Michigan University**
Paul E. Szarmach